Managing and Supporting Student Diversity in Higher Education

CHANDOS
INFORMATION PROFESSIONAL SERIES

Series Editor: Ruth Rikowski
(Email: Rikowskigr@aol.com)

Chandos' new series of books is aimed at the busy information professional. They have been specially commissioned to provide the reader with an authoritative view of current thinking. They are designed to provide easy-to-read and (most importantly) practical coverage of topics that are of interest to librarians and other information professionals. If you would like a full listing of current and forthcoming titles, please visit our website, www.chandospublishing.com, email wp@woodheadpublishing.com or telephone +44 (0) 1223 499140.

New authors: we are always pleased to receive ideas for new titles; if you would like to write a book for Chandos, please contact Dr Glyn Jones on gjones@chandospublishing.com or telephone +44 (0) 1993 848726.

Bulk orders: some organisations buy a number of copies of our books. If you are interested in doing this, we would be pleased to discuss a discount. Please email wp@woodheadpublishing.com or telephone +44 (0) 1223 499140.

Managing and Supporting Student Diversity in Higher Education

A casebook

ROBYN BENSON, MARGARET HEAGNEY,
LESLEY HEWITT, GLENDA CROSLING AND
ANITA DEVOS

Oxford Cambridge New Delhi

Chandos Publishing
Hexagon House
Avenue 4
Station Lane
Witney
Oxford OX28 4BN
UK
Tel: +44(0) 1993 848726
Email: info@chandospublishing.com
www.chandospublishing.com
www.chandospublishingonline.com

Chandos Publishing is an imprint of Woodhead Publishing Limited

Woodhead Publishing Limited
80 High Street
Sawston
Cambridge CB22 3HJ
UK
Tel: +44(0) 1223 499140
Fax: +44(0) 1223 832819
www.woodheadpublishing.com

First published in 2013

ISBN: 978-1-84334-719-4 (print)
ISBN: 978-1-78063-385-5 (online)
Chandos Information Professional Series ISSN: 2052-210X (print) and
ISSN: 2052-2118 (online)
Library of Congress Control Number: 2013939099

© R. Benson, M. Heagney, L. Hewitt, G. Crosling and A. Devos, 2013

British Library Cataloguing-in-Publication Data.
A catalogue record for this book is available from the British Library.

All rights reserved. No part of this publication may be reproduced, stored in or introduced into a retrieval system, or transmitted, in any form, or by any means (electronic, mechanical, photocopying, recording or otherwise) without the prior written permission of the publisher. This publication may not be lent, resold, hired out or otherwise disposed of by way of trade in any form of binding or cover other than that in which it is published without the prior consent of the publisher. Any person who does any unauthorised act in relation to this publication may be liable to criminal prosecution and civil claims for damages.

The publisher makes no representation, express or implied, with regard to the accuracy of the information contained in this publication and cannot accept any legal responsibility or liability for any errors or omissions.

The material contained in this publication constitutes general guidelines only and does not represent to be advice on any particular matter. No reader or purchaser should act on the basis of material contained in this publication without first taking professional advice appropriate to their particular circumstances. All screenshots in this publication are the copyright of the website owner(s), unless indicated otherwise.

Typeset by RefineCatch Limited, Bungay, Suffolk
Printed in the UK and USA.

Contents

Acknowledgements	*ix*
Preface	*xi*
About the authors	*xvii*

1	**Setting the context**	**1**
	Introduction	1
	International trends supporting widening participation in higher education	6
	Theoretical perspectives underpinning social inclusion	12
	Opportunities and challenges	13
	Strategies for improving access and retention	14
	How students from diverse backgrounds succeed in higher education: an overview	16
	Using participatory research and the student's voice to inform decision-making	19
	An introduction to the cases	20
	Summary	21
	Notes	22
	Chapter 1: discussion topics	23
2	**Finding the way to higher education: Miranda and Rochelle**	**25**
	Introduction	25
	Miranda's story	26
	Rochelle's story	36
	Implications for managing and supporting student diversity: transition to higher education and the first year experience	44
	Summary	46
	Chapter 2: discussion topics	49

Contents

3 This time it's different: Sesh and Shannon — **51**
- Introduction — 51
- Sesh's story — 53
- Shannon's story — 68
- Implications for managing and supporting student diversity: student retention — 85
- Summary — 89
- Chapter 3: discussion topics — 91

4 The international experience: Lam and Zelin — **93**
- Introduction — 93
- Lam's story — 94
- Zelin's story — 105
- Implications for managing and supporting student diversity: international students — 120
- Summary — 124
- Chapter 4: discussion topics — 125

5 Coming to education later in life: Alex Carole and Virginia — **127**
- Introduction — 127
- Alex Carole's story — 128
- Virginia's story — 135
- Implications for managing and supporting student diversity: mature age students — 154
- Summary — 157
- Chapter 5: discussion topics — 159

6 Finding my voice at last: Lillian, Marie, and Harriet — **161**
- Introduction — 161
- Lillian's story — 162
- Marie's story — 172
- Harriet's story — 190
- Implications for managing and supporting student diversity: encouraging transformative learning — 200
- Summary — 204
- Chapter 6: discussion topics — 205

7	**Helping students to succeed**	**207**
	Introduction	207
	How the students from diverse backgrounds succeeded in higher education	208
	Overall implications of the cases for managing and supporting student diversity	214
	Summary	222
	Chapter 7: discussion topics	223
References		**225**
Index		**233**

Acknowledgements

We are grateful to the Australian Department of Education, Science and Technology's Higher Education Equity Support Program for funding the project that led to this book, and for the research support provided by Cathi Flynn and Yolande McNicoll. We thank Kate Kirk from Manchester Metropolitan University for the research design, which we adapted for the project at Monash University. We especially thank Alex Carole, Harriet, Lam, Lillian, Marie, Miranda, Rochelle, Sesh, Shannon, Virginia and Zelin for sharing their stories for the benefit of others.

Preface

Recently, the recruitment and graduation of an increasingly diverse student population has emerged as a key challenge for higher education institutions. It has also become a topic of global interest. Governments in both the northern and southern hemispheres have embarked on policies that extend higher education beyond massification to universal access (Trow, 2000). A major driver of government policies is the perceived need to develop a more educated workforce to increase the participation of nations in the knowledge economy through increasing the number of people with undergraduate degrees. As a more socially inclusive higher education sector is seen as an important aspect of achieving this goal, university staff in many countries are responding to government imperatives and implementing a social inclusion agenda.

Policies and practices to promote affirmative action, equality of opportunities, and international education are in place in these countries, contributing to increased diversity of student populations in higher education institutions. This is occurring in the context of a dynamic and complex global environment. The development of a globalised higher education market, in which universities compete for students from other countries, generates income for institutions and nations, and helps students, staff and, more generally, the community, to develop international and globalised perspectives. Students are also increasingly mobile, leaving their home countries to enrol in the courses of their choice, and reaping the personal, academic, career and linguistic benefits that an international education experience can bring.

If you teach or support students, or recruit prospective students in a higher education institution, you are probably increasingly aware of the diversity of students' backgrounds. Students may have a smooth pathway into higher education from school, or one that is affected by family difficulties, disrupted schooling, health problems, or the impact of migration or low socio-economic background on prior educational opportunity. They may be the first generation in their family to enter higher education and hence be unfamiliar with the system. They may be mature age students who are single parents or carers, and they could be care leavers themselves. Students may come from minority ethnic or language backgrounds and, depending on the context, could be indigenous students or students from rural, regional and remote areas where educational opportunities are limited. Many of them will have experienced more than one aspect of having a 'non-traditional' background in the context of higher education. Increasingly, they may be students from other countries, often with English as a second or foreign language, who have enrolled in your institution to pursue educational and work opportunities.

The factor that all these students have in common if they are to succeed in their studies is the need to adapt to an institutional climate, and meet institutional requirements, in a context that is not historically organised to meet diverse student needs, and which may be very unfamiliar to them. This, in turn, has implications for the way higher education institutions manage the inclusion of students from diverse backgrounds, and the approaches that they put in place to support them, which is the main concern of this book. At a more specific level, our emphasis is on considering strategies for managing and supporting student diversity that you, as a practitioner, can implement to assist students or prospective students. The focus for our consideration of these issues is a selection of case studies in which learners from some of the diverse backgrounds introduced above describe the factors that affected them and how they were able to succeed in higher education.

The case studies provide a rare opportunity to hear what students with non-traditional backgrounds who have succeeded in higher education tell us about the system and about what works for them. The cases provide a space in which they tell their stories of challenge and success and how they can be best supported to succeed. In their own words, the students explain the types of support and strategies, both administrative and academic, which have helped – or hindered – them in their journey towards achieving an undergraduate degree. Overall, the cases provide an authentic account of factors affecting the student experience. They are a rich primary resource from which university staff can draw as they discuss and make decisions about approaches for working with students from similar backgrounds. They can also be used with prospective students from diverse backgrounds to inspire, motivate and inform them about how others have succeeded.

The study that informs the book

The case studies are derived from a longitudinal research study of the factors that contributed to the success of a group of students from diverse backgrounds studying at Monash University, Australia. Participants told their stories during semi-structured interviews, following an initial questionnaire in which students were invited to self-identify if they considered themselves to come from diverse backgrounds such as those noted earlier, or they thought of themselves as coming from a non-traditional background for another reason. Participants included students who were studying on-campus and some who were studying off-campus as distance education students. Interviews were undertaken three times during their course. At the start of their course, participants discussed their pathways into higher education. While their studies were in progress, they commented on how they were managing. Finally, they reflected on their experiences at the end of their course.

Reflecting the nature of the case study approach, the students' stories provide an in-depth understanding of complex social phenomena. Many students from diverse backgrounds experience a similar range of issues when they enter higher education, and it is these common issues that extend the relevance of the cases beyond the local context. The project was concerned primarily with inclusive education by investigating the factors that contribute to successful study by students such as these. Our definition of student success is provided in Chapter 1.

The structure of the book

In this book we explore the issues facing students from diverse backgrounds as they embark on and engage with their higher education studies, and identify the factors that contribute to their success. The book is primarily intended as a practical resource within the framework of recent literature on strategies for supporting social inclusion in higher education. It is structured as follows.

Chapter 1 provides the context for the cases that are introduced in the following chapters. We begin by defining some of the key terms and concepts used in the book and then provide an overview of international trends in widening participation in higher education. This is followed by an explanation of some theoretical perspectives underpinning the concept of social inclusion. We then outline the related opportunities and challenges, and consider strategies that have been suggested for improving access and retention, as background to summarising some of the ways that universities can facilitate successful study by students from non-traditional backgrounds. As you progress through subsequent chapters, you may find it useful to compare these ideas with the implications emerging from each student's story.

We then discuss the role of participatory research, and of the student voice, which were used in the preparation of the students' stories, to highlight their value as a means of informing decision-making about the management and support of student diversity in higher education. Finally, we provide a brief introduction to the cases that follow, before summarising key points made in the chapter and suggesting preliminary discussion topics to help you prepare to explore the issues raised in the book.

Chapters 2–6 all follow the same structure as we introduce the cases and consider the implications of the students' stories. Chapters 2–5 each contain two stories and Chapter 6 three stories. Each story begins with an outline of the particular student's pathway to higher education, then explains how they managed their studies, and concludes with their reflections and plans following graduation. *The names used for the students are pseudonyms, which they selected themselves.* Each student's story highlights a range of factors relating to social inclusion, but we have used the stories in each chapter to explore a particular aspect of managing and supporting student diversity in higher education. All of these chapters end with a summary and some discussion topics for your consideration.

In Chapter 2 we present the stories of Miranda and Rochelle, both of whom were the first in their families to enter higher education. There are differences as well as similarities in their stories, which we use to focus on the complexity of their routes to university. We then consider some implications for managing the transition to higher education and supporting the first year experience of students enrolling from backgrounds such as these.

In Chapter 3, the stories of Sesh and Shannon illustrate how students may have one or more previous attempts at undergraduate study before they find a course and a set of circumstances in their lives that allow them to progress. Their stories highlight the significant challenge of retaining students in higher education when features of their backgrounds may mitigate against successful study, and when students may have had inadequate guidance in their selection of a field of study. Students who withdraw from their initial attempt at university may not enrol again.

Shannon's story also demonstrates the risk that extra university fees and charges, and course requirements such as practicums, pose to students whose financial situation is fragile. We focus on student retention when considering the implications of these stories for university staff.

Chapter 4 addresses issues related to the international experience of students who leave their home countries to study overseas. Lam and Zelin are Chinese women in their early twenties. While they did not experience the social disruption to their education that characterises the backgrounds of students in other chapters, studying in a different culture and unfamiliar education system with English as a second language is a significant challenge for them. Their stories provide a basis for considering the implications for managing and supporting student diversity relating to these aspects of their experiences, and whether or not these implications are the same as those for students from other non-traditional backgrounds.

Chapter 5 presents the stories of Alex Carole and Virginia, who are older than the students considered in the earlier chapters, both enrolling in their courses in their forties. Part of the reason for their enrolment was that 'it was the right time' – the circumstances in their lives made university study feasible for them. Through their study they also discovered new dimensions of themselves. We use their stories to consider particular implications for managing and supporting the experience of mature age students.

Lillian, Marie and Harriet were also in their forties when they commenced university study. We consider their stories in Chapter 6. We have grouped these students' stories together because of the powerful impact that the experience of study had on them, resulting in significant personal transformation. Each of these students refers to major shifts in the ways they understand their identities. While there is evidence of perspective transformation in other students' stories, the intensity of the changes experienced by Lillian, Marie and Harriet provides an opportunity to consider the implications for staff of supporting perspective transformation in students who have entered higher education via non-traditional pathways.

Finally, in Chapter 7 we review what the participants' stories have told us about how students from diverse backgrounds succeed in higher education, reflecting on the approaches for helping students succeed which we introduced in Chapter 1. We then discuss the overall implications of the cases for university staff, concluding with a summary of suggested strategies for managing and supporting student diversity in higher education.

About the authors

Robyn Benson is an Adjunct Senior Lecturer (Educational Design) in the Faculty of Medicine, Nursing and Health Sciences at Monash University, Australia. She has a background in adult education, distance education and the use of educational technologies in higher education. The focus of her research activities has been on how the learning experiences of students can be improved using practices informed by a range of theoretical perspectives, with particular reference to implications for educational design and academic professional development. She is an Associate Editor of the international peer-reviewed journal, *Higher Education Research and Development*.

Margaret Heagney, Adjunct Research Fellow, Faculty of Education, Monash University, was National Student Equity Convenor for the Australian Group of Eight Universities and, before that, Coordinator of Student Equity in the Equity and Diversity Centre at Monash University. Her recent research and publications focus on global trends in student equity and widening participation, student retention and equitable selection practices. She is co-editor of *Widening Participation and Lifelong Learning*, an international peer-reviewed journal and Australasian Ambassador for the world Congress on Access to Post Secondary Education.

Lesley Hewitt is writing a history of sexual assault service development in Victoria, Australia, for the Victorian Centres Against Sexual Assault (CASA) Forum. She was a lecturer in the Department of Social Work at Monash University for 20 years where her teaching and research interests included human development, ageing, violence against women and social work education.

Glenda Crosling is Professor and Senior Academic Advisor at Sunway University in Malaysia, and Adjunct Associate Professor, Office of Pro Vice-Chancellor Learning and Teaching, Monash University. She has extensive Australian and international experience in educational quality assurance, improvement and policy development in higher education. She led the institutional audit from which the Monash campus in Malaysia was granted self-accrediting status by the Malaysian Government, and developed the campus course self-accreditation system. Glenda has published widely in scholarly journals and books on quality issues in teaching and learning. Her current research interests include transnational education, student diversity, the assessment of student learning and the development of creative thinking.

Anita Devos is an Adjunct Senior Lecturer, Faculty of Education, Monash University, where she taught in adult and workplace education, and held leadership roles in graduate student administration. Anita continues to research, publish and supervise research students in higher education and related areas. She has published widely on women and mentoring, doctoral education and, more recently, gender, migration and learning. She has a particular interest in the politics of post-secondary education, and the gendered dimensions of education and training reform globally. Anita has served on the editorial boards of leading higher education journals, and has been the recipient of major grants in her area.

Setting the context

Abstract: This chapter sets out the key terms and concepts used in this book, and outlines the international background for social inclusion and widening participation in higher education policies and practices. We introduce some theoretical perspectives underpinning the concept of social inclusion, exploring related opportunities, challenges and strategies for improving access and retention, before providing an overview of existing ideas about how students from diverse backgrounds succeed in higher education. We then explain the participatory research project from which the book's cases are drawn. As with each subsequent chapter, this chapter concludes with some discussion topics, to stimulate thinking about the best ways to support the participation and success of students from non-traditional backgrounds in higher education.

Key words: disadvantage, diversity, equity categories, higher education, indigenous, low socio-economic status (SES) background, narrative enquiry, non-traditional, participatory research, regional, rural, social inclusion, student success, study modes, widening participation.

Introduction

In this chapter, we review international trends and perspectives relating to social inclusion in higher education to contextualise the cases that we consider in Chapters 2–6. Following some definitions of terms and concepts used in the book, we begin with an overview of international trends, drawing on a range of relevant literature from Europe, North America, the United Kingdom, and Australia, before considering some theoretical perspectives underpinning the concept of social inclusion in education. We then explore opportunities and challenges relating to social inclusion and strategies for improving access and retention, before documenting some ideas about how students from diverse backgrounds succeed in higher education. As you progress through Chapters 2–6, you may find it useful to compare the implications for university practitioners emerging from the students' stories with approaches that have been suggested in this chapter and, on the basis of these, to derive ideas for your own context.

Next, we turn to the role of participatory research and use of the student's voice to inform decision-making about social inclusion in higher education. We explain how this approach was used with student participants to develop the cases on which this book is based. Finally, we summarise the key points that have been made in the chapter as a basis for highlighting issues relating to social inclusion in higher education that transcend the Australian setting of the cases. The implications and discussion topics presented in Chapters 2–6 will build on this background to generate principles and strategies that may be applied in a broad range of contexts to assist the success of students from diverse backgrounds in higher education.

Some definitions

In this book, we use the terms 'higher education' and 'universities' interchangeably. We define social inclusion as involving processes or actions to ameliorate the impact of disadvantage and/or to counter the processes that create it (Ferrier and North, 2009), in contrast to definitions that focus on the state of being socially included or excluded. This is called *widening participation* in some countries. In Europe, key aspects of widening participation are reflected in the social dimension of the Bologna Process where the nations involved envisaged a European Higher Education Area (EHEA) aimed at:

> equality of opportunities in higher education, in terms of: access, participation and successful completion of studies; studying and living conditions; guidance and counselling; financial support, and student participation in higher education governance. This implies also equal opportunities in mobility, when it comes to portability of financial support, removing barriers, and providing incentives (Bologna Process Website, 2007–2010).

In the UK, widening participation was identified with social mobility in the 1990s. More recently, it has come to be associated with the role of universities in 'enabling non-traditional learners from diverse cultural and socio-economic backgrounds to access HE as a stepping stone to professional employment and improved socio-economic advantage' (Butcher et al., 2012: 51). We include the concept of widening participation within the term 'social inclusion'.

We also use the terms 'diverse' and 'non-traditional' interchangeably when referring to students' pathways to higher education. 'Non-traditional' can refer to the pathways students took to access university, such as those admitted to university on criteria other than results of their final year of schooling. It can also refer to students themselves; that is, students from groups under-represented in higher education. As well as these different meanings, Hockings (2010: 2) comments on other problematic aspects of the categories 'traditional' and 'non-traditional':

> First, while there is some overlap between the groups considered to be non-traditional, it does not mean that all these groups are necessarily disadvantaged, although the evidence suggests that many are. Second, an individual may identify with both non-traditional and traditional groups.

We associate the term 'non-traditional' with disadvantage, which is another problematic term. 'Disadvantaged' students are those whose life circumstances, such as poverty, poor health, or other factors, have prevented them from demonstrating their academic potential and from accessing higher education. This term has fallen out of favour in recent times, as it characterises *the student* as disadvantaged. The current preference is for a more critical examination of the *processes* or *circumstances* that exclude or discriminate against individuals or members of certain groups. These processes or circumstances are frequently structural factors, such as inequitable selection policies, conditions of study that favour those with middle-class forms of social capital, or inflexible regulations governing extensions for assignments or access to libraries and computers. When these factors interact with personal circumstances such as work and family responsibilities, then students are at risk of withdrawal from their studies (Long et al., 2006).

Students in groups under-represented in higher education are sometimes referred to as belonging to certain 'equity categories'. This term has come into the lexicon because entrenched patterns of under-representation of some groups relative to their share of the population have prompted governments, particularly in the UK and Australia, to engage in a wide range of student equity policies and programs. In the UK, these categories encompass students who have black or minority ethnic backgrounds, disabilities, disadvantaged social and economic backgrounds, no prior family background in higher education, a background in the care of Local Authorities, opportunity to study only part-time, and non-traditional qualifications (Butcher et al., 2012). In Australia, the equity categories comprise students from low socio-economic, non-English-speaking,[1] Australian Indigenous, and rural backgrounds, those with a disability, and women in non-traditional disciplines. These groupings were first established in the 1990s. More recently, institutions have included students who are first in their family to attend university (sometimes called 'first generation' students) in their widening participation activities.

Equity categories can be effective in directing equity effort within universities, and the collection of statistics on the access, participation, retention, and success of students in these categories provides a basis for monitoring the equity performance of universities and of the higher education sector as a whole. However, students experience disadvantage beyond the boundaries of the designated categories. For example, many people from low socio-economic backgrounds are disadvantaged for other reasons, such as being a sole parent, being unemployed, or being a trauma sufferer (Clarke et al., 1999). Categories can also mask internal diversity within a group. For example, the Australian Indigenous student category includes students living in urban and rural areas, and individuals with differing degrees of numeracy and literacy (Ferrier and Heagney, 2000).

The use of equity categories hence overlooks the fact that multiple group membership is common. When students are members of more than one disadvantaged group, the barriers they encounter compound to increase the effects of their disadvantage (James et al., 2004). Thomas and Quinn (2003: 90) found that 'socio-economic status and the linked question of first generation entry need to be posed as the most central and pressing factor in addressing under-representation in higher education'. In an Australian study, Dobson et al. (1998) showed that 60 per cent of rural students were also members of other equity groups, as were more than 80 per cent of students from low socio-economic status backgrounds. They noted that low socio-economic status is a common central component of the disadvantage experienced by students, which affects the impact of other forms of disadvantage.

Low socio-economic status is defined in Australia as coming from the lowest 25 per cent of income-earning households, as determined by postcodes using Australian Bureau of Statistics (ABS) census data.² In the UK, low socio-economic status is indicated if a student receives free school meals, receives an Education Maintenance Allowance, or comes from a Low Participation Neighbourhood (LPN) (defined as an area for which the participation in higher education is less than two thirds of the UK average) (Skyrme and Crow, 2008).

In the Australian context, 'rural' refers to students whose home postcodes are deemed to be rural, based on distance from cities and services, geographic area grouping derived from ABS census data, and Ministerial Council on Education, Employment, Training, and Youth Affairs (MCEETYA) mapping. In Canada and some European countries, rurality is defined in terms of distance from a higher education institution. 'Indigenous' refers to those students who identify as belonging to a First Nations or First Peoples' grouping, which in Australia is referred to as being of Aboriginal or Torres Strait Islander descent.

In this book, the terms 'distance education' and 'off-campus study' are used interchangeably to refer to a mode of study that requires little or no on-campus attendance and frequently involves online learning. 'Full-time' and 'part-time' are on-campus study modes. Part-time students undertake less than the defined maximum course load and therefore take longer to complete their degrees. Student success is identified by graduation, together with evidence of students' commitment to and satisfaction with their study which suggests that it will impact on changing the direction of their lives. This draws on the definition by Kuh et al. (2006: 7), who explain student success as 'academic achievement, engagement in educationally purposeful activities, satisfaction, acquisition of desired knowledge, skills and competencies, persistence, attainment of educational objectives, and postcollege performance'.

When we refer to managing and supporting students from diverse backgrounds, our focus is on you, as a practitioner, involved in teaching or supporting these students. You may not necessarily have a formal management role in your institution but, in undertaking your duties, you will be involved in bringing people (including students) together to achieve the goal of social inclusion efficiently and effectively. Similarly, your primary role in the institution may or may not have a direct focus on students, but you will be involved in helping them in some way, for example, through providing academic support, financial assistance, or support related to their social backgrounds or circumstances, or through the support you provide while teaching them. Depending on your role, you might be closely involved in enacting your institution's social inclusion policies, and you may be very much aware of the national and international trends underpinning them; or you may have some general awareness of these developments but be more specifically focused on assisting the students with whom you engage. The cases in this book will show some of the ways that students reported that they could be best supported.

International trends supporting widening participation in higher education

In many parts of the world, governments have reacted to the global financial downturn by placing further pressure on higher education institutions to manage larger student numbers with reduced public funding. At these times, many universities are focused on financial survival yet higher education institutions continue to enrol students from a widening range of backgrounds. Higher education has become globalised; students move from one country to another to access the university course of their choice, bringing financial and cultural rewards to the institutions that enrol them, while also increasing the complexity of teaching, learning, and administration.

While increasing the enrolment of international students continues to be a priority, a more diverse domestic student population has emerged as a key challenge for universities. New economic drivers at the centre of national and global policy discourses have repositioned the social inclusion agenda, elevating its importance in the eyes of national policymakers and university administrators. Widening participation has become tied to economic objectives such as increasing national competitiveness in global markets. Many countries are aiming to produce a better educated workforce to support innovation in the knowledge economy, and they are looking to universities to provide these workers.

Widening participation and productivity

The link between having a more diverse student population and achieving economic objectives is evident in Australian government policy. Working on the premise that 'strengthening our human capital is the key to continuing Australia's economic and social progress' (Gillard, 2009: 1), the *Review of Australian Higher Education* (Bradley, 2008) argued that national productivity can only be increased if the proportion of the population with higher degree qualifications is also increased. The participation of Australians with degree-level qualifications was seen to be lagging behind that of other countries; in 2009, Australia was rated ninth on this Organisation for Economic Co-operation and Development (OECD) measure, falling from seventh in 1996.

The Bradley Review found that increased productivity derived from an increase in people with university-level qualifications could not be achieved without a change in the student cohort. Students from high and intermediate socio-economic backgrounds were already participating at rates well in excess of their representation in the population. Increased productivity would flow from inclusion of students from low socio-economic backgrounds – that is, by bringing in the groups who were not already in higher education. To achieve its goals, the Australian Government (2009) decided to introduce a target of 40 per cent of 25- to 34-year-olds to attain a higher education qualification by 2025, and a 20 per cent target for enrolments from low socio-economic background students by 2020.

In the UK, the Higher Education Funding Council of England (HEFCE) linked higher education with economic competitiveness and the knowledge economy in the context of meeting the global challenge for higher level skills, research excellence, and knowledge transfer (HEFCE, 2009). In Europe, similar arguments are being made. Skills shortages in the context of social, demographic, and economic changes are driving knowledge-based societies to increase their global competitiveness by producing more university graduates. As a result, European higher education institutions are aiming to widen access to include new target groups such as those with vocational qualifications and work experience (Moissidis et al., 2011). While there appears to be acceptance in many countries of the economic benefits of widening participation to groups hitherto under-represented in their higher education systems, each nation's response to these challenges varies considerably.

Variation in national contexts

A complex mix of social, political, and cultural factors helps shape national responses. The importance of the widening participation agenda is very often based in a particular national context.

Germany

German youth have high participation rates in vocational education and training (VET), but the number of young people accessing higher education institutions is low. Although it has set a target for 40 per cent of its young people to attend university, the German government is a long way from achieving its goal (Leichsenring, 2011a). In addition, the country's population is declining and ageing, making it more difficult to replace those retiring from the workforce (Leichsenring, 2011b). Academically trained staff are in short supply. Although it is imperative that more educated workers are produced and universities need to meet that demand by producing more graduates, the system itself remains highly selective and socially stratified, and struggles to include disadvantaged students and those from non-traditional backgrounds (Leichsenring, 2011b). For example, approximately one per cent of students with VET qualifications enter higher education (Moissidis et al., 2011).

Social stratification is further exacerbated by tuition fees levied by some of the states. The majority of students are supported by their parents, although there is federal student support.

Finland

Moissidis et al. (2011) report that although higher education is free in Finland, other factors such as a lack of cultural capital and being first in the family to attend university work against equitable access. Most higher education participants are recent school leavers. Finnish students with vocational education and training qualifications are seen as 'underprepared' and less than one per cent of students in this group participate in higher education. As there are no fees, there is little interest in widening participation, except in university departments where enrolments are low. And as there are no maintenance grants, 61% of university students and 59% of polytechnic students have to work while studying (Statistics Finland, 2013). Timely completion rates are also an issue (Moissidis et al., 2011).

Scandinavia

In Sweden, the state funds almost 100 per cent of the tertiary education system. The state also provides funds to support students through their courses. About 40 per cent of young people up to the age of 25 years participated in higher education in 2003, up from 25 per cent in 1992. Participation was skewed in favour of students from upper-class backgrounds; they comprised 27 per cent of commencing students compared with their population share of 18 per cent, while students from working-class backgrounds made up 36 per cent of the general population and only 24 per cent of those who entered Swedish higher education institutions (Forneng, 2003).

Although tuition is free and there are good maintenance grants available for Danish students, geography is a barrier to equal access for students in rural areas. High school and university level educational facilities are concentrated in urban areas so that students in more remote areas of the country have to leave home to continue their studies (Moissidis et al., 2011). Research suggests that students from low socio-economic backgrounds who live in rural areas are doubly disadvantaged. Heggen and colleagues (Heggen, 2000; Heggen et al., 2003) have demonstrated that in Norway lower socio-economic status and regionality are linked, as they are in Australia (see Clarke et al., 1999) and Canada (see James, 2008).

Canada

In Canada, rurality or regionality (defined in terms of distance from a higher education institution) works against the participation of students from low socio-economic backgrounds much more than it does for students from high income backgrounds. As James (2008: 96) reports: 'low SES [socio-economic status] students are less likely than high SES students to attend university if no university is located nearby', and participation rates of high SES students in rural areas are only marginally lower than high SES students who live near universities. In other words, high SES background cancels out the effects of rurality.

Responsibility for education rests with Canada's provinces and national data on students' characteristics and participation in higher education are not collected from a variety of sources. Despite this, many of the trends affecting higher education around the world have been reported in Canada. For example, the link between an increased number of university graduates with improved productivity is clear, and the number of young people in Canada is declining. However, 55 per cent of its 25- to 34-year-old cohort have a post-secondary school qualification (Berger et al., 2009) compared with 29 per cent in Australia. Students from low SES backgrounds, First Nations students, and those who are first in the family to attend university are all under-represented (James, 2008). In contrast to students from rural and remote areas for whom high socio-economic status outweighed rurality when it came to gaining access to university, having parents who had been to university is more important than financial considerations even among poorer students (Thomas, 2006).

United States

It is not easy to gain a clear picture of how US institutions have responded to the pressures on them to admit a wider range of students. The population of the USA is very ethnically diverse and, as a result, university populations in some states are also diverse.

Access to university is unequally distributed between various groups, and different cohorts of students are to be found in different types of higher education institutions. For example, highly selective research institutions – both private and public – tend to be populated by students from white, high-income backgrounds enrolled in four-year bachelor degree programs. Students enrolling in two-year programs in community colleges tend to be those traditionally under-represented in higher education and include students from low income groups, those who are first in their families to enrol in higher education, and some racial and ethnic groups such as Latinos and Chicanos (Handel and Herrera, 2003). People from these two ethnic groups make up nearly one-third of the population of the state of California, yet their access rates to higher education are well below their representation in the general population (Ferrier et al., 2010). Multiple forms of disadvantage are common among these groups; low socio-economic background combines with race and ethnicity to work against access to higher education.

Recently, there has been increased awareness of the benefits of having a diverse student population (Ferrier et al., 2010). The need to have a more highly educated workforce to participate in the global economy has also been acknowledged. President Obama's *American Graduate Initiative* was established to restore the USA from tenth to first place in OECD rankings that chart the proportion of a country's citizens with post-secondary degrees (Marr and Jary, 2011).

Recent policy changes have put these gains in jeopardy. Increased student fees, shifts from needs-based to merit-based scholarships, and major cuts to funding and financial aid for students have been accompanied by a fall in the number of students who graduate. Only one in three students graduates from two-year public community colleges in three years and less than half of the students enrolled in four-year university courses graduate in six years (Marr and Jary, 2011).

United Kingdom

As in other parts of the world, the push for more skilled workers for the knowledge economy is driving the continued focus on widening participation in the UK, though the policy context is very different. Following the Browne review of higher education (Browne, 2010), UK universities are free to improve their financial position by charging students tuition fees of up to £9000 (14,480 Australian dollars) per annum. However, not all countries that make up the UK have gone down this path. Both Scotland and Wales have decided not to increase their tuition fees (Marginson, 2011).

Universities that do increase their fees are required to enter into an Access Agreement under which they must engage in widening participation programs to recruit and support under-represented students. This policy change signals a shift in responsibility for widening participation from government to higher education institutions themselves – a move that was clearly evident in the government's axing of the national widening participation program *Aimhigher* in July 2011 (Ferrier, 2012).

Universities left 'on their own' to achieve national goals and targets

Like their UK counterparts, Australian universities in receipt of government funding must contribute to the national social inclusion policy agenda: 'Social inclusion must be a core responsibility of all institutions that accept public funding, irrespective of history and circumstances' (Bradley, 2008: 33).

There is designated funding for equity activities and institutions can bid for funding for collaborative outreach programs linking universities, schools, and other sectors such as the community sector to raise students' aspirations and build attainment. Universities also receive a loading based on the number of low socio-economic background students they succeed in enrolling. In its budget response to the Bradley Review, the Australian Government (2009) suggested some strategies such as targeted academic support, greater financial assistance, counselling and mentoring that universities could employ to assist in the retention and graduation of students from low socio-economic backgrounds. However, the main focus was improved equity performance as shown in the participation rates of low SES students, leaving the institutions to decide how best to bring about these outcomes.

Despite the fact that UK universities are free to increase their tuition fees and Australian institutions have access to designated equity funding, recent research suggests that universities are 'on their own' in trying to serve their diverse student populations (Leichsenring, 2011a: 53). In the context of the abolition of the national widening participation program *Aimhigher* in the UK, Liz Marr (2011: 5) reported that:

> the English government has asked universities to soak up the work that *Aimhigher* has been doing so effectively in partnership with them…

It appears that universities are to take on this work when direct funding has been reduced. While it is clear that universities' social inclusion and widening participation activities are driven by the need of the global economy for more educated workers, concerns about social justice, the transformative power of education, and the need to cater for international students, continue to motivate universities and their staff to address the challenges of educating a diverse student population.

Theoretical perspectives underpinning social inclusion

Although government imperatives to widen participation in higher education have gained impetus as a consequence of economic developments and to a lesser extent social justice principles, these initiatives are consistent with established theoretical perspectives that shape educational practices.

The interpretive and critical social theory paradigms in scientific thought (Foley, 2000; Soltis, 1992) provide substantial support for encouraging social inclusion in education:

- *Interpretivism* acknowledges the social construction of reality, recognising that reality only exists from the perspectives of those who perceive it. This worldview underpinned developments in the field of humanistic psychology during the 1950s and 1960s, which focused on the holistic development of fully functioning (Rogers, 1969) or self-actualising persons (Maslow, 1970). It is a concept which supports values that are important for social inclusion because it acknowledges the lived experiences of people, from their point of view.
- *Critical social theory* is of particular importance because of its focus on social justice and empowerment. Emanating from the Marxist-oriented Institute for Social Research in Frankfurt and New York, this theory places social justice and the relationship of knowledge, power, and ideology at the centre of the learning experience (Habermas,

1971). Brazilian adult educator Paulo Freire was an important exponent of critical social theory in education, rejecting the 'banking concept of education' (Freire, 1972: 46) where the taught are seen as dehumanised objects, and power and knowledge are in the hands of the teacher. He favoured a humanising pedagogy where a permanent relationship of dialogue is established so that both parties become subjects in unveiling reality. This approach has a number of parallels with current theorising in education which supports social inclusion and the active involvement of the learner in the learning process.

Freire's ideas were widely taken up by feminist educators and scholars (among others) in the 1980s and 1990s as a means of exploring issues of unequal opportunity and power in access to and participation of women and girls, in particular, at all levels of education. Recent decades have seen the development of ideas from critical social theory to explore questions of gender and power, and how gender intersects with ethnicity, race, able-bodiedness, social class, and other forms of difference to disadvantage certain groups of women and of men. From this work has emerged a distinctive feminist scholarship in education concerned with working towards social justice. This work pays attention to the ways individuals understand and negotiate their identities, particularly in the context of globalising times (e.g. Devos, 2011; Jackson, 2011; Leathwood and Francis, 2006).

Opportunities and challenges

Ideas and initiatives supporting social inclusion in higher education offer opportunities for access to education by people who may not have previously considered studying at this level. They also facilitate the enactment of inclusive practices by teaching and professional staff, countering other institutional priorities relating to outcomes such as prestige that encourage restrictive entry criteria and discourage a broader student base.

Social inclusion also offers a number of challenges for institutions and for teaching staff. For many institutions, having increased numbers of students from non-traditional backgrounds is a new phenomenon. In the main, universities are geared to serve homogeneous populations. For example, in 2010, the ratio of low SES Australian students under 25 years (the bottom 25 per cent of income-earning households) participating in higher education to high SES students (the top 25 per cent of income earning households) was 0.42 (DEEWR, 2011a); in 1993, the participation ratio was 0.40 (Martin, 1994).

In the UK, young people from 'higher social groupings' are five to six times more likely to attend university than those from the most disadvantaged backgrounds (DEEWR, 2011b), while in Canada students drawn from high income backgrounds are likely to participate in higher education at almost twice the rate of those from the lowest income quartile (DEEWR, 2011b). In many countries, lack of relevant data makes it very difficult for universities to understand the structural practices that contribute to their homogeneous recruitment outcomes and their less than optimal retention of students from non-traditional backgrounds (DEEWR, 2011b).

For practitioners, social inclusion highlights the need for staff development and the provision of quality teaching and student support. Burke and Hayton identified the need to pay more attention to developing higher education pedagogies that are accessible and participatory and move away from concepts such as 'delivery' and 'styles'. They suggest that there needs to be dialogue between lecturers about new approaches to teaching and learning that 'promote excellence and value diversity and difference' (Burke and Hayton, 2011: 22).

Strategies for improving access and retention

For students entering higher education from non-traditional backgrounds, gaining access is an achievement in itself, but successfully completing a course involves a combination of personal and structural factors. The factors influencing access to higher education may not be the same as those that affect students' success at university once they enrol (James, 2008). In this section, we draw on some of the literature on access and retention to focus on how strategies relating to these can contribute to students' success.

Much of the literature on access deals with sector-wide practices and the principles that underpin them (Marks et al., 2001; Palmer et al., 2011). James (2008), for example, provides an inventory of faculty- or institution-based access programs, designed to assist non-traditional students to enter university. Other studies consider the equity implications of various selection practices based on prior school achievement, aptitude tests, and students' equity characteristics, all of which are used by

Australian universities to select their students (Dobson and Skuja, 2005; Heagney, 2011; Levy and Murray, 2005; Palmer et al., 2011; Wheelahan, 2009). Thomas and Quinn (2003) reported on an international study into widening participation which includes a summary of the issues affecting mature age students in various countries. In a comprehensive Australian study, O'Dowd (1996) examined access and retention issues for mature age students such as lack of confidence and feelings of isolation. She argued that mature age students who do gain access to university show great determination and have to overcome the feeling that university is not for them.

Mature age students entering university face many issues that their younger peers do not. Some feel they are too old to be successful in their studies, and that university is a strange and perplexing place. Greer and Tidd (2006) suggest that a targeted induction program, including a campus tour, meetings with staff and fellow students, and information about academic expectations and support services, can help to alleviate students' anxieties and overcome feelings of isolation.

Social inclusion is the focus of a handbook of good practice (Cook and Rushton, 2009) in which the links between recruitment, transition, and retention made by some UK universities to improve outcomes for students from diverse backgrounds are documented. Strategies discussed include providing quality pre-enrolment information which outlines the hours needed to be devoted to study, information on transport to university and what it costs, and other basic information. Other pre-enrolment initiatives include internet sites for prospective students to ask university staff about courses and what is involved in studying at university. Peer support programs, both pre- and post-enrolment, are also canvassed.

Research on student retention indicates that students withdraw from their studies for a variety of reasons (Crosling et al., 2008). Summarising UK research in this area, Jones (2008) suggested that students withdraw because of: poor preparation for higher education; weak institutional and/or course match, resulting in a lack of commitment; unsatisfactory academic experience; lack of social integration; financial issues; and personal circumstances. These reasons support the previous findings of an Australian study of student attrition (Long et al., 2006).

There is increasing support for the view that institutional practices should not differentiate between students taking non-traditional pathways into higher education and school leaver-students, and that support should be integrated with students' learning experiences. Thomas et al. (2002: 17–18) drew on responses in a UK study of student services to note the importance of being proactive in supporting all students, rather than offering services as a last resort for students with 'problems'. They saw the link between student support, teaching, and learning as 'the heart of the issue'. Warren (2002) argued that a mix of semi-integrated and integrated models of curriculum provision offers better prospects for helping a wide spectrum of students to succeed at university than the 'separate' provision of academic support. This is consistent with evidence that many students are reluctant to approach specialised support services (Clegg et al., 2006; Dodgson and Bolam, 2002). A longitudinal Australian study linking student diversity to resilience and successful progression (Kinnear et al., 2008) emphasises the relationship between teaching staff and students in enhancing academic endeavour, successful progression, and students' help-seeking behaviours.

The recent emphasis on the importance of student engagement, with particular reference to first year students (Krause and Coates, 2008), suggests a number of strategies that teaching staff can implement to improve engagement and provide a supportive learning and teaching environment. We address many of these strategies when we discuss the implications of students' stories in subsequent chapters.

How students from diverse backgrounds succeed in higher education: an overview

Just as many factors combine in complex ways to prevent students from non-traditional backgrounds from accessing higher education, the personal and structural factors that influence or hinder their success at university work together in ways that are similarly complex. If students are to have a successful experience at university, then both the individual and the institution need to be involved 'in a two way active process of change and development involving a complex interplay between personal, psychological, financial and educational factors' (Murphy, 2009: 7). Similarly, May and Bridger (2010: 5) found that 'sustainable and effective inclusive cultural change will only come about through institutions focusing simultaneously on both institutional and individual factors'. Beyond the university, the complexity of the factors affecting students is illustrated by the fact that quite often serendipitous events or encounters influence pathways to higher education that eventually lead to success (e.g. McGivney, 2006; O'Shea, 2007; Stone, 2008).

Numerous studies have identified factors that contribute to student success. To provide an overview of these factors, and a context for considering in Chapter 7 what the students in this book tell us about how they succeeded, we refer below to a small number of recent Australian studies, an American review of the literature on what matters to student success (Kuh et al., 2006), and a UK synthesis of research on inclusive learning and teaching (Hockings, 2010).

In their longitudinal study of resilience and successful progression at one Australian university, Kinnear et al. (2008) identified personal goals or career aspirations as 'overwhelmingly' important, together with various forms of support, including family support, financial support, employer support, staff support, and peer support, with peer support networks being particularly valued. The role of personal goals is mirrored in another study at an Australian university by Devlin and O'Shea (2012), where motivation was the most frequently mentioned factor reported by students, with student time management and family attitude also playing major roles. The most frequently mentioned institutional factor was teacher availability/approachability. In their review of what matters to student success, Kuh et al. (2006) refer to pre-college experiences (including academic preparation, family and peer support, and motivation to learn) and then to the college experience itself, with the two central factors determining student engagement being students' behaviours and institutional conditions. Contributing factors include work off campus, financial aid, and policies.

Focusing on institutional factors, an Australian study encompassing three universities (Devlin et al., 2012) identifies five areas of focus for institutional leadership to help students from low SES backgrounds to succeed:

1. inclusive curriculum and assessment design;
2. promoting students' engagement with and support from others;
3. encouraging 'help-seeking' by students;
4. minimising financial challenges for students; and
5. resourcing and supporting teachers of low SES students.

They also provide six areas of focus, specifically for teaching staff:

1. knowing and respecting students;
2. offering students flexibility, variety, and choice;
3. conveying expectations clearly, using accessible language;
4. scaffolding students' learning;

5. being available and approachable to guide student learning; and
6. engaging in reflective practice.

Many other studies also highlight the part played by institutions in student success and, within this, the role of teachers both through their personal support and through the way they design and implement teaching strategies and provide feedback, including their use of the online environment. The synthesis of research by Hockings (2010) encompasses a similar range of factors to those mentioned by Devlin et al. (2012), organising them into four main areas of attention:

1. inclusive curriculum design;
2. inclusive curriculum 'delivery';
3. inclusive assessment; and
4. institutional commitment to and management of inclusive learning and teaching.

The strategies relating to improving access and retention in the previous sub-section can be added to the approaches outlined above. Further strategies to help students with the practical aspects of making success possible have included:

- providing basic information on courses such as how much time needs to be spent in study, how many basic texts need to be purchased and their cost (Ferrier et al., 2010);
- providing book vouchers for low SES students (Ferrier & Heagney, 2000; James, 2008);
- providing grants for professional placements to cover accommodation and travel (Ferrier et al., 2010; James, 2008); and
- considering students with work and family responsibilities when developing timetables, attendance requirements, and assessment (Ferrier & Heagney, 2000; Ferrier et al., 2010).

Thomas et al. (2002) suggest that academic and support staff can work collaboratively with student unions and associations to help students to overcome isolation and integrate successfully. Inviting office bearers of student associations to talk about the clubs and societies they run for students and for specific groups such as mature age students (Greer and Tidd, 2006) and international students can help link them into these peer support networks. Ferrier (2012) provides a list of UK universities whose student unions engage in widening participation activity.

Using participatory research and the student's voice to inform decision-making

Although decisions about strategies for promoting social inclusion are frequently determined by top-down policies within the framework of existing practices of universities, there are strong arguments for drawing on the experiences of students from diverse backgrounds themselves to inform directions for achieving inclusion. This approach helps to ensure that the practices put in place are appropriate to meet the students' needs.

Participatory research

One way of developing an understanding of the needs of students from non-traditional backgrounds is to engage in participatory enquiry consistent with the goals of collaboration and empowerment embedded in critical social theory. Patton (2002: 185) comments that the fundamental element of participatory enquiry is a 'commitment to involving people in the setting being studied as co-inquirers', as opposed to conducting research *on* people. While acknowledging that the degree and nature of involvement may vary widely, Patton identifies a number of principles which guide participatory enquiry:

- involving participants in learning enquiry logic and skills;
- real, rather than token, ownership of the research by participants;
- participants working as a group, with the researcher supporting group cohesion and collective enquiry;
- conducting all the aspects of the enquiry in ways that are understandable and meaningful to participants;
- a relationship between participants and researcher that is co-equal, with the researcher acting as a facilitator, collaborator, and learning resource;
- recognising and valuing participants' perspectives and expertise, and assisting them to value their own and each other's expertise; and
- minimising status and power differences between researcher and participants.

The stories of the students in this book emerged using a process that aimed to reflect the above principles, while recognising that there were some limitations. Publication would be undertaken by the researchers, with the consent of the participants and with reference to the texts produced collaboratively with them based on their stories. The particular method used was narrative enquiry because this provided a way of hearing the students' stories, in their own words.

The student's voice

Our commitment was to engage with students and to work with them in a participatory research project, to co-produce stories based on their words. Listening to and engaging with students' voices are integral aspects of emancipatory research (Corbett, 1998). Narrative enquiry enabled us to produce 'richly-detailed expositions of life as lived', which offer 'insight[s] that befit the complexity of human lives' (Josselson, 2006: 4). Tedder (2007: 26) notes that 'understanding an individual's learning career depends crucially on understanding the wider biography within which it is located'. To see the experience 'through the learner's eyes' (Marton and Booth, 1997: 179), we needed to move away from traditional researcher–researched relationships, towards a more relational view (Pinnegar and Daynes, 2007). Connelly and Clandinin (1990) refer to the storying and restorying that occurs as researchers engage with participants' stories, producing a mutually constructed account of enquiry.

An introduction to the cases

The cases in this book were developed over the course of a longitudinal research project that investigated how students from diverse backgrounds succeed in higher education. In this project, students entering an undergraduate degree and studying either on-campus or off-campus (by distance education) were invited to participate if they self-identified as being from non-traditional backgrounds. Participants included students from low socio-economic, non-English-speaking and migrant backgrounds, regional and remote areas, as well as students with a medical condition, or who were first in their family to enter university. While participants' backgrounds and experiences differed, they shared interrupted educational biographies with no clear pathway into higher education.

The students were drawn from a social work undergraduate course, but students from any course might report similar experiences. What perhaps characterises *these* students is the vocabulary and sociological perspective their academic training afforded them in articulating their experiences.

In semi-structured individual interviews, participants discussed their pathways into higher education at the start of their course. While their studies were in progress they commented on how they were managing. Finally, at the end of their course, they reflected on their experiences. The project was undertaken at Monash University, Australia following approval from the University's human ethics committee, which required the informed consent of student participants. It adapted the research design of a similar project at Manchester Metropolitan University (MMU) in the United Kingdom (Kirk, 2006).

The interview questions, focusing on how students succeed, were adapted to the Australian and institutional context from those used in the original study at MMU. The interviews were audiotaped and transcribed, and then sent to each participant for verification. When each set of three interviews was completed, the transcriptions were combined into a single document, again sent to participants for verification, and became the basis of a 'life and learning story', in which each participant explained the challenges she or he had overcome and how they had succeeded in higher education. Initially, course completion (graduation) was used as the primary indicator of success. Subsequent insights gleaned from some of the students who had completed degrees but not regarded their study as successful, led to the inclusion of commitment, satisfaction, and the likelihood that the outcomes of study would change their lives as indicators of success.

These life and learning stories form the basis of the cases presented in the following chapters. They are written in the third person, each with a similar structure based on the three interviews conducted with each participant. We have retained liberal quotations to capture the words of the students as they worked toward successful completion of their studies.

Summary

This chapter has provided a conceptual background for the students' stories that we present in Chapters 2–6. We have defined the key terms that we use in this book, including social inclusion and widening participation, our interpretation of diverse or non-traditional backgrounds, and what we mean by student success. We have provided a broad outline of the trends supporting social inclusion in higher education that are evident in a number of countries, and have shown how these trends are consistent with current educational viewpoints that emphasise the perspectives and empowerment of learners. We have outlined some of the key theoretical influences on the development of this study and acknowledged some of the opportunities and challenges associated with increasing student diversity in higher education, noting some suggested strategies for improving access and retention and some evidence about how students from diverse backgrounds succeed in higher education.

We then discussed the importance of participatory research and of using the student's voice to inform decision-making about managing and supporting student diversity in higher education, showing how this approach was used in developing the students' stories which are included in this casebook. As you read these stories, it is important to bear in mind the background and principles that we have outlined in this chapter in order to consider the relevance of the issues raised by students in your own context, and the implications for your own management and support of student diversity in higher education.

Notes

1. We use the term 'non-English-speaking backgrounds' (NESB) in this book but note the increasing preference for the expression 'culturally and linguistically diverse' to encompass students from a range of backgrounds.
2. In response to widely held dissatisfaction with the postcode method of identifying students' socio-economic status (SES), the Australian Government introduced a blended identifier for low SES people in 2011. The new measure is a mixture of personal financial disadvantage identified by being in receipt of welfare benefit or government income support, and living in a low SES status Census District (a small area of approximately 500 people) based on data collected by the national census. Officially, this is an interim measure. In 2012, the Australian Bureau of Statistics replaced Census Districts with Statistical Areas Level 1 (SA1). The Department of Industry, Innovation, Science, Research and Tertiary Education (DIISRTE) is yet to assess the impact of this change on targets for low SES student participants.

Chapter 1: discussion topics

1. How aware are you of the backgrounds, previous educational experiences, and other interests of students that you work with? What methods do you use to find out about these issues? What additional methods could you use to make you more aware of the issues facing students?
2. How did the students that you work with enter higher education? What were their pathways into university?
3. What effect do you think the entry modes you have identified have on students?
4. What are four strategies that your institution implements to support access to and participation in higher education of students from diverse backgrounds?
5. How could these strategies be improved? (We will return to your response to this question at the end of Chapter 7 so that you can consider whether your views have changed after reading the stories in this book.)

2

Finding the way to higher education: Miranda and Rochelle

Abstract: This chapter highlights the impact of family background and geography on access to higher education. We introduce Miranda and Rochelle, two women who completed their studies as mature age, off-campus (distance education) students living in rural locations at some distance from their university. Their comments draw attention to the different ways that disrupted early schooling experiences affected these women's sense of themselves as learners, and inform their commitment to completing their studies once they enter higher education. Following their stories, we consider the implications for managing the transition to higher education and supporting the first year experience of students enrolling from pathways such as these.

Key words: first generation, first year experience, off-campus study, rural, transition.

Introduction

We begin with the stories of Miranda and Rochelle, using their experiences to focus on the complex pathways to higher education that are often encountered by students who come to university from non-traditional backgrounds. Miranda's and Rochelle's stories, like those that follow in later chapters, provide a wealth of information regarding issues related to managing and supporting student diversity. You may wish to return to their stories as you consider further issues in later chapters.

There are similarities and differences in the ways that Miranda and Rochelle found their way to higher education, and in their perceptions of themselves on this journey. Both were from rural areas, were the first in their families to attend university, and their stories illustrate how serendipitous encounters can have a crucial effect on key decisions that lead to higher education. Miranda, from a single-parent family, developed early confidence in her abilities as a learner, which helped her through various further education courses, eventually resulting in her enrolment in an undergraduate university course. In contrast, Rochelle, from a background where 'everyone's a tradesman', received considerable practical and financial support from her parents but did not perceive herself as a good learner, and her route to university was characterised by lack of information, unsuccessful applications, and a variety of work experiences related to her love of animals. As you read their stories, consider the implications of the experiences revealed in them for managing and supporting the transition of students from similar backgrounds. We will consider further implications for assisting transition in Chapters 3 and 4.

Miranda's story

Pathway to higher education

Miranda was in her mid-thirties and the parent of a school-aged daughter when she started her course. She was the first in her family to attend university. She lived in a rural area, and studied as an off-campus (distance education) student.

Family background

Miranda's parents separated when she was two and she described herself as coming from 'quite a line of solo parents'. She has an older sister and a younger half-sister. Miranda often moved from place to place with her mother when she was young, attending nine different primary schools (the first seven years of school – age approximately 5–12 years):

> I don't really remember a whole lot about primary school – my primary school life or age was marked by my home life, and that was where my focus was.

This constant moving left Miranda feeling as if she was always the 'new kid':

> *... because we always moved, nothing was ever long-term. There was a huge feeling of temporariness about everything that we did ... we knew that we didn't have to worry about things for too long because that would change. So commitment was very difficult.*

As a consequence, Miranda learnt to be independent and to interact 'superficially' with people. With every move to a new location, Miranda's mother would throw out their old possessions:

> *I have one childhood toy – we could take one thing and she was constantly getting rid of our things. She thinks that if you hold on to something for more than a year . . . you're hoarding it. She has like a phobia – she's very much a clean freak.*

Miranda recalled her mother resisting the stigma of single parenthood:

> *... she had a very sterile environment. She fought the assumption a lot that 'single parent – kids probably feral'. And I was born in '69, so it wasn't common to be in a single parent family. Unless the father had died.*

Miranda was aware that she and her family were 'different':

> *I remember when I was about in Grade 5 [the penultimate year of primary school] . . . we were playing chasey [chasings] up the stairs and I remember telling a girl who was in my class that my parents were divorced. And she didn't know what that was.*

Miranda's older sister was 'so rebellious and just so contrary to everything – she was very feisty and fiery':

> *You couldn't say boo – she'd create an argument out of that. She left us when she was 13. She spent a lot of time homeless and couch-surfing . . . [She] still has never held a job and she's 40 now. She's now married. She did have a child. The child was removed through the state when she was 17.*

The removal of her sister's child and the baby's experience of abuse and neglect led Miranda to reflect on her own life experience and developed her awareness that she wanted to contribute to child protection in her later life. She learnt from this 'that safety should be a right, not a privilege'.

Miranda's younger half-sister was born with significant learning difficulties:

> My sister was born with the cord wrapped around her neck several times, and it was quite tight and she was quite blue. And the doctors told my Mum that she does not have the full brain capacity, and it has affected her ability to remember things and stuff like that . . . I don't know if that's environmental or innate . . . [M]y mother's response to that was . . . 'Oh, well . . . don't expect too much from her – she's got this problem.' And I don't know if it's because my sister was told that, plus because she's the baby of the family . . . and so she believed it . . . But she did struggle a bit through school. She passed her Year 11 exams [in the penultimate year of high school] and that was it for schooling. And my Mum was ecstatic about that . . . my sister had to really study hard.

Miranda felt that her family situation contributed to her own stability:

> . . . my Mum and my sister needed me – that's why I was stable. I was the next in line . . . when my Mum was out of action . . . I remember being the adult . . . I had an obligation to my family to stay or what would happen?

Miranda's mother married three times and also had a long-term *de facto* relationship. Miranda did not get along with any of her stepfathers: 'we were happiest without them around. Like when there was just us girls, we were happier then.' Poverty was a continuing issue for this sole-parent family at a time when welfare benefits were not available.

Miranda's mother 'had a nervous breakdown' when Miranda was in her final year of primary school. She relied heavily on Miranda:

> . . . because I'd been the adult of our family unit for a while, she saw me, I think, [as] older than I was . . . she saw me as someone she could soundboard off-against. And that sort of thing.

Miranda had several strong female role models. Her paternal grandmother, who Miranda resembled physically, was a stable, nurturing, warm figure:

> My Nanna was everything. She was the sweetest, kindest woman. She was the only one in my family who – aside from me – has blue

> *eyes ... Nanna ... brought out the importance of nurturing and caring for people and she would take in anyone.*

Miranda's paternal aunt was a determined career woman, who had strong political views:

> *... she has been a very supportive role model in that she's let me see that women can do anything ... you just need to be determined enough ...*

Miranda's mother also taught her the importance of 'manual working skills':

> *... to contribute to society ... you need to get up in the morning, you need to be committed to a job, and go to it and come home at the end of the day and feel you've done a good job.*

Miranda's younger sister demonstrated this family work ethic:

> *Mum's saying that my younger sister ... she's got these problems with memory, she's not going to achieve, go ahead and stuff ... but she's a real good, strong manual worker ... she's been working in the hospitality industry for years now. In the same job. And she's happy and successful in that.*

As role models, all of these women contributed to Miranda's sense that if she was determined enough, she could achieve what she wanted.

Educational experiences

Miranda always believed that she was 'smart'. This perception was reinforced by her mother and various primary school teachers:

> *I did well in primary school. I've always done well in school. No one's ever worried about me, because they all know, 'Oh, she's so smart, she'll be fine, don't worry.' And I always was.*

Her mother constantly stated that she did not have to worry about Miranda and that Miranda 'would be fine':

> *[She] left me to my own devices ... and when she spoke of me, to me, or about me, it was always, 'Miranda's fine. Miranda's fine.*

> *She's smart. She'll catch on and she gets it – she gets things straight away and she lands on her feet.'* . . . *They probably thought I would end up somewhere – like I would do something. I think they expected some further study, some sort of career, but I don't know that they ever thought I would have gone to university. Because I am the first one in my family to go to university.*

Miranda had few memories of primary school because of the constant moving. The possessions that her mother was constantly throwing out included school books, so Miranda and her sisters were never able to take books from one school to the next.

After her itinerant primary school education, Miranda stayed at one secondary school. She refused to move:

> . . . *even though my Mum made us move house, and we moved a significant distance from my high school, I still would not leave my high school. I had a really great bunch of friends there and [was] doing really well academically . . . And I was not prepared to give it up. So I would . . . leave home at six in the morning, catch two buses – a bus into the city and a bus out to my high school, to get there by nine, or ten to nine. And I wouldn't get home till after five at night, but I was determined I was not changing schools. I refused to change high school.*

Miranda felt accepted by her peer group at secondary school, was academically competent, and successful at sport and drama. In contrast to her primary school experiences, '[h]ighlights were all the time. Getting boyfriends and feeling accepted by my peers, and all that stuff.'

In the first year of high school, Miranda wanted to be a psychiatrist, but this ambition was quashed by her friends who said 'you'd have to be crazy, because you have to deal with crazy people.'

Miranda left school at the end of her penultimate year of high school to escape a family life of conflict with her latest stepfather. She worked at a supermarket full-time for a year, and then started studying hospitality and tourism at a further education college to 'see what else there was to life'. She was too young to work in hospitality when she completed the course, so she worked in a department store, and then in a restaurant. At 19, Miranda went grape-picking with her husband-to-be, and then they moved into a house together. Miranda returned to further education and completed a women's studies course, which gave her insight into her own and her family's circumstances. She also 'started volunteering':

> ... my Mum had been volunteering ... she ... went into community services too ... in her forties ... [through her nervous breakdown] she gained a lot of information, through counselling, about self-help.

Miranda then undertook a community studies certificate. She married and gave birth to her daughter and this led her into early childhood studies at a further education college and then a diploma at a regional university:

> I worked in that for a while. But at the same time I was having my child and seeing to my child and she was little, and then my own marriage ended when my child was nearly three. So there was a bit of a pattern, perhaps. From there I ran a crèche for a while at a local gym.

Encouraged by a Salvation Army officer she met at a job network, Miranda applied for a 'government job' as a Rural Youth Information Service Officer. Without that encouragement, she would not have had the courage to apply:

> ... fate dealt a hand or something. I don't know. We just got talking about the position, about what I'd done, and he said, 'Just try!' ... [I] would never have considered even looking at a job like that. It had a government stamp on the top.

After 'a couple of years' in this job, Miranda felt the need for further information on the issues confronting the young people she worked with. She gained admission to a degree in community welfare, which she completed by distance education. Miranda then became aware that she was ineligible to work in child protection in her home state without a social work degree, so she applied for and was accepted into her current course.

Miranda believed that her mother's ability to change and move taught her determination and pluck to take chances and meet challenges as she worked towards achieving her educational goals:

> I think I got some foundations for entering university ... Mum, with all her faults, she's never afraid to move on and to try something new. We always embraced change. Newness. So that's where I get my pluck!

Miranda commenced the course believing that she was a capable learner:

> *I think that the expectation that I was smart ... went a long way into me getting here, because I believed them.*

Managing study

Planning

Miranda stated that the key to her success in studying was planning:

> *I needed to have a chat with my daughter. I always sit her down at the beginning of the year. And let her know my work plans and my responsibilities to her as well as to my workload and my employment and whatever else – other commitments. And I check in with her to make sure she feels that's OK, or whether she thinks she's going to need a little more of my time.*

She also 'had a chat with my fiancé ... because he's not really used to what my workload might be'.

Miranda acknowledged that there are sacrifices in studying:

> *... my daughter has just made school captain ... and I missed it, because I'm here [at a residential workshop]. And you know, I felt like I've missed a milestone ... so it's one of the sacrifices that I make to do this, and in the long run she'll see that this is what you have to do – you have to work hard and do things to reach the goals that you've set yourself.*

For Miranda, part of her planning involved balancing commitments. This involved juggling her part-time workload and her financial commitments, including her mortgage repayments, as well as her responsibilities to her daughter.

Managing

Miranda studied in the evening after her daughter was in bed, on weekends, and occasionally at work. To manage the demands on her time, she was assignment-focused:

> *I look at the question ... and I'll write out as much as I know about it already and I try to make a plan of the things I'm going to need to look up, and I'll just get to the point. I don't read anything I don't*

> *have to read ... If I have to research a particular thing, I will break that down. I will look at the things that I don't know and I'll research those and then I'll look at the things that I do know and I'll find supporting academic references for that.*

These demands required her to be 'very efficient in [her] time management', developing strategic reading skills:

> *I think you learn to cull things a lot – you're a lot harsher as you get older. Well, I have been. I'll cull out the things I don't need and then wade through them to see what I can take ... I read the end of [a book] first, like backwards, and I'll only read the relevant bits. I can't remember the last time I read a whole book, cover to cover ... I don't think I have since I was pregnant, I think, which was 13 years ago, 14 years ago ... I never read an entire book: I only read what I need.*

Miranda used a computer as she studied:

> *I need to be taking notes because it's solution-focused reading, it really is. It's not reading for the pleasure or the fun of it. I need to be able to make notes there and then and I don't like to deface books.*

While she was studying, Miranda had become engaged, bought a house, and her daughter got a puppy. She refused to let these life changes impact on her study:

> *... you have to have the attitude of, 'it's a priority'. It's like work. It's like my daughter – it's up there – it's important to me ... I've never thought of giving up. I won't. Difficult times come and go, but that's life, I think. Nothing ... [has] made me want to give up.*

Miranda did not face any particular problems with her study, seeking clarification 'on the odd occasion' from the appropriate subject adviser, and reporting that she received the advice that she needed.

She studied by distance education:

> *I'm very used to being an off-campus student. In fact, I prefer it. I don't think I could work as well, as efficiently, within the confines of attending daily ... I need the flexibility to be able to work and pay*

my mortgage now and to support my daughter – I really need the flexibility of external studies.

Support

Miranda received support from family, friends, university staff, and her employer. Key sources of support were her mother and her fiancé:

I have to admit that I would be dead in the water without my Mum and my partner – my fiancé. They just help out here, there and everywhere . . . like my daughter will walk to my Mum's house two nights a week, because I know I'm working back . . . That sort of thing . . . she goes there after school and stuff like that because she hates going to out-of-school hours care . . . [My fiancé], he'll give up his weekends to come out and watch her in the rain – play netball and stuff like that . . . and you know I might take a book out and he'll tell me, 'Oh, she's got the ball, she's going for a goal,' or something so I can check and see the good bits.

However, there were some limitations to family support:

. . . my family are supportive but I'm the first one in my family to pursue tertiary education so the support was there, but the level of understanding wasn't.

Miranda appreciated the support of one particular friend because she shared a similar experience of off-campus study:

. . . I've got a very close friend who has also studied externally in a different course . . . our friendship entailed something different than I had with anybody else around here because she was studying at university level and so was I. So she could relate to me a lot better and we supported each other quite a bit and she's also a sole parent too . . . and working part-time as well, so up against the same sort of things . . .

Miranda felt that university staff supported her learning:

I think that they offered me as much information as I needed to fulfil my requirements as a student . . . and they conveyed that

> *information to me fairly well, so ... I haven't really got any complaints about my education and support.*

She did not seek additional support from the university:

> *I didn't really know that there would be any there that would be appropriate for me. I didn't think I really required additional support. So I didn't really look into it.*

Miranda summed up her sources of support as follows:

> *I have a supportive team at work. I've had a really supportive boss ... he's been wonderful. And the fact that I get study leave to come to residentials – it means that there's no interruption on the income flow. A really supportive family, they're all proud of me. And supportive university staff, so yeah, I'm getting support from everywhere. I feel really supported.*

Reflections and future plans

Miranda completed her degree in the minimum time, continuing to work part-time while she studied, from two and a half to four days per week. At course completion she continued her half-time position (two and a half days per week) and began another position with an identical time commitment.

Reflecting on her experience at the conclusion of her degree, Miranda stated that though her studies did not change her as a learner, she became more efficient in her time management skills and increased her knowledge and her status in the workplace. These increased her confidence in herself as a professional:

> *I am more confident in the workplace now because I have an entitlement to do certain things that I didn't have before ... if you're not a [graduate] ... you can't write certain reports and you don't have these certain duties and responsibilities, and so that certainly boosts my confidence ... knowing that I have an entitlement to do these things that goes along with the role.*

Miranda appreciated 'the learning that [she] gained' from the course, particularly her ability to apply it in her workplace ('I love doing that').

As a result, she planned to undertake postgraduate study in the near future:

> ... probably ten years ago I wouldn't have said I would have had the courage ... to actually go out and study ... I mean ten years ago I didn't have any degrees ... I've done ... quite a bit of [further education] study and stuff like that but, as far as university study, ten years ago, I wouldn't have thought to – I wouldn't have had the courage to.

Miranda also felt she needed to spend the next few years providing stability for her now adolescent daughter:

> ... [I'll] then review where I'm at once she's off to uni and I've got more time on my hands, I suppose. I would be looking at doing some community development work in a developing country. I would love to do that.

Miranda felt that the key to her success was that:

> I'm extremely stubborn and I would just keep going ... I take a long time to make a decision, but once I do, I don't tend to move from it ... I've got a bizarre competitive streak ... that's quite motivating in itself ... [competitive] with just myself ... to [achieve] my new personal best.

Rochelle's story

Pathway to higher education

Rochelle, a mature age student in her early thirties, came from a regional town in a remote part of Australia. She lived there with her parents until her final year of secondary school, when she moved several hundred kilometres away to a school near the capital city of her state to undertake her last year of schooling.

Family background

Rochelle was the first in her family to go to university. Neither of her parents had any experience of education beyond high school. Her father was a tradesman, and her only brother was also a tradesman:

Finding the way to higher education

> ... I come from a town where everyone becomes a tradesman ... everyone's a tradesman, everyone's hands-on. My brother's a tradesman, my Dad's a tradesman ... it's really sort of earthy you know ... I just reckon all the girls are hairdressers and all the boys are boilermakers.

The 'tradesman story' is a recurring motif in Rochelle's narrative.

Educational experiences

During her primary school years, Rochelle was 'always a middle of the road student':

> I was never really interested and if I felt like I couldn't do something, I ... just sort of snuck away from it ... I never thought I was bright enough. I never thought I had the ability to learn, or the ability to get any better, and so I chose not to try very hard.

Neither her parents, nor her teachers, had any expectations of Rochelle and they did not challenge her about her perceptions of herself as a learner. She, too, did not challenge this view of herself:

> [I] just didn't think I was smart enough. Just thought, 'That's it. That's how I am. That's how it is.'

Rochelle was content to be a 'bit of a daydreamer', and thought more about horses than school work when she was at school. She had always loved animals and thought she would work with them when she grew up.

Rochelle attended the Catholic secondary school in her home town, although she found the presence of boys at her co-educational school a distraction. She enjoyed this time, as she liked being around people, but once again, she did not really try hard at school, and continued to be a C or D grade student:

> ... you went there and hung [out] with your mates and came home. You didn't worry about studying. It was a tradesman's town.

Rochelle's parents were disappointed in her approach to school work and thought she was 'hanging around with the wrong people'. When her parents sent her to boarding school for the final year of high school, she was happy – she was able to take her horse with her, and she could study agricultural science subjects. Again, Rochelle said she did not do any work. Having decided that she did not need to achieve a high final year school examination score, Rochelle concentrated on the agricultural science subjects that she enjoyed:

> ... I don't know how I passed ... I didn't need a [high tertiary entrance] score. I didn't need one of those. So I just didn't bother ... I never thought I was smart enough to be a vet. Never, ever, ever, thought that. But I liked that industry and I liked working with animals ...

Rochelle tailored her academic performance to suit her goal, which was to work with animals as a veterinary nurse. However, she had underestimated the entry requirements for veterinary nursing courses offered at further education colleges, and failed to gain a place:

> ... I didn't get in. So I was devastated ... I couldn't believe that I didn't get in, so I went back ... home.

Upon moving back to her home town, Rochelle enrolled in an environmental science course at her local further education college, and lived in a caravan. Again, she 'didn't really study'. Her grandmother died, and she withdrew from the course after the first semester. This affected her deeply:

> ... I felt like a real failure ... I've never pulled out of anything! And it still bothers me that I pulled out ... I still don't like telling that bit of the story – that I pulled out. I didn't like pulling out ... [when you] start something you should finish it.

Even through this difficult time, the desire to be a veterinary nurse stayed with Rochelle. She returned to study to get a better tertiary entrance score, while working one day a week as a volunteer at a veterinary clinic. This time she succeeded in gaining entry to a veterinary nursing course and moved back to the city to study.

Once again Rochelle's parents were very supportive of her education, funding her attendance at a university residential college for the first years of the veterinary nursing course.

> They have been really good – my parents basically. They're the ones that funded it all.

Initially, she did not want to go to the residential college in the city, feeling:

> *I wasn't as good as them [the other students]. They're uni students and I'm only a [further education] student.*

In time, Rochelle came to appreciate what the college offered her in terms of a supportive study environment, particularly through her friendships with fellow college students.

These friendships helped to boost Rochelle's self-confidence and override the influences of her home town:

> *They just made me feel like I could do it. I could actually walk into a uni. Because it's **terrifying** , that stuff . . . You've never been smart in school, you never thought of doing . . . a uni subject and you thought that you would never do one.*

Rochelle obtained a job in her home town and completed, with difficulty, the remainder of the course by distance education. She 'didn't have the right attitude' and it took a long time. She then worked for five years, including some time on cattle stations (large outback cattle farms), and travelled overseas. On her return, she moved to an isolated city in another part of Australia and again worked as a veterinary nurse.

About this time Rochelle began to feel frustrated that she wasn't 'using her brain':

> *I don't know why I decided I wanted to study. I don't consciously know why. I just thought I wanted to study something . . . even though I still didn't think I had a brain.*

Rochelle was living by herself in another part of the country, and began to consider re-enrolling in the environmental science course she discontinued when her grandmother died:

> *. . . because I liked cattle stations and I liked cattle and horses and . . . hands-on stuff, that's why I think I thought environmental science was the way to go.*

Although Rochelle was clear that she wanted to enrol in a course so that she could be 'using her brain', her knowledge of her options was limited to the careers she had seen in her home town, and in the isolated city where she worked as a veterinary nurse:

> *And I never thought [about] anything – you know, on the other side. Humanities, or anything like that. And [I] didn't even know what humanities were, you know.*

During this time, Rochelle had one male friend who 'was really inspirational' and had studied at post-secondary level. He and a female friend encouraged her to believe she had skills and abilities. Rochelle applied to enrol in the environmental science course and moved back to her home town and lived with her parents. Her application was not successful. Once again, Rochelle was 'devastated':

> *So I just went, 'Oh my God! What am I going to do now? I didn't get in. And I'm back at home and I'm nearly 30, and I live with my parents and I don't know what I'm doing.'*

Her parents persuaded her to visit a branch of a regional university in her home town. There Rochelle met a staff member who was 'so . . . energetic and inspiring', and helped her to see what was possible:

> *. . . 'You can do it!' That's what she said to me. Just having that inspired you and then also empowered you, I suppose . . . And she made it sound fantastic . . . 'You do some study . . . live at home . . . [It will] be fantastic' . . . so she made a positive out of living at home.*

Reflecting on the skills that this woman had, and on the impact of meeting someone who really inspired her, Rochelle recognised that she had reached a point where she was ready to be inspired, admitting, 'I was obviously receptive to that at the time, too.' Persuaded that what she had to do was 'just start somewhere', Rochelle passed an English competency test and started studying social science in her home town.

During this time she was supported by a mentor who 'really looked after' her. Rochelle was working in a government department where she met a woman who went to university when she was 50. This woman provided support and encouragement, and most importantly for Rochelle, helped her understand better her experience of study:

> *If you're in that environment I feel you're all right. You get encouraged. And you don't lose heart. But if you end up out of that*

environment, where no one understands you, and you can't relate to anyone [it is difficult].

Soon afterwards, a part-time community work position became available in another regional town, which she commenced. This led Rochelle to think she would like to study social work. She enrolled as an off-campus student, which meant she could continue to live at home with her parents.

Managing study

Planning

Enrolling as an off-campus student in a remote area of the country, a long way from the university, provided Rochelle with some challenges.

First, she needed to re-organise her work schedule. She took up work as a track rider, exercising race horses for three and a half hours per day, six mornings a week. She also had to re-organise her responsibilities at home and her finances. In addition to arranging travel and accommodation for her visits to the university so she could attend the compulsory on-campus residential workshops, she had to meet the considerable costs involved. Because of the large distance between her home town and the university campus, the cost of Rochelle's airfares was high. She also had to find the money to pay for accommodation while she was on campus.

Managing

As well as riding track work six days a week, Rochelle developed a routine of going to the local library and treating this study time as a working day:

> *I'm flat out from 4.00 [am] on, then I crash – [I] have two things – family and study. I manage by locking myself in the [municipal] library and by treating study as a work day. [My] family don't necessarily understand this [i.e. that study is work].*

In addition to managing the costs associated with the mandatory course residential workshops, Rochelle had to purchase expensive text books, as there was no library access for students from that university in her remote regional town.

Self-doubt was another barrier Rochelle felt she had to overcome, especially the feeling that 'you're doing it but you don't really believe that you are'. She felt that university was somewhere she did not belong:

> *You just don't even know the language, the uni language. You just don't know anything when you're not part of it. You're not part of the culture. I've never been part of uni culture.*

Juggling study and work was also a challenge for Rochelle, particularly accommodating two 70-day compulsory unpaid work placements. In spite of this, she commented that there were no really difficult times. Midway through her course, Rochelle reported that she had never felt like giving up because:

> *I'm more confident, more aware of values. I feel there is light at the end of the tunnel. I'm more than half way through the course.*

Support

As she was first in her family to attend university, Rochelle's family were not able to share or understand her experiences as a student:

> *Because I studied ... those heavy subjects ... that challenged my thought processes ... I had no one to talk to, because I studied by myself.*

Nevertheless, her parents supported her to live at home with them, although they were not altogether comfortable with her choice of course:

> *Dad really questions – especially social work, you know. 'Why would you want to hang out with those people?'*

Rochelle was supported during her first professional placement by her placement supervisor and peers and friends. She felt very affirmed when she was offered a position with the host agency. This helped her to maintain her confidence both in herself and in her decision to study social work.

Rochelle felt she would have benefited from contact with the university during both placements. She missed the opportunity to tell her lecturers how she was faring: 'I was really disappointed with the lack of contact during my 14-week placement.' There was no contact from her supervisors: 'No one [from the university] asked, "How are you going?"

I could have done anything.' Rochelle also felt that assessments could have been better timed and organised, so that they did not clash with finishing the placement: 'Instructions were not written down. It was very stressful.'

Rochelle did not access any of the university's support services. She was able to get some library books through the regional university, which had a study centre in her home town and she also used their facilities.

Reflections and future plans

Rochelle successfully completed her course and found professional employment soon after. Looking back over her student experience, she considered that the most important gain for her during her course was her belief in herself as a competent learner and the accompanying growth in confidence. Prior to the course, she had 'no confidence in my ability to learn', but this grew as she progressed:

> *I started passing subjects, so started to grow in confidence . . . in the end [I] would give anything a go! It's not rocket science! . . . After first year, once you have passed Year 1, you're OK . . .*

Some of the challenges she faced as an off-campus student from a remote rural town, such as going to the university for residential workshops, built her confidence: 'having to come all the way to [an interstate city] was a big spin out'.

Having access to the library of the regional university's study centre in her home town was of great assistance. This university provided study space and did not charge for materials posted from the main library. On the continued lack of support from her own university during her placements, Rochelle commented:

> *[There was] no follow up – didn't improve on the second placement . . . [there were] no checks on how I was going or what I was doing.*

She was sad to finish the course, and thought she might undertake further study, perhaps a Diploma of Education, sometime in the future. Having graduated, she felt she would 'give anything a go if I want to do it'.

Implications for managing and supporting student diversity: transition to higher education and the first year experience

Miranda's and Rochelle's stories of entering higher education illustrate a number of factors that may affect students from diverse backgrounds. Among these are the varying levels of confidence in their learning ability on entering university and the complex routes they undertake in getting there, compared with school leavers. This, in turn, means that such students are often older; their age may be the only feature that visibly distinguishes them from other (school leaver) students. The barriers they have overcome to enter higher education, and which may continue to affect their studies, are not always evident. Those who do reach university tend to be well-organised and highly committed. These women's stories also show the value of sometimes serendipitous expressions of support by others outside the university or the immediate family or friendship circle, in contributing towards participation and success.

Both Miranda and Rochelle were first generation students – that is, first in their family to experience a university education. This played out in ways which were evident even before they enrolled. Their stories show the importance of family support, which can take the form of emotional support, affirmation, financial support, and child care, among others, but their families did not understand what university study involved. Rochelle, herself, had no prior understanding of how university worked. This situation highlights the role of cultural capital in students' alignment and adjustment, or lack of adjustment, to educational values and ways of operating (Bourdieu, 1986). A student's family background can mean that they have no affinity with academic approaches, or feel unentitled to participate, as reflected in Rochelle's comment, 'I've never been part of uni culture.'

Studies undertaken in the UK (Leathwood and O'Connell, 2003; Read et al., 2003) found that students from non-traditional backgrounds were surprised at how little supervision they were given at university, as Rochelle experienced during her work placements. Not knowing the 'uni language' and not having anyone she could ask made her transition to university more difficult. Successful transition is also compromised for students when they don't know what is expected in assignments or how to structure academic writing. As Rochelle observed: 'Instructions were not written down. It was very stressful.'

Miranda felt that she gained all the support she needed for her studies. Her employer gave her study leave to attend the residential workshops, she had good support from teaching staff, and she did not seek assistance from the institution beyond this, but Rochelle identified some gaps in university support. A noteworthy characteristic of both these students was that they were studying by distance mode, which gave them flexibility to study successfully while remaining in their local communities, close to their families, local employment opportunities, and other forms of support.

So what implications for managing and supporting student diversity are suggested by Miranda's and Rochelle's stories, particularly to assist students in their transition to higher education and support them during their first year of study?

As entry to higher education becomes more accessible to greater numbers of people, the pressure on institutions to prepare and support students towards success has increased. There is a growing body of literature exploring the particular needs of first year university students (e.g. Crosling, 2003; Kift et al., 2010; Krause et al., 2005). Students like Miranda and Rochelle, who face additional pressures associated with their path to university, highlight the importance of management and support by practitioners within higher education institutions. Yorke (2008) confirms differences in the first year experience of relatively advantaged and disadvantaged students and the impact of factors such as ethnicity, lack of financial security, and cultural capital on the latter group's experience. Klinger and Murray note that language is a factor affecting students from non-traditional backgrounds. Even though most of them are native speakers, many 'exhibit language that does not align with the academy's expectations' (Klinger and Murray, 2012: 27).

Emphasising the importance of the link between teaching and support which we noted in Chapter 1, Kift et al. (2010: 1) suggest that it appears particularly important for institutions to adopt a 'transition pedagogy' where the first year experience is regarded as 'everybody's business' and addressed through 'an intentionally designed curriculum by seamless partnerships of academic and professional staff in a whole-of-institution transformation'.

Some enablers to successful university transition include the availability of student support services, accessibility of information technology services, the usefulness of resources, and the relevance of study material and study skills support, as well as creating a strong campus culture and atmosphere, and encouraging peer and academic learning communities (McInnis, 2002). These activities can be incorporated in the holistic 'everybody's business' approach to transition pedagogy proposed above, which has the benefit of including proactive support for students from all backgrounds.

Crosling et al. (2008) suggested that academic staff consider such strategies as:

- establishing early engagement with students through pre- and post-entry induction activities;
- finding out about students so that this information can inform the program and curricula;
- developing authentic and relevant curricula building on students' experiences, using inclusive language and relevant examples;
- designing and implementing student-centred active learning;
- integrating study skills (as above) to support the success of all students, with signposting to other support services as necessary; and
- providing relevant, timely, and constructive formative feedback.

The involvement of academic and departmental professional staff appears to be particularly important in guiding students to appropriate support services (or bringing support services to the students) because, as we have seen from the stories of Miranda and Rochelle, students may not seek these out. While many students may be sufficiently persistent to succeed without additional support, it is the students who are at risk who are likely to benefit. Simply finding out about students that you come in contact with, and adopting a friendly and approachable manner, are important strategies in themselves, especially during students' first few weeks at university. Note how Rochelle responded to the people who mentored her prior to her enrolment.

Summary

Miranda's and Rochelle's stories illustrate the diverse pathways that students might take into higher education. The factors that make their pathways into higher education so complex – such as low socio-economic background, having no one in their family with experience of higher education, and living in a rural or remote location – influence their studies in an ongoing way. Factors such as these must be explicitly addressed to support students' participation and success. Students draw on a range of personal qualities to succeed, but structural issues need to be addressed and adequate support provided by university staff to maximise students' potential for success.

We have focused on some of the implications for managing and supporting students from non-traditional backgrounds during their transition to university and their first year. You may think of others that may be particularly relevant for you in your institution. As we noted earlier, we will refer to some further implications in Chapters 3 and 4. Consider the discussion topics that follow.

Chapter 2: discussion topics

1. Think about your role in your institution. What strategies are you and your colleagues already using to manage and support students from non-traditional backgrounds in their transition to higher education? Are they working? How can you tell? If you don't think they are working, why not? What else could you do?
2. Now consider the questions above but specifically in relation to first generation students. Are there any issues that these students face which you have not addressed? If so, what could you do to assist these students?
3. If you are teaching students such as Miranda and Rochelle, what additional teaching and support strategies could you consider using in the first weeks of the course? If you are in a student support role, or another role where you come in contact with students regularly, what additional strategies could you use?
4. Make a list of the demands students face in coming to university that are relevant for your role. Are some students better able to meet those than others, due to their life circumstances? How can you and your colleagues support *all* students to meet these demands?

Chapter 3: discussion topics

3

This time it's different: Sesh and Shannon

Abstract: This chapter provides further perspectives on the impact of family background and geography on access to higher education. In it we present the stories of Sesh and Shannon, a woman and a man who both initially commenced university as school leavers but did not proceed to graduation. Their comments show how their subsequent experiences led to their current, successful enrolment as mature, self-reliant learners, proceeding without the assistance of university support services. We use their stories to focus on the implications for retention of students from diverse backgrounds. We consider whether Sesh and Shannon could have been assisted to continue during their earlier attempts at study, and what this means for your own practice.

Key words: first generation, gender, low socio-economic status, off-campus study, student engagement, transition, retention, rural.

Introduction

In this chapter we introduce Sesh and Shannon, a woman and a man with rural backgrounds and similar pathways to higher education: both commenced university study as school leavers but did not finish their courses. Their reasons for discontinuation were different. Sesh made three very brief attempts to begin a university course but withdrew each time, despite having been a good student at secondary school. She considered that her efforts at secondary school related more to escaping pressures at home than to natural ability. She was the first in her family to attend university and this, together with other factors such as her rural background, contributed to her withdrawal from university. Shannon regarded himself as a good student throughout his schooling and his first attempt at higher education continued into the second year of study but ceased when he became a parent at a young age.

Sesh and Shannon then worked for several years before becoming students again. For Sesh, this involved finding a clearer sense of direction in her life and overcoming family pressures, though before her success in her current course she reluctantly completed another degree. Shannon's sense of direction also became clearer before he returned to study. He was motivated by the need for qualifications to increase his income and, with a partner and two young children, by the need to 'set myself up'. Like Sesh, he returned to study via another course, though for him it was a positive experience which enabled him to meet prerequisites for the course he eventually completed.

As with the stories of Miranda and Rochelle, Sesh and Shannon throw light on a range of factors influencing the success in higher education of students from diverse backgrounds. You might consider the implications for managing and supporting student diversity that emerge from Sesh's journey, particularly relating to strategies she put in place to overcome adverse factors from her background. Or you may find it helpful to consider the implications for other students of the detailed information Shannon provided about how he combined his study, work and family responsibilities, and managed to finance his university studies.

Like Miranda and Rochelle, neither Sesh nor Shannon depended on university services for support in successfully completing their degrees. Sesh's peers were her primary source of support, while for Shannon support came mainly from his workplace and his family. You could think about what this means for managing and supporting student diversity in higher education. In particular, you might consider what their stories tell us about retention of students from diverse backgrounds, as this will be the focus of the implications that we address later in the chapter. If you had encountered one of these students during their initial attempts at university study, is there anything you could have done to prevent their withdrawal? Or were the factors adversely affecting their continuation outside the control of university staff?

Sesh's story

Pathway to higher education

Sesh was a young woman in her twenties when she enrolled in the course that she successfully completed. She was the first in her family to attend university.

Family background

Sesh has a younger brother and her mother is from a small island nation. Gendered stereotypes impacted on her family's expectations of her. In her primary school years, '[t]here was a lot of expectation on my brother to perform really well. There wasn't so much on me.' The attitudes of both of her parents reflected these traditional gender roles:

> *[My mother had] . . . a really strong expectation that whatever he [my father] says goes . . . my Dad is very strong and has always been the sort of person where he's had to rely on himself. So making sure that my brother had those skills . . . was very important for him. Whereas me, he probably thought . . . I should be following my mother's role. Like it's the Mum's job to look after the daughter . . .*

As a result, 'it's not like I was ignored – it's just . . . do what you want'. All Sesh wanted to do was ride horses.

Her life changed when her parents separated just before the start of secondary school:

> *. . . my brother lived with my Mum for a while, so it was just me and my Dad. And because we lived in a country town then, I was given a horse to look after . . . So I had the horse . . . but . . . coming home from school, I needed to be home at a certain time. If I wasn't . . . I was in a **lot** of trouble. And I usually had to be inside the door . . . straight after school . . . So, yeah, it was just me and my horse and my Dad.*

Further changes occurred when her brother moved back home, and then she acquired a stepmother who 'wasn't very nice':

> *. . . while it was just me, him and [my brother] it was . . . all right . . . we learnt to get along. Because Dad was always so hard it was*

> *... a matter of working out how to compromise with him and stuff like that. But when she [my stepmother] ... entered the picture ... she was supposed to be the person that we negotiated with. Not with him any more. And she wasn't up for negotiation. She would say what she said and that was it. She ... [went] to my Dad with a different story. So I learnt ... at that point, to play by her rules.*

Sesh began to work hard and achieve well at secondary school to avoid the problems at home.

Educational experiences

Sesh began primary school at a 'big school' in the city but then moved to the country. The experience of a big school 'meant that I was used to having lots of people around' with the later result that going to university 'was still confronting, but it wasn't nearly as bad as it could have been'.

Sesh did not recall much about her primary school days, or what she wanted to do when she grew up:

> *... there was no real stress at all. I wasn't an outstanding student or anything like that ... I don't think I ... lagged behind – but I certainly wasn't up with the main group ... I just wanted a horse. That was my main focus all the way through primary school and a lot of the way through high school. That's all I wanted was a horse.*

But she remembered differences in the expectations and aspirations of children at her city and country primary schools:

> *... in the city ... [t]hey had dreams, whereas in the country ... you're expected to get married and have kids and become a farmer's wife or something like that.*

Due to the changes in her family life, secondary school became very important to Sesh for social support. She worked hard:

> *... because I didn't want to get too involved with what was going on with family, the main excuse I had was to do my homework. So when I didn't have a horse, or when there was no horse there, I would be staying in my room and I would be doing homework in there, just to avoid everything else.*

Her father also placed a lot of emphasis on her academic progress:

And my Dad [would say] . . . 'Why didn't you get an A+ for science and why didn't you get an A+ for maths?' So he was really maths and science focused . . . so I just excelled at that, because . . . I had to – if you didn't, you got into a lot of trouble for it . . . I wasn't a high achiever through being intelligent. I was a high achiever just because I put the time and the effort in. . . .

Sesh's achievements at secondary school then increased her parents' expectations of her, which was a change from their expectations in her primary school years:

My Mum was very much, 'You're the smart one' . . . it became obvious during high school – she wanted me to get the money up. Because I think she felt that I was the most responsible one out of me and my brother and that I would be the one to look after her. Because, being from her background, the kids look after the parent. And because our family was poor I think she would have been – she still is – a bit concerned about where she's going to go. So . . . from probably about the stage when I was 14, 15, she was like, 'You've got to work hard so you can get a really good job and buy a house.' She didn't actually say, 'Buy a house' . . .

Friends and teachers at Sesh's secondary school helped her deal with her problems at home. One friend suggested that she 'write a diary to deal with all the stuff at home', and as a result, her English improved. Sesh was referred to the school counsellor at the end of her fourth year of high school (age 16) to help her cope with the pressure of expectations that she felt from her parents to achieve good grades:

Everyone knew – because it was like a small town – so everyone knows everyone else's business. So . . . the teachers knew that I'd be worried about getting a [good] grade because . . . they'd met my Dad before . . . everyone [including my friends] was like . . . 'If she wants to do her homework during the lunch break then let her do it. And then when she wants to . . . come out with us, then she can.' So it wasn't a big deal.

At the end of that year Sesh's peer group consisted of a number of girls who wanted to do well at school. Sesh found this group very supportive ('we got very competitive ... we were supposed to be the smart kids'). The group found the demands of the last two years of secondary school more difficult, and some struggled:

> I just didn't get too emotionally involved ... You know that you're trying your hardest anyway ... I'm already getting it from home, so there's no point in taking it to school as well ... up until that point, no one else had really been struggling to ... get the best grade, whereas I had been doing that ... most of the way through, so it was ... more comforting having them there, who were also struggling to get the best grade because ... I was normal then. I felt like ... these guys are actually getting what I'm getting.

Sesh continued studying maths and science to appease her father, even though 'I just couldn't get the concepts' and 'English was my best subject.' At that stage, with her experience of horses, she wanted to be a veterinarian:

> ... [but] that required ... really high grades ... And looking back I think that was too much of a pressure ... I don't think I was ever going to be a veterinarian.

Sesh regarded her teachers and friends as role models. Her physics and maths teacher 'was a massive support', driving her on weekends to visit her mother who lived in another country town 'because he used to drive down to [the city] every weekend, so it was on the way'. This teacher would discuss the physics concepts that Sesh found difficult. Another teacher drove Sesh and another student to attend a university 'taster' program where students went to lectures and experienced university life for a week.

Sesh later became aware of the obstacles to success of attending a country school:

> ... we didn't really have that many resources. I really only found [that] out when I first came to uni ... Everyone here knew how to write. I'm not a very good writer. How to form an argument in an essay. Didn't really know how to do that ... I had no idea what they were talking about. I remember getting my first essay back and them saying, 'Where's your argument?' And I thought, 'What are you talking about? It's all an argument.' So skills like that, the English teacher didn't really focus on.

Sesh considered her parents to be another obstacle to success:

> ... They were a big pressure ... The teachers never put a lot of pressure on me to do well. It was my parents. I don't think they realised how much pressure ... there were quite a few times when I'd get a grade that wasn't the best and it would actually affect how I felt about myself really badly. It was when I got home, whether I should tell Dad about it or not ... If he'd pushed much more, I probably would have just packed it all in.

Attitudes towards gender also impacted on Sesh's experience of secondary school:

> ... particularly the girls – it was just, 'Oh, why do you have to try?' One girl was happy to get a C ... and it wasn't that she wasn't smart – it was just ... 'What am I going to do with this after school anyway?' ... because there was always the expectation that we would all end up getting married and having kids by the time we were 25 anyway. So ... it was just, 'Well, what's the point?' The boys were a little bit different. They were expected to do a little bit better, only because the teachers said they needed to be able to read because of the catalogue they must use on the farm ... So it was ... more of a country thing, I think!

After completing school, Sesh was offered a place in a science-based course at a university in a regional city, but she left after only three weeks:

> ... I look back and ... it was bound to happen ... I'm in this weird city, I don't know anyone. No one really seems to be that interested in me ... I had to hand in my assignment. I didn't get the grade that I thought I would get. And it was my fault ... the expectation ... from the lecturers was different. The social environment was different. And just being in a big city and feeling like I didn't have the support of my family. I basically said to my Mum, 'Look I've got into [ ] University' ... And she says, 'Oh good.' 'And so ... how am I going to get down there?' She goes, 'I don't know. Take the train?' 'Well, where am I going to live then, Mum?' 'I don't know, where do you want to live?'

Sesh went to the university student services office where she was given a list of houses:

> ... so I just called up one of them and it was with an elderly lady and another student in this house. But that in itself was really confronting ... because I'd ... never thought I'd see myself living in a house with people I didn't know. That was a bit scary for me at that stage ...

Sesh went back to her mother after three weeks:

> And she was very angry with me. She was [saying], 'Get back to uni. Go back to uni.' And I was [saying], 'No, what for?'

Sesh contacted another university in the town where her mother now lived:

> ... they said, 'Oh, we've got a place in arts if you want to do arts' ... So I lasted probably about another three weeks in that. Dropped out of that and then Mum [was] ... not very happy with me at all. My Dad said, 'Oh, well I told you so!' ... because I moved down to my Mum's place. As opposed to my Dad's place ... The next year I still felt that pressure to go to uni. Tried doing a science degree. I think I finished a semester of that. Before I dropped out. Because it was still all this science stuff ... Like I had to keep on doing what my Dad told me to do, and I didn't feel like I could do anything else.

Sesh then moved to the city 'for work, not for school', which helped her to adjust to city life. On the problems of transition to university, Sesh commented:

> ... in a country area everything's relaxed. You've got more supports there ... it's easier to make friends because everyone's close together ... you're seeing them all the time, every day. So it's mainly the social aspects. But it's not only that – just the sheer size of ... the buildings [at university] and the busyness of it – you just can't get away. You don't have your moment of peace. As much as you would out in the country. So there's no real down time ... at most of the unis that I've been to, even if you do go into the library ... there's always stuff going [on]. ... unless you locked yourself in a classroom when there was no one there, you would still have people going around.

Sesh believed that the teaching style in her country secondary school did not prepare her for the transition to university, and that the low expectations, particularly of girls, constrained their aspirations:

> . . . [the teachers] were supportive in any way that they possibly could. But I think the teaching style . . . wasn't really what we needed to make . . . the grades . . . There was a jump in [expectations].

Sesh noted that 'one or two' of her friends from secondary school had also been unable to make the transition from school to university and had returned to their home town.

Sesh started working at a large gambling venue in the city, then went to Europe and worked in casinos there. She also worked at other jobs, including a child care centre, at 'a place where lots of refugees came into'. One day her supervisor there 'pulled me aside and said':

> 'We're creating a position for you for custody disputes . . . If they've got a problem they can contact you and you can support them.' And I [said], 'Oh, OK, well why are you giving me that?' And they said, 'Because you're . . . the best person we've got that doesn't cause arguments . . . You calm things down, you don't get them all fired up.'

This was a turning point in Sesh's decision to pursue higher education:

> I was still wondering at that point . . . about what was my next step. What was I going to do? Where am I going to go? And then they said this, and I thought, 'Right, then I'm going back home and I'm going to study.' I could actually do something.

Sesh returned home and 'did volunteer telephone counselling':

> I thought that if I could do that, I'd take the next step. I wouldn't just jump into a degree . . . all the way through primary school and high school, I'd always loved animals. And it was like I loved animals more than humans . . . And then going to Europe and seeing the stuff that was going on transferred just being empathetic [to humans] and wanting to help out . . . anyone that needed it. I wasn't going to be judgemental . . .

Sesh explored her options while working as a volunteer telephone counsellor and decided to pursue psychology:

> I spoke to my Mum about it . . . and she . . . [said] . . . 'Why don't you get a degree so that you can get a decent job . . . like psychology?

> ... there's lots of famous psychologists out there!' So I did the psychology degree ...

There were many times when Sesh 'just wanted to quit' but friends encouraged her to continue:

> ... during the second last semester I was totally burnt out. And went and saw my Dad then and he's just turned around and said, 'You've done ... two and a half years of this degree, you're not going to quit. I'm not going to let you. It's not going to happen.' And he [gave] me that look that he used to give me when I was a child ... [and I said] 'Ohh, OK, OK, I'll go and finish it off.'

When she completed the degree Sesh's family expected that she would 'get a job', but she decided to study social work, rejecting her family's views and marking a shift away from her father's influence:

> I don't really care about my family ... what they think ... they all hate social workers ... My parents had bad experiences with [social workers] ... when they first got married. They saw a social worker. The social worker said that they should have kids. So they had us kids and ... that didn't save the marriage at all. So they're sort of blaming the social workers ...

At the time she made the decision to study social work:

> I don't think I really realised how much they were pushing. And then when I did it ... my Dad just looked at me and [said], 'Well, it's your life. You're over 18. You can do what you want.' And my Mum ... well, her attitude was made clear ... I went, 'OK, so they don't really approve at all, but they're willing to [go along with it].'

Sesh commented that:

> I could have got a job doing anything beforehand. I was earning more money than probably [I will be] when I'm doing social work ... It wasn't about that for me ... it's pure determination now ... [as] a mature aged student ... basically you've got to give up your life. Just to do it.

Managing study

Planning

As Sesh had finished a psychology degree, she understood academic arrangements and requirements, and how to manage the costs associated with studying at university. She planned for text books and internet costs, and applied for the government student allowance. She lived at home with her mother to keep her living costs down, knowing that this would help her to achieve her long-term goals: 'I wanted to get out – I wanted to be able to have a career where I can reliably get out of there ...' She was confident that she would complete the social work degree:

> *I was more flexible but also I knew that I could do it ... It didn't matter how hard it was going to get, I knew I was going to be able to do it ... I had more of an idea about my ability to achieve ...*

Managing

Sesh did not undertake any paid work during this course but did voluntary work with an indigenous community organisation during the summer breaks. Her decision not to work during the semester was based on her experience in her previous degree where working interfered with her ability to study:

> *Not working means I can focus more on my assignments and what needs to be done, but working as well as the study also enriches – you need that break away – you have to get away, whereas at the moment I am just so involved in doing assignments that I can't think of anything else ...*

In her psychology degree:

> *There was a few times where ... I forgot about a deadline or something like that and I'd stress out and go up to the boss and say, 'Look, can I have the day off, because I'd better get this assignment done?' And they'd [say]... 'What for?'... after those sort of experiences, you just sort of learn to get your assignments done as quickly as possible.*

Sesh clearly benefited from her experience in her first degree. Friends found that she was unavailable during semester due to study commitments. She became focused on study and '[e]verything else fits around' that.

The electronic resources at the library assisted Sesh with research for assignments. Referencing was a skill that she had learned during her psychology degree:

> *Referencing is a big thing that I learnt from the first one. I'd never had to reference before . . . just the logic of it. The logic of you have to write their surname, then the initial of their first name, then the year, then the journal article name . . . And then it's different for online articles . . . I understand now why, but at the time . . . I never really thought about it before . . . that you could actually be stealing someone else's ideas that way. It was a new concept.*

Support

Sesh found it 'weird' that at 28 she was still living at home with her mother, relying on financial support and help with daily living tasks such as cooking, washing, and cleaning. Sesh's family had become more understanding of the demands of a degree. Initially her family expected Sesh to be available for errands and household tasks while her brother, who had also started a degree, was allowed time and space to study:

> *He's sort of like the alpha male because he's the only one . . . and there's a cultural thing with my Mum . . . so, him being the male, what he says . . . is taken as law. . . and also because he's got a girlfriend there as well . . . Whereas . . . I'm the female and I don't have a partner living there . . . it was a bit of a struggle last year. But it's all sorted itself out now . . . just them sort of walking into your room . . . forgetting that you're actually engrossed in something . . . and just turn[ing] on the TV really loud because they hate the fact that there's no noise . . . little things like that . . . end up slowing you down.*

Sesh described feeling isolated:

> *. . . because there's nothing else in my life. I've made uni such a central process . . . people my age at 28, they're out there, they're*

> *working ... they go out on weekends ... that stuff that normal people do ... I don't understand any of that. I don't have any of that.*

She was able to discuss some of her studies with her brother, although he argued from 'a different perspective'.

Peer support was significant for Sesh. She approached other students in her course for help, using online technology to keep in contact with them, and valuing the collaborative learning that can occur through sustained peer contact:

> *We usually work on similar assignments at the same time, so it's reciprocal ... Whereas with the teachers, [if] you go up to them and say, 'Look, I'm having a problem with this essay' ... it's more of an, 'OK, where are you at? Yes, that sounds like a good idea,' and then off you go. Whereas when you're discussing it with a student ... there's a bit more brainstorming, I think.*

During her previous degree, Sesh had approached university student support services for assistance with forming an argument in her writing, but this '[d]idn't help':

> *... she just kept on just asking questions like, 'What's another way of saying this?' And I obviously had no idea what she thought was wrong ... She was saying things like, 'There's no structure.' And I'm like, 'There are paragraphs there. What do you mean by structure?' So that's the sort of stuff that I'm sharing with students now which she didn't really help me with ... It was just three years of trial and error ... And she'd sort of speak in another language and not be able to see where you were.*

The friends that Sesh made during the course were 'definitely' her biggest support in completing the degree:

> *... they also helped me out with personal stuff because my family ... didn't really have an environment that was supportive of me studying. So when it got to the final semester I actually moved out just before the semester started and one of my friends said I could stay there to finish the finals ... they quite literally believed in me. It was weird. It was weird how it all happened.*

After her attempt to obtain support during her previous course, Sesh did not approach university support services again. She did not think that her current department could have done anything to better support her learning:

> *I wouldn't ask for things to be any different . . . because I learnt what I learnt through what happened . . . I still think they did a bloody awesome job . . . There's two people [I know] . . . one has graduated from psych and another one has graduated from social science and I'm just looking at both of them [thinking] . . . 'I feel sorry for you mate. You've got a bit of learning to do there' . . . they're a bit green . . . I just sit there and go, 'Yeah, didn't you know?' but that was just because we had placements. We had two placements that they didn't have.*

Sesh enjoyed the course because:

> *I've got freedom . . . I can't think of a job that I'd be qualified for at the moment where I'd have as much freedom to choose the subjects that I want to do, assignments that I want to do, and learn what I want to learn . . .*

Reflections and future plans

Sesh completed her degree in the minimum time. Reflecting on her experiences as a learner, she commented:

> *I thought that I was really motivated to get out there and just absorb things and it didn't matter what it was; I was open to anything. But I don't think I really was as open as . . . I thought I was. I think I felt a bit arrogant about it all.*

She thought this 'arrogance' related to the fact that she was the first in her family to attend university and this was her second degree.

Feedback on an assignment in the first semester of her first year changed Sesh's view of herself as a learner:

> *I think the depth of the assignments and the different spin that they had on it [made me realise that] . . . you can't be sitting there all high and mighty about it. You've really just got to get focused in*

on what you're actually doing . . . After my first few assignments . . . I was sort of thinking, 'Oh yeah, I'll get a good grade for these' and I obviously hadn't done the work that I could have done . . . I didn't have the attitude to go in there and give it everything that I've got . . .

The assignment 'was on an area that I thought that I would have been pretty good at'. When it was returned:

. . . it wasn't that bad. They were just saying, 'You could have done more.' And I was [thinking] at the time, 'What more? What else is there?' . . . now I know. . . I got angry for a little bit . . . I think it was just me realising that I really didn't give it my all . . . to begin with I was really upset.

The comments on the assignment motivated Sesh to start thinking about what she was learning:

I was here for a reason . . . I've already got one degree. If I don't fulfil this then everything is wasted so I've . . . just got to do it. But at that point I [thought], 'Well, don't worry about how good you are or whatever, just do it . . .'

Sesh completed a field work placement at the end of her first year, working in drug and alcohol assessment. This placement also had an impact on Sesh's view of herself as a learner:

I still had a bit of that cockiness in me because I actually put my name down . . . not even knowing what it was. I just [thought], 'OK . . . I don't want to do disability services, and I don't want to do hospitals so I'll just get one of the other ones.' And everyone said . . . 'My God, Sesh, why have you picked that one?' And then afterwards I've gone in there and I've just [thought], 'Oh, man. OK, I can do this.' Writing . . . five page assessments and stuff . . . it was the same thing again. You get that knock back at the beginning and it got me motivated. So I think it was a theme . . . motivation increased heaps after [that placement] . . . it just went through the roof.

Sesh was so motivated that she asked her parents to fund her attendance at a conference about working with sexual offenders. She was the only student at the conference:

> *I ended up getting approached by some people . . . and they were . . . saying, 'Well, how about a job? Do you want a job?' And so . . . from the placement, I really . . . began to find my feet about what I liked doing.*

The conference also reinforced some of her learning from the course:

> *. . . there was someone who came over from Oxford . . . talking about multi-systemic therapy [MST] . . . And then when I went up to the . . . conference, I actually met someone from Missouri in America and they were all big into the MST as well . . . And I ended up getting a really good grade for that assignment . . . obviously, I must have learnt something because I never knew about MST beforehand . . .*

Sesh's second year was 'just about solidifying that . . . passion':

> *It was quite a huge year . . . I went out on another indigenous volunteer thing during the break and then I came back all feisty again and this time . . . all my assignments were all on indigenous stuff. I was really passionate . . .*

In the first semester of that year, Sesh recalled some bullying during student group work which she considered the lecturer did not deal with appropriately. This made her angry and led her to question what the social work course was about:

> *So I stood up in a lecture and [said] . . . 'I don't think for anyone to be a social worker should they be ganging up on [someone]' because it was. It was . . . one girl being surrounded by five others that are just attacking her.*

This experience changed Sesh's attitude:

> *. . . after that I decided . . . I was going to focus more on what I wanted to get out of it rather that what the year wants to get out of it. And that was good because it meant during the next semester . . . I was more focused. I got the assignments done really quick[ly] and I was helping others with their assignments as well, which is weird when . . . I'd made the decision that I was going to focus on my stuff but it ended up being that in focusing on my stuff it meant I was more [collaborative].*

Sesh achieved High Distinction grades in all her subjects in her final semester, after which she gained employment in the prison system. This was another new start:

> *I think I'm back at stage one again ... new job, all that sort of thing. So I've done the training for it, it is just a matter of going in there and doing it. So there is a part of me that is going, 'Yep, I've learnt it all. I can go in there and just rock.' But I know very well that I don't know ...*

Sesh commented on her most important learning from the course:

> *It wasn't how to write essays ... It was more the challenges that I was faced with during the course. The things that challenged me to either quit or to stay ... I don't know how to explain it. But when you fight for something so much, you end up ... determined and passionate and all those things. You roll them all up and that is what I learnt. I don't think I was ever passionate about anything before. I mean I was, but not like this ...*
>
> *I think beforehand I didn't know where I was going, what I was doing and why I was doing what I was doing. Then doing the placement, meeting the girls that I met and I hung out with who were similar minded to me ... these girls that I'm going to stay friends with from here for a long time ... and having the opportunity to meet them and for us to work together in a group and the way we worked was just fantastic. And the motivation and beliefs that they had in me ... And the sparking of that passionate drive to just keep on going.*

On her graduation, Sesh also reflected on the impact of her family's background and response to her success:

> *I look back now ... at my Dad and my Mum in particular, and my brother ... and my Mum is still exactly the same and my Dad ... he 'got it' sort of half way through this degree, but after graduation yesterday it finally clicked in with him because he'd never been to a graduation before. He'd never seen anything like it. We were packing our bags to come down here and he was saying, 'So what do I wear?' and I'm [saying], 'What do you mean what do you wear? It's a graduation.' And he goes, 'Oh, so do I wear a suit?' I'm [saying], 'Well, I think other people will be*

> *wearing suits. I don't want to say you've got to wear a suit but there will be some people there.'*
>
> *So ... he's got all dressed up and then after the graduation ceremony he was bouncing ... Yeah, he got a real kick out of it. So ... looking back ... I think the lack of support on my Dad's side is not from being intimidated or anything like that, it's about just not knowing ... the perceptions I get from my parents is what I'm still going to get out in the field anyway so it is preparation if nothing else. The fact that it can change is awesome on my Dad's side ... I'd never thought about why my parents reacted in certain ways with study. I never understood before ... And now you come back and you think about it and you put all the pieces together ... This is about their perception of learning. So it is not my stuff. That's what was enlightening. I loved that.*

Sesh's graduation had a huge impact on her, leading her to reflect on her experiences in the course:

> *... it's all been good ... I think I'm heaps more grateful because I had graduation yesterday ... and I'm ... still bouncing from that ... I so didn't like my psych degree. I so didn't respect it that I wrote myself off the night before graduation so I was there going, 'Yeah, whatever.' But this one I was actually really excited. I knew that I got something out of this, whereas ... I got some stuff out of psych but it hadn't answered any questions for me and this one did because now I'm working ... I'm like that brand new teenager kid in a new workplace, bouncing round and going, 'Yep, I can do it all.' So it's good to have that ... it's very rare that someone can get to do a job that they absolutely love ... it's just amazing.*

Shannon's story

Pathway to higher education

Shannon has a rural background. His family moved around frequently when he was at primary school but he was always a capable student. He commenced university study in the city when he finished high school but did not complete his degree and returned to live with his partner and baby son in the country. He worked initially in a timber mill, gradually moving into jobs that led to his enrolment in his current course.

Family background

Shannon's father was a mechanic and his family moved around because of his father's work. Then his mother, 'when she was 35 decided to go to university to be a teacher so then we moved because of that'. They moved from the country to the city and then back to the country. He has two younger sisters.

When Shannon was young he enjoyed 'being outside, climbing trees, going for a ride'. He did not think about what he wanted to do when he was older:

> *I don't remember ever wanting to be anything. I remember being told what I could be . . . I was living in the moment. I really didn't think, 'This is what I want to do' . . . I was good at computing but I never even really wanted to do that when I was older. I really didn't think about doing anything until the end of high school.*

Other people (parents, family friends, teachers) thought:

> *. . . I'd be a writer or a politician, something like that [because] I was really good at reading. I'd always be in the top group or reading books that I shouldn't have been.*

Because his mother was studying to be a teacher, 'family friends . . . were often teachers'. Shannon was 'just finishing primary school' when his mother began teaching in the town where he has lived most of his adult life:

> *I finished primary school as she finished uni . . . my younger sister basically grew up at the university . . . She was with Mum while she was studying. She was there every day with her.*

His mother had a successful teaching career, becoming a School Principal and then 'a Coordinator across hundreds of schools'. His mother's brothers were also 'fairly academic':

> *. . . only one of them went to uni, but they were quite . . . intellectual. And so they'd often encourage that intellectual side. And you'd be arguing theories for the sake of arguing theories.*

Shannon commented that:

> ... it's funny ... I didn't know until well after I was already at ... university that my Grandma was the first woman to graduate through the Conservatorium [of Music] there.

Shannon's mother's sister attended university, but his own sisters did not. It '[n]ever really interested them'. His 'middle' sister did not finish school, but his younger sister did. Shannon thought that his mother's decision to return to study 'definitely' influenced him:

> ... my thinking was that if my Mum could go to uni at 35 and now she's a Principal ... then I could do it at 27 or 28.

His mother left Shannon to make his own decisions: 'that was our family dynamics ... you make your own decisions':

> I guess when I went to uni straight after school ... everybody just did that ... you just applied for uni and went. But I only stayed there two years.

When he moved to the city to attend university after high school, he lived with his aunt in the first year, and then in a house. He discontinued in his second year following the birth of his son:

> I stopped going to university because I met somebody and we had a child – young ... and it was too difficult to be in a big city from the country with a young child ...

His partner was a student, 'but she stopped going to school'. She came to the city to have the baby and, as she did not have a family who could support her, she stayed at a place that supported young mothers. Three months after their son was born she moved back to the country and lived 'in an Anglican community ... for a little while'. Shannon then returned as well, and with his partner and their baby, lived with his parents until 'we eventually got a house'. He needed a job and in the town he came from 'just about all the jobs are in the timber mill':

> So I worked in the timber mill and I was fairly bored doing it ... So whenever a different role came up I would take it.

He took on the roles of occupational health and safety officer and trade union representative, which involved negotiation and work-based training activities. Acquiring these skills led to a change in employment:

> ... [it] was actually when my second child was born that I decided I didn't want to do that any more. Shift work didn't suit and I started to look for other work. And I went to a supported employment facility – which was a timber mill which people with physical and intellectual disabilities worked in. And I got the job because I could train them. I knew nothing about ... disability but I knew how to train people to do a timber job. So I did that. And quickly got interested in the disadvantaged [people] that I saw ...

When his contract ended, an encounter with a student friend of his younger sister led to his next position:

> ... she worked in disability ... actually doing the job I'm doing now – she ... said there's an opportunity for a job working with people with disability in community health. So she linked me into [that]. . . I think it was significant that it was at the start of an agency beginning in the town. Previous to that, there hadn't been any government agency which was providing care to people with disabilities.

With the manager who was appointed, Shannon helped to set up the agency:

> That was a real good learning curve. As that grew, I guess I took on more responsibilities within that because I was lucky enough to be there ... that was the impetus really to change ... it was still shift work. And ... because I was good at setting up programs and negotiating with people in the community ... I was able to negotiate just [to] work day shift. And solely concentrated on that. But because I didn't have any qualifications, I couldn't do much beyond that.

Knowing that he was 'stuck there' with the skills but not the qualifications to progress, eventually led Shannon to return to study:

> ... [At] an inter-agency training day ... [others] recognised ... that I noticed that there were things in the community that could be changed, a better way of doing things ... they were strangers

> *basically ... I spoke to somebody who said, 'Well, hey, I'm recognising this trait, but you're not going to be able to do much with it unless [you qualify]' ... I don't know the person's name and I've never seen him again. And I took it away and thought ... well, at barbecues and ... family events or sitting around on the weekend, you're talking about those social issues and putting forward your opinion so argue it on paper and get something out of it.*

Shannon could not enrol directly into his current course because he was not qualified, but he enrolled in another degree that would allow him to transfer later.

When he returned to study, Shannon continued to work for the same government agency. He enjoyed the job, though he would have preferred to work in a non-government organisation:

> *I don't like the constraints of working for government. I think it's too limiting ... But I don't want to move to a non-government organisation without a degree, because I won't get paid very much ... Inside government, [the pay's] reasonable [if you're] unqualified. Outside of government it would be a pittance. So if I can be qualified before I leave the government, then I'll be OK, I think.*

Shannon's children were 7 and 11 respectively when he began his current course, and Shannon was 30. Pursuing university study and his ambition to move into more senior positions in his field were driven by his need to provide for his family:

> *I guess if I didn't have children, I probably wouldn't have been driven to set myself up ... I'd probably be just quite happy doing what I was doing. I probably wouldn't have that reason to secure everything.*

Educational experiences

Shannon attended five different primary schools, which provided him with 'different experiences of learning':

> *... some were in one-classroom schools. Some were in brand new schools. Some were in schools in low socio-economic areas.*

This 'didn't seem to bother' him. He remembered:

> *. . . writing stories in recess and lunch and having to be told to leave. And carrying too many books for a little kid to be carrying into school.*

Shannon enjoyed reading and as the oldest child, 'I had time to be read to.' He also remembered 'getting in trouble in the school yard' and 'running around' but '[n]othing stands out', though he recalled a teacher he found supportive:

> *. . . because we'd moved schools so much, having one teacher for two years in a row was quite significant . . . And so he inspired me to read more and argue. Challenge things and negotiate meanings . . . I think the thing I remember most about that teacher was . . . whenever there was a question, I'd always put forward two sides of the story. And he'd keep saying, 'You've got to come to a decision' and I'd say, 'No, I won't. I'm going to sit in the middle.'*

Shannon did not recall much about high school: 'it was a new town, new people, and a new school.' He was 'good at study': 'I remember I didn't try very hard but I achieved well.' However, he was 'falling behind' in his penultimate year and he then moved to the Catholic school his sisters attended. The change was prompted because in the first part of the year he had 'decided I didn't want to go to school, I wanted to go swimming'. The change provided the opportunity to:

> *. . . have a fresh start at the next school where the rest of my family is . . . I thought it was a good way to make up for six months of making mistakes.*

At high school his interest was 'very clearly [in the] arts':

> *I knew that I was a people person. I knew that I could . . . influence people and I could influence situations . . . like at debating and those arts sort of things . . . It's kind of a funny story . . . [At] the public school . . . in science we had to do biology and chemistry and physics and . . . agriculture I think. And I remember I did physics and agriculture . . . and when I went to the new school in the second semester, I said that I'd already done chemistry and biology. Because I really didn't want to do them, and so I never actually did chemistry and biology at school . . . I only did physics. I . . . talked my way out of doing them. [It] might be jumping ahead, but when I worked at a*

> timber mill later on in life I got interested in ... the way chemistry worked and so I went and bought ... books from the second hand shop and on night shift at the timber mill, I would go through the exercises and do the test and I say to myself, that I actually finished [high school] chemistry. Because I did it by night shift.

At the Catholic school Shannon 'did really well':

> I came top of the school, but they didn't like me at all. I challenged them a lot. In particular in terms of religion and things like that ... But I did well and I got along with people.

When Shannon finished school, he studied psychology at university:

> ... we had to put our preferences in, and a couple of us sat in the library on the computer and looking through the books and [said], 'Oh, let's do psychology, that'd be cool.' That was all it was ... 'It's a people subject, let's do it.' Now I recognise that I didn't like psychology. Because I thought it was too objective to actually achieve anything. Couldn't take a stance on anything ... values had nothing to do with it.

He was doing 'fairly well' and passed first year and the first half of the second year, but his son was born on the day of his mid-year exams. In the second half of that year, 'I still went to exams, but I didn't pass.'

Prior to this his life had been organised around his study:

> I was only 17 and I didn't do much else ... I treated [university] like school. I went there and I came home and I studied each night and I'd get up the next day with my packed lunch and caught the train home at the end of the day. So I didn't have any other distractions.

Following the life changes that took Shannon away from study, the development of his interest in helping people, and the realisation that he needed a qualification to progress in his chosen career, he began a three-year undergraduate degree, studying off-campus and attending weekend residential schools. He did not finish this course as he only needed two years of previous university study to qualify for his current course. He then transferred and continued to study as an off-campus student. Hence, these two years of study provided the bridge he needed into the course and career he wanted to pursue.

Managing study

Planning

In making plans for his studies, Shannon

> . . . had to make sure that I kept a workspace . . . in the house . . . [I] tried to keep organised with my computer – tried to keep things as orderly as possible for ease of access . . . I guess preparation was more about just telling people what I was doing so that they were prepared for the fact that I'm going to be studying and some things might be different.

In creating a workspace, Shannon did not have 'a particular room':

> Our lounge room's quite long and I have a desk next to a window facing the wall . . . so the kids can be doing stuff in the same room and I can be facing the other direction.

Because he had a laptop as well as a home computer, Shannon was able to develop other ways of working:

> . . . the laptop has wireless networking. Most of the time it evolved into me sitting . . . out the back under the pergola doing my work, rather than in the house . . . Basically just being able to switch off from everything else and get things done. Sometimes I'll be doing it in the kitchen so that I can be studying while my partner's preparing tea . . . basically I found although I'd prepared a space . . . sometimes I need to be near my family and sometimes I need to be away from my family and having a laptop and wireless made it possible . . . there was an expense associated with that.

Despite his mobile study habits, Shannon still made use of the workspace at home:

> I still have the computer there and . . . I've got my working books there. There's too many things to keep in one place. I've got a bookshelf in another room where things go when I'm not using them . . . but I still keep things there, like all of the filing, books I'm using at the present time. But essentially I pick those up from there where I know they are . . .

Sometimes his mobility extended beyond the household environment:

> *I take four hours a week study leave off work. And rather than be at home and do study, with the dishes to be done and the washing to be hung out . . . I'll drive up to the local lake and sit there under a tree with my laptop. Until the battery runs out . . . I actually have four hours that are completely about study that way.*

Shannon's partner worked full-time so he reduced his working hours:

> *I dropped back my hours so there was more time for other things. So I only work till 3.30[pm] now, whereas I used to work . . . till 5.00[pm] . . . if I worked full-time I would be getting five hours [paid study leave] a week, but because I work . . . till 3.30[pm] each day, I get four hours.*

Shannon's computer was central to managing his study:

> *Basically over time I've used [Windows] Outlook and the different Task Manager functions and calendar functions a lot more, in terms of having reminders pop up to say, 'This needs to be done' . . . I've learnt to break down semesters and subjects and assignments into very small parts. For example, once residential school's over, I will go home and I'll look at the dates and I'll put those in the calendar . . . on the computer. And then once I've put those dates in, then I'll work back . . . I might move the dates around – I mean, never past their due date. But sometimes I'll put when I think I need to be finished that, so that they're reasonably spaced and then I fill the gaps . . . for example, do a quarter of the readings for this essay . . . over four days, an introduction over two, next paragraph over two. And basically try and space it out so that every morning when I turn the computer on, a task pops up or the calendar pops up and says, 'Today you need to do this small task' . . . I don't think I would have done it any other way, just because there are so many competing demands on my time and knowing that today I only have to spend half an hour of my time on uni as opposed to four hours [makes it manageable]. I might have given myself a goal of reading a chapter and if I happen to get it done before six o'clock in the morning, then I've done my study for the day.*
>
> *If I know what I have to do, I can fit it into places you wouldn't think you could fit into study . . . I can just keep that little amount*

> *with me, everywhere I go that day, perhaps if you're waiting outside a shop ... There are so many different places if you've got it with you – then you just pick it up and read it.*

The computer also helped Shannon to organise his day:

> *I've taught myself to get up at five o'clock and that took a long time! ... the first thing I'll do is I'll have breakfast ... but if I turn the computer on, then I'll see what I have to do. If I have not planned to do exercise that morning, then I'll get stuck into it. And more often than not, I'll get done what I need to get done. I get ... [the children] up at seven. So normally, I've got two hours of my own time, with no one else up.*

For the two years Shannon was enrolled in the earlier course, he studied in the evenings but early morning study fitted better with his other responsibilities. This routine was sustained six days a week, with Sunday his only day for lying in. On weekdays when he finished work at 3.30pm:

> *Usually, it's taking the kids somewhere to a sport. The scouts or tennis training or organ lessons or ... just hanging out with the kids.*

He recognised the importance of this time:

> *... there are times when ... an assignment becomes due, sometimes you've got no choice and you have to do the work in the time, but even then I recognise that I shouldn't be doing it there. It should be their time with me. And ... I'll just put my pen down and deal with them ... Ten minutes and then I'm able to go back, whereas if I try and persevere and just try to block it out, I probably wouldn't achieve as much as if I didn't put the pen down.*

When Shannon began his current course he set up the system of alerts to deal with the workload. His previous course had involved a lot of work but:

> *... it was at a different level ... of professionalism ... or a different level of reading, or a different standard of work ... you seem to step up a bit for this course ... it was just basically such an overwhelming thing, I thought I need[ed] to work out a way to tackle it.*

He went to bed at 10.00pm, 'so we have an hour or so after the kids are asleep'.

Because Shannon was studying off-campus and working he studied part-time, with each year of the course taken over two years. At the beginning of his second year, his children were aged 8 and 12 respectively. Study was 'getting easier' as the children grew older:

> ... they both tend to equate my study to work. I'm always telling people that I'm studying what I'm working with and I'm working with what I'm studying and they obviously have absorbed that in the sense that my daughter says, 'Have you finished your work?' But I said, 'That's not work, that's my study.' But she says, 'But it's work' ... I feel a bit sad in the sense that she thinks I'm working at home. And I don't want to ... model that sort of behaviour ... she'll grow up thinking that it's OK to bring your work home!

Financial management was also important in organising Shannon's study:

> ... again it's about using calendars and things as wisely as possible ... I'm no good with finances so ... I compensate ... [by] just being really open and informed ... [as] soon as I know what subject booklists I've got, I'll print them out and put them in our invoice folder, so that I know ... that it's an upcoming expense. I don't tend to get them until the last minute, but that's just a bit longer to prepare for the expense.

Shannon stopped borrowing books from the university library because he could not afford the costs involved. The library paid 'for the books to be sent ... and I have to pay for them to come back'. He also found that he got 'into strife' using old material from the library so he began buying new books.

In addition, Shannon had to find the money for travel to the residential schools:

> We have two cars but we tend not to register one unless we have to. And we had to register the second car simply because I have to take the good one away ... so there's lots of inconveniences and expenses that you wouldn't normally associate with a two and a half day residential school.

Shannon drove the car to the city for university residential schools but he still had to cut costs while there:

> *I even rode my bike ... from my friend's place where I'm staying for free to here, simply because it saves me the eight dollars a day in parking.*

Taking unpaid leave from work for two 70-day professional placements was itself 'a big expense', which also impacted on others in his work team. He managed to negotiate 20 days paid leave for his first placement:

> *... they'll be able to get a replacement for the part of the time that I'm not getting money ... But if they want to replace me for the two and a half months, that means I don't get any money. So it's a Catch 22 in a sense. So, I'm saving money now in preparation for that. It's quite tricky!*

He took on an extra job to supplement his income:

> *I'm going to use one of my sibling's farms to earn a little bit of cash money while I'm on the placement. He has a dairy farm so I'll do some work there. I'll work his early morning weekend shifts which he doesn't like, milking cows ... it'll be $150 a weekend that I didn't have.*

As well as affecting work colleagues, study also involved managing time with family and friends. Shannon's parents lived about 400 kilometres (248 miles) away:

> *And they might invite us up for a weekend and sometimes we just say, 'No, I've got something to do.' Or sometimes it suits me to take the kids up and just let Mum and Dad deal with the kids and I'll spend a weekend studying away from home ...*

In terms of relationships with friends:

> *... they get used to the fact that if they're having a barbecue or an event, I still rock up, but I'll leave early and I won't sit around and have a few beers. I might have one and then leave, and then come back, once I've achieved my goal.*

The computer also helped Shannon to balance study with these other aspects of his life:

> *It sounds like I do a lot of time studying but . . . before I dropped back my hours, I did a lot of thinking about balancing my commitments. And whereas in the previous two years . . . I threw myself into study a lot and I got results . . . I really wasn't balanced. And I started to think, 'Well, I need to get some more balance to make it achievable.' And so . . . rather than do a lot of work less organised, I'm trying to do less work but be more organised.*
>
> *I've got a six month [gym] membership. So that was good fun and I'd go three mornings a week for an hour, from six to seven. And I started playing tennis, and I started playing hockey . . . to exercise I actually have to put down the books . . . And that was purely the reasoning behind joining the clubs . . . because it's costing me money, I've dropped back from the gym, but I've . . . worked out a different program, riding and running and home exercise routine . . . essentially if do exercise more I can study better.*

Shannon also undertook community responsibilities which involved a few hours of his time each week. As well as being treasurer for the scouts, he was on the hockey committee and managed his children's tennis team. These activities took about five hours per week.

A change in Shannon's circumstances after he began the course was the need to 'look after my health a bit more':

> *. . . but that's only made [it] easier to organise and refine things . . . I had really, really, really high cholesterol . . . it was 8.9 and things start shutting down when you're 10. So . . . I had to spend my time preparing food and things like that. But . . . I've managed that within three months – got it really good . . . I've got more energy and [am] feeling healthier.*

Shannon did not cook but he shared the housework with his partner:

> *I'm a terrible cook so I just make sure I do all of the other things around cooking. Wash the dishes and just make sure the kitchen is clean before cooking . . . do the washing and do as much cleaning as possible . . . It is a little bit of a time waster in the fact that I finish at 3.30[pm] and she'll finish at 5.00[pm], but I just can't cook.*

Sometimes work demands made study difficult, but he organised his study times to cope with the stress:

> *... quite often I don't want to turn on a computer when I get home or I don't want to have to deal with complex situations through uni after work which is a lot of the reason that I will do it before work.*

Overall, Shannon managed his study by combining rigidity with flexibility:

> *Really it's all about balance ... it sounds like I'm really rigorous and into routines and things like that, but really, I've been flexible.*

He had never seriously thought about giving up the course:

> *Sometimes I've thought it hasn't been relevant ... I'd rather just put my energy into getting on with my job, but then I think, well, you know, that's being a bit arrogant, I need to be open to learning and taking new things in. Really it's just, 'Have I got time for this ... in terms of stress?' But then you discover something new and read something interesting or talk to someone about something interesting that recharges you, but ... it could be easy to let yourself let it go.*

These times of thinking about letting it go were rarely when an assignment was due ('because they're usually the times you're energised'), but rather when:

> *... you're expected to plod through chapter after chapter and do your own independent sort of learning ... I prefer lots of little assignments to keep me going rather than a few big ones.*

To Shannon, managing study was sometimes more important than what he studied:

> *Not always, but generally the achievement of, 'Well, I handed that up and I got an OK grade.' Sometimes that's more important than the content ... And other times the content's more important than the achievement of the grade.*

He felt that this was all part of 'keep[ing] yourself motivated':

> ... everyone finds at the end of the semester sometimes you just don't care whether you get a very good grade, as long as you get it in. Well, I've actually always got really, really high grades ... I got the top marks in the [previous] degree, for the [time] that I did it ... [Each year] I got an award and I keep those on my desk. But basically what I told myself was that ... at the end of the day I've got to survive it and it doesn't matter if I get the best mark or whether I've got a pass. It's still a pass ... that's why I thought, 'Well, I've got some room to move.' I can spend less time studying, and I can lower my quality a bit, and have more quality in the rest of my life.

Shannon had looked forward to his first placement, though it presented financial challenges:

> ... the money will be hard, but I'm looking forward to the fact that I imagine the work placement isn't going to be anywhere near as stressful as my normal workplace ... it'll be the first time ... where work isn't added onto my study. It's just study really. Because I'm not being paid – I'm there doing my placement and I can focus on study, and although there's a pressure of money ... it's just uni ...

Support

Shannon commented that 'supportive workplaces and supportive family have best supported my study'. As an off-campus student, he had reservations about the use of online forums for feedback and support:

> I think some people can do it freely. I can't ... there was actually an instruction in our last semester that we needed to make a comment of our own and then give someone else feedback and I found it really difficult to give feedback to someone, just words on a page, rather than someone there and then ... you can't gauge reactions. You might be completely off track ... and it might be completely misinterpreted.

Telephone contact with fellow students raised other problems, such as time zone differences, and access at work to a phone to make long-distance calls. He did not contact other students in his town for support either, seeing them as having a support role '[o]nly in the sense that I see that they're either nearly finished or they've finished', which made him feel '[t]hat I need to get there'. He did, however, take on an informal support role himself in mentoring students in his region.

Apart from contacting the lecturer for advice 'once or twice a year', and asking a tutor to look at a draft assignment on occasion, Shannon did not feel the need to use any university support services and thought that those provided were adequate:

> *I think they always offered and they made it really clear what support was there and I also saw other people accessing those supports, so I don't think they could've done anything differently.*

Shannon did emphasise the point that '[f]ree postage for books' would have better supported his learning. Because he could not afford costs involved in using the library, such as fines for late books and paying to post books back to the university, he relied more on the internet and journals.

Reflections and future plans

Shannon completed the course after four years of off-campus study. He regarded himself as a capable learner who had always been interested in learning. Reflecting on his development as a learner during the course, he commented:

> *I think if I was to describe myself as a learner before I started it might have been as . . . trying to absorb as much as possible. I guess I saw learning as trying to take in as much information as possible, and devote as much time as I could . . .*

During the first half of the course:

> *I threw everything into it by doing as best I possibly could, and that gave me confidence that I could do it . . . As I gained confidence, I probably didn't devote as much time but still put the effort in to get what I needed out of it.*

He managed his studies by becoming more efficient at studying:

> *I guess I let learning come more naturally... I didn't necessarily try and extract all of the major dot points, and all of the essential elements. I started enjoying it more and just reading and questioning and liking, and the learning came from that, rather than trying to extract it.*

He began to notice these changes at the beginning of the second half of the course while talking to peers at a residential school. During the second part of the course:

> *I became an easier learner, a more relaxed learner. I was able to integrate my learning more because I was better at my work...*

Shannon changed jobs during his second year of study, and started working at the agency where he completed his first placement. Although he noticed the changes to his development as a learner at the beginning of his third year, he considered that it was his first placement during the previous year that brought about these changes:

> *I think that's because I'd had my first placement, and I took my learning into practice a little bit more, so I got more confident ... I could see the value in the learning more, but I could also see that I had a good grasp of it, so I felt a bit more relaxed about it.*

He regarded the most important learning for him during the course as:

> *(a) ... the first placement and (b) ... the second placement ... because ... reflecting back on all of the different things I'd learnt in my second placement, it really tied it together ...*

Having completed the course, Shannon was a 'bit over' formal study but still referred to his pleasure in learning. Although he had no immediate plans, he thought he might do some further study in the future. After confirming his career direction following his first placement, Shannon was 'not planning to do anything different'. Confirmation by the university that he had completed the course allowed him to be paid more as a qualified employee: 'I was stuck at work for a while. The only thing that's changed is the piece of paper.'

Implications for managing and supporting student diversity: student retention

Sesh's and Shannon's stories illustrate the strong sense of self-reliance that some older students bring to their studies, coupled with limited use of university support services. Despite this, their stories point to a range of ways that universities can better support students from diverse backgrounds. In reflecting on these, we focus on the issue of student retention to encourage you to consider ways that university staff could have assisted them to achieve success during their previous attempts, and the implications arising from their subsequent successful experiences.

In Chapter 1 we noted that research indicates that students withdraw from their studies for a variety of reasons (Crosling et al., 2008), including poor preparation for higher education; weak institutional and/or course match, resulting in a lack of commitment; unsatisfactory academic experience; lack of social integration; financial issues; and personal circumstances (Jones, 2008; Long et al., 2006). You can see how some of these factors affected Sesh's and Shannon's original attempts at university study. Successful transition is the first stage in student retention and because Sesh and Shannon both initially enrolled as school leaver students, their stories raise some additional points about transition that we did not consider in Chapter 2, as Miranda and Rochelle did not enrol until they were older.

Among these points is the importance of the link between schools and universities in preparing students for higher education. Although Sesh had attended a week-long university 'taster' session, this was not enough, and her comments indicate that although she was doing well at school, the resources and expectations at her rural high school were not sufficient to provide adequate preparation. As part of an 'everybody's business' approach to transition (Kift et al., 2010), you might consider whether this issue is being adequately addressed at your institution and, if not, what you could do in your role to address it. If you have a teaching role, then bridging courses and their equivalent are clearly important here.

Note, too, that both Sesh and Shannon lacked advice about courses and careers (as well as Rochelle in Chapter 2). Help in this area may have assisted Sesh in countering the influence of her father 'pushing' her towards maths and science and provided guidance in course selection, while for Shannon the choice of psychology, because 'that'd be cool', was obviously based on limited information. This is another important aspect of the relationship between schools and universities.

Sesh's first study attempts were compromised by several factors stemming from her rural background. Among them was a lack of information designed specifically for rural students about both academic and practical matters. As well as lacking information on course selection, it appears that she was not provided with pre-enrolment information about what to expect at university, the differences between university and school, what to do in a lecture and a tutorial, assessment, fees and charges, and living-away-from-home issues such as food and shopping facilities near the campus, the cost of living, how to rent a flat, use public transport and get a job. She found university very big and overwhelming and felt her rural schooling had not prepared her adequately for university study. Sesh's status as a first generation (first in family) student was also a factor in her withdrawal from her first course. Her family had little understanding of what was involved in moving from home to attend university, and she was left on her own to deal with social isolation as well as the academic and practical issues noted above.

This contrasts with Shannon's family background. From his extended family he gained social capital in terms of 'love of reading, belief in the value of education and encouragement of critical thinking' (McLean and Holden, 2004: 4). This was pivotal, as was the influence of his mother, and his initial withdrawal was primarily the result of the practical challenges of early fatherhood. Shannon was subsequently successful in his studies.

The financial challenges Shannon encountered during his course were not sufficient to derail his goals. His story points to the social capital he gained from his mother and extended family, and his motivation to 'set myself up' given his family responsibilities. Finances were an enduring problem for him though, particularly the 'hidden' costs associated with university study such as posting books back to the library, attending residential schools, and participating in work-based placements.

It is important to be aware of the services offered in your institution and consider whether these are sufficient to help retain students (and if not, what you could do to improve them), along with what part you could play in improving students' awareness of their availability. Assistance in the form of equity bursaries and practicum or placement bursaries, emergency grants, travel and conference grants, as well as government and institutional scholarships, are important examples of the financial supports that students may not know about. Scholarships, however small in monetary value, can be affirming for students (Aitken et al., 2004). If some of these do not exist in your institution, consider whether you and your colleagues should be advocating for the provision of bursaries or similar forms of support.

Research on students' use of support services reveals that their 'help-seeking' behaviour is complex. One US study found that 'low income' students differed from their 'higher income' colleagues in their use of the support services set up to assist their retention, mainly because they were not aware these supports existed or how they could benefit from them (Engle and O'Brien, 2007). Kinnear et al. (2008) found that individual students' background, attributes, beliefs, behaviours, values, goals, and experiences coalesced to create either 'proactive' or 'reluctant' help-seekers. The student/staff relationship determined whether or not students sought help. Students rarely sought help from unfamiliar or unapproachable staff and needed to 'feel confident in the helper's interest and ability to assist them' (p. 10). There was also evidence that students of non-English-speaking backgrounds and first generation students may be particularly reliant on effective help-seeking strategies, while international students generally rely more on support from teaching staff and distant family than on peer support from local students.

Similarly, Clegg et al. (2006) reported that students seek help from a wide range of university staff with whom they come in contact (e.g. technicians). Frequently reluctance to seek help is 'combined with an immense determination to succeed', and students may 'appear to preserve their esteem by using informal supports and by digging deep into the self and their own sense of personal project in coming to university' (p. 102); they may not want to be seen as 'not coping' (p. 111). Family support is often seen as 'natural', not needing to be asked for. Note, for example, Sesh returning to live at her family's home to save money. Clegg et al. suggest that institutional policy should build on what is known about the strategies and resources already available to students rather than appearing to individualise or pathologise problems. Students' choices about help-seeking hence need to be respected; the key responsibility of staff is to ensure that students know of the range of services available to them.

The nature of students' help-seeking behaviours again reinforces the importance of a proactive, 'everybody's business' approach (Kift et al., 2010; Thomas et al., 2002), because students are more likely to seek help 'from staff and their immediate learning community with whom they have developed a working/positive relationship' (Kinnear et al., 2008: 10), if they seek assistance at all.

Sesh and Shannon were both students who did not use this support, in Sesh's case because of previous adverse experiences. Her comments on academic literacy issues (gaining help in forming an argument, and understanding the importance of referencing) have important implications for ensuring this assistance is provided in ways that are meaningful for students.

While university strategies to assist transition or support retention can help avert attrition, there may be times when such intervention is not enough. As Kuh et al. (2007: 3) note: 'There are limits as to what colleges and universities can realistically do to help students overcome years of educational disadvantages.' They see retention in terms of student engagement and while engagement consists of a combination of student behavioural and institutional factors among others, they suggest that most institutions can foster greater levels of student engagement and success by implementing promising policies and effective educational practices based on research (Kuh et al., 2007). The important relationship between retention and student engagement is supported by Australian studies on student engagement (e.g. James et al., 2010; McInnis 2001; Radloff and Coates, 2010), as well as studies elsewhere (e.g. Tinto, 2012; Yorke, 1999).

By the time Sesh and Shannon committed to the study outlined in their stories they had developed clear goals and organisational strategies to support them, suggesting their increasing maturity as adult learners. For Shannon this involved juggling work and family responsibilities, a feature that often characterises these learners. We will focus further on adult learning in Chapters 5 and 6. In addition to the implications for student support considered above, Sesh and Shannon's stories highlight strategies that can be undertaken by teaching staff to increase student engagement and improve the likelihood of retention. For Sesh, peers in her course were important as a source of support, information, and guidance, rather than formal university services. Building group work into classroom and study activities provides a forum for students to develop relationships with each other. Both Sesh and Shannon also found work-based placements integral to the development of their identities as learners. You might think about what work-based learning opportunities, or other authentic learning experiences, are available to or possible for your students. Sesh also comments on the value of freedom to choose subjects and assignments, which provides further avenues for tailoring students' learning to their interests and increasing their engagement. In addition, her experiences of feedback highlight its importance in guiding and directing students. Prompt feedback, sensitively delivered, can play an important role in supporting students. This can extend beyond the classroom to broader aspects of their progress and involve both teaching and professional staff.

Summary

In this chapter, we introduced Sesh and Shannon as two highly self-directed learners, neither of whom drew on university support services. Both had previously attempted university unsuccessfully as school-leavers, prior to enrolling and successfully completing their current course. Both students lived in the country some distance from the university and enrolled to study as off-campus students. As adults, and in Shannon's case, with family and financial responsibilities, the advantages of studying by distance also involved considerable expenses, in addition to the stress of organising work and life to complete long unpaid work placements for the course. Both students report the central role of family in their educational success. For Sesh, parental pressure to succeed was initially critical in driving her. She also received practical support in the form of accommodation from her parents. In Shannon's case, his mother's decision to study as an older adult, and then her achievements in her new career, made her an important role model.

A question raised by their stories is whether the institutions they attended earlier responded adequately to their situations so that they could have continued and successfully completed their initial studies. We have encouraged you to think about this in terms of the transition issues facing many school-leaver students from non-traditional backgrounds, along with other implications of their stories relating to retention and engagement.

Chapter 3: discussion topics

1. As part of an 'everybody's business' approach to student support, what could you do in your role to improve student access to assistance with the practical aspects of coming to, and remaining at, university, such as accommodation and financial support?
2. How are students currently assisted with academic skills, such as writing essays, in your institution? What could you do in your role to improve the way that academic support services such as these are offered so that they are better organised to meet students' perceived needs?
3. If you have a teaching role, what are three (or more) strategies that you are not using now that you could implement to increase students' engagement?

4

The international experience: Lam and Zelin

Abstract: Lam and Zelin are two young women, from Hong Kong and mainland China respectively, who travelled overseas to study as international students. Their stories foreground the kinds of issues faced by many students studying in the current globalised educational environment, including grappling with English as a second language and adapting to a different society and culture. While Lam and Zelin did not experience the socio-economic difficulties faced by some of the students in other chapters, the international context presented comparable challenges that they needed to overcome in order to succeed in their study. Like some of the other students, factors relating to gender also played a part in their educational background. Their stories highlight issues relating to the management and support of international students in higher education, which we consider in the final part of the chapter.

Key words: culture, English as a second language, first generation, gender, international students.

Introduction

The stories of Lam and Zelin provide an opportunity to focus on the implications for managing and supporting student diversity emerging from the experiences of students who move to countries with a different language and culture to further their study. Lam is from Hong Kong and Zelin from mainland China. Both travelled abroad to increase their educational opportunities, Lam at the end of high school and Zelin after completing an undergraduate degree in China.

While Lam and Zelin are both from stable socio-economic backgrounds, you may find it interesting to consider these backgrounds and the role of family expectations and support in their educational experiences, as compared to the students we have met so far. Despite family support for education, their mothers' expectations of them as female students were lower than their fathers', probably reflecting their mothers' own experiences. Although they had direct educational trajectories from school to higher education, they both experienced 'false starts' after travelling abroad for study, before enrolling in the course on which they focus in their stories. They also faced similar issues relating to language, culture, and teaching and learning approaches, which differed from their previous experiences, and yet they gained only limited assistance from university support services. You might consider, in particular, the implications for managing and supporting student diversity relating to these aspects of their experiences, and whether these implications are the same as those for students from other diverse backgrounds.

Lam's story

Pathway to higher education

Lam was in her mid-twenties when she commenced her course. She had completed her school education in Hong Kong and become an international student by undertaking a foundation year at a major Australian university. She followed this with an undergraduate degree at that university and then worked for two years for the Chinese community in her new city, before becoming a permanent resident and enrolling in her current course.

Family background

Lam was the first person in her immediate family to attend university. Her father is a 'business-oriented person' who gained his qualifications through an apprenticeship. Her mother is not from an educated background and did not think it was important for a girl to be educated. As a result, she would disturb Lam's study:

> She comes to see me and to chat with me and so I say, 'No, I have to study' because I'm the person who is quite [a] self-disciplined girl . . .

Lam did not think much about what she wanted to do as an adult when she was a child. She loved drawing and family members told her 'you're a genius in drawing'. Lam noted that '[m]ost Asians' are conscious of 'how successful you can be in the school', but neither of her parents pushed her 'to do much'. Her father had more expectations of her than her mother but 'he didn't really care about my progress in study'.

Lam had a lot of discussion with her father when she was choosing subjects to study at university. This led to conflict because she had decided that she would be 'better off to work with people in the community', but he felt that 'you can earn more money in business'. He also thought that Lam would be 'not good at handling' people who were 'homeless, drunk, alcoholic'. An important family experience that influenced her was that her brother developed schizophrenia when he was at secondary school. She felt that she was a 'caring person' and 'not really money-oriented'.

Lam's mother's attitude to education for girls did not change and she did not offer any suggestions about career directions:

> *She always told me, 'If you feel stressed in your study, don't go for it. You stop if you get stressed.' She didn't see the point of further education . . . and she think about where I can get a good husband . . .*

Consequently, Lam's father was 'the main person for me to be influenced by', and she stated that '[despite] a bit of conflict with him . . . I still respect him'.

At the time she was considering options for university study, she was influenced by a campaign in Hong Kong promoting overseas education and applied to study in Australia, arriving with her boyfriend. They had studied at the same high school and both enrolled in the same foundation program in Australia. Initially, her parents were not happy about her boyfriend accompanying her, but Lam was becoming more independent and although she felt that it was not good to be away from her home, there were 'a lot of difficulties' in her family, including her brother's illness and the stress involved in the conflict with her father. She felt that she 'couldn't handle it' and that it was better for her to leave, acknowledging that maybe she wanted to 'escape from my family'. Although her father did not initially agree to her moving overseas with her boyfriend, 'he still allowed me to go with him at the end'.

She took a further step in escaping from her father's conditions by doing 'a very naughty thing' when she began the foundation course: she enrolled only in arts subjects and did not take mathematics, with the result that she 'couldn't choose any type of business course'. She confessed that 'I did it deliberately!' Her boyfriend was an arts-oriented person and gave her a lot of support.

Educational experiences

Lam attended three years of kindergarten and then six years of primary school in Hong Kong, where there were about 30–40 students in a class. She was 'dropped off at school, and got academically fair to average marks'. She considered that she was not 'that smart' but was happy because of her friends: 'I . . . still have those primary school classmates and still keep in touch now.'

Lam started at the same primary school as her brother: 'In our system when you live in the suburb you would probably choose the school around the suburb.' However, her family considered that this 'very low band school' was 'not particularly good in reputation' so she changed schools at the end of the first year. This required an examination to gain entry to another school. She did not achieve her first preference, but was accepted by another school and she and her brother moved schools.

Later, Lam was accepted into her first choice of a prestigious girls' secondary school based on her primary school results. The social aspects of her educational experience were still important to her and this was where she met her best friend:

> *We still keep in touch with each other and I think it is a most valuable friendship that we can still understand each other, although we are apart . . .*

She completed five years at this school, but was not able to stay there for the two additional years required for university entrance, owing to disappointing results at the intermediate level public examinations. Lam's commitment to education was evident at this stage because, although '[t]he perception [in Hong Kong] is that after five years you will have the minimum requirement to get the job', she wanted to continue to complete her sixth and seventh years.

Having to change schools was difficult for her:

> *. . . it was a hassle at that time, because I have to find another school and I was very desperate because my marks, even though is not that poor, but doesn't meet the requirement . . . to stay in*

> *the school, and I have to leave my friend as well. We were like bosom friends and I'm desperate and I have to go to the other school...*

Prior to this, Lam had experienced a setback at the end of the third year of secondary school when students were streamed into arts or science. Although she was better at science subjects than arts subjects:

> *...unfortunately because of all the competition in my secondary school I couldn't get into the science class. I have to move and [was] forced to be an arts student.*

She was 'not that good at writing ... at that time', but she thought that her future was still 'pretty good', although she 'didn't know what I can do and what things I would like to do'. She was not a 'genius' at science and mathematics, but she had thought about becoming a nurse, before confronting another obstacle. Lam needed to study human biology if she wanted to become a nurse, and this would have been possible within the arts stream. However, on entering her fourth year, '[t]hey cancelled ... human biology' and only computer programming was available, so she enrolled in that. It was after this that Lam began to think about community work.

Lam (and her boyfriend) were accepted into the one year accelerated foundation program in Australia on the basis of their seven years of high school. They did 'quite well' in this course and Lam's result was 'quite nice', allowing her to enrol at university.

Her objective at this point was to get to university ('I didn't think too much about courses I have to take ...'). Although she had already ruled out business studies, Lam was still aware of her father's conditions and so she chose psychology, partly because her brother's illness gave her an interest in mental health, but also because

> *... psychology will be more like high prestige and position ... [and my father] he's really happy ... psychology is a really honourable career in Hong Kong.*

She enrolled in the three year course but subsequently realised that this was not a well-considered decision:

> *... I choose it before thinking about other university course[s]. Because when I think back ... I think I would be better to see what*

> *I really want to do before I decide to just jump into [that] university ... [but]at that time a lot of people say ... if you go to university, your aim is to go to a very good university and [that Australian] uni is a really big name in Hong Kong. So I went for it, but without thinking about how they structure the psychology course ... and I thought at the time, 'Yes, I can finish in three years and then I can be [a] psychologist.' But it doesn't work like that!*

Lam did not realise until the second year of the course that she would need to complete Honours and Masters degrees as well (a total of six years) to become a psychologist.

Her choice of psychology, while pleasing her father, was not proving to be the right path for Lam. As a result, on completing her degree, she decided to find a job to reinforce her eligibility for further education related to community work. She found it 'rather amazing' that she was able to find a position as a coordinator at an Asian community elderly day-care centre. She worked there for two years:

> *And after these two years ... I have my ambition to be further educated in this area because I really find it is my ... career pathway.*

While working, Lam was aware of her need for further study to 'enrich my knowledge, to enhance my skills to work ... for the people'. She 'felt satisfied with what I did' but also considered that she lacked knowledge in the area:

> *... unfortunately, the agency couldn't give me much more opportunity for me to grow. So that's why I stopped.*

Lam gained access to her current course on the basis of her psychology degree. She felt that her two years' experience had given her 'more confidence to work in the ... area' and she was keen to adapt to Australia and join 'the mainstream society'. Her approach to her new course was different from her previous study. She did not see it as 'just assignment[s] that I have to submit ... and pass the marks' but rather was keen to 'gather all the knowledge and skills that I can acquire' to become part of 'this Australian society'. Developing her knowledge and putting it into practice were important now. Consequently, she was 'pushing' herself to work harder, though she was aware of the need to improve her spoken and written English.

Managing study

Planning

In her immediate planning to make the transition from work to study, one of Lam's first challenges was to write 'a good resignation letter', as she had not written such a letter before. Another aspect of her preparation was the enrolment application, requiring 'full-on essays', which she found 'quite daunting' wondering, 'What should I focus on – things the department would like to hear about?'

Lam gave up her paid work, but continued with some voluntary work. Planning how she was going to manage financially was a concern ('I still need to find another job so I was kind of struggling in the beginning') as she embarked on study involving full fees. However, she gained permanent residency and became eligible for a government funded place, which allowed her to defer her tuition fees until her income reached a certain level.

Managing

Lam felt 'quite shocked' in the first week of her course:

> *I couldn't think how I can handle it . . . And I felt like, I better go back to work. And stay in [a] normal job and have a normal income rather than be a student with not any income at all . . .*

But she also recognised that 'this . . . is my aim and this is what I choose; I couldn't go back.' Her emotional distress at this stage was also related to her problems with the English language. Although Lam found the course interesting and thought she was suitable for this area, starting the course was a 'struggle' as after working full-time in a Chinese-speaking environment, she suddenly had to 'talk in English' again. Despite a lot of contact with the 'outside world' in liaising with other agencies, she found the need to 'pick up my English' for the course was 'really different', involving 'quite a bit of struggling' to adjust to 'all the emotional change'. Written English was also difficult:

> *[There are a] lot of essays and I have to translate it from Chinese into the English and it's still hard.*

Lam had found it easier to study during her previous course – she was more equipped to study immediately after completing her foundation year than returning to study after working ('when you go to work you forget').

She did her best to cope with the assignments. As well as problems with the grammar and general writing skills, she was also challenged by managing time, including studying and reading and '[t]rying to pick up more of the thinking – the critical analysis'.

To address her need for income, in the first three months of her course Lam worked at a girls' high school as a kitchen hand, initially for two days per week, from 8.30am until the end of the school day, but she dropped back to one day 'because I find it's too hard to cover my study and work'. By mid-year, Lam had found a casual paid job in a community health centre, usually for one day a week, which, in her second year, increased to two days per week. This posed an additional challenge in time management.

However, as she embarked on her second year, Lam was 'quite OK' about her management of the previous year. She was 'not satisfied with everything' but felt that she could 'learn . . . from my past experience' and 'manage it better this year and try to make the most of the time'. Lam hoped 'not only [to] focus on the study but also try . . . to give myself a break – going out with friends – trying not to focus on the study during the weekends'. She felt that 'sometimes I need contact with my friends' and was 'trying to balance my life. Have a social life and a study life together.'

Lam also continued the voluntary work she had commenced before starting the course 'because it's . . . my interest and also the way of contributing to the community'. This involved visiting an elderly lady for two or three hours a week. Other demands on Lam's time included her involvement with her church, which began during her course, and sometimes attending a parish group on Tuesday nights.

Lam continued to be concerned about her writing skills into her second year. Her lecturer recognised her 'argument in the essay', but encouraged her to 'check the grammar and refine some of the words'. Consequently:

> . . . even though this year things have improved, I still find it so difficult to manage the work at times – heaps of assignments coming – having to actually sit down and look at books and just commenting on the side. And most of my friends really like to think about it like that. Although they are English-speaking, I think I need to put more effort in writing – to write a good essay, although I can see that they've still got difficulty and sometimes I feel, 'Oh, I'm not that . . . bad!' I feel a bit better that all the friends at uni come across the same obstacles.

To manage her study time along with her other commitments, Lam tried to be as efficient as she could. Having learnt from her experience the previous year, she tried to plan ahead using a year planner on which she highlighted all the assignment due dates. Her new study plan was a significant shift away from the previous year, in light of her work demands:

> *I always . . . study at night because I have to work until late every day from Monday to Friday, so now I prefer to study at night and I concentrate my work during the weekend.*

Following her plan to have a social life and a study life, and also to get away from home, Lam sometimes went out at weekends to 'meet some people rather than isolate myself' or 'have a walk . . . just [for] a few hours and then get back to study'.

The number of nights Lam studied per week depended on how many assignments were due:

> *. . . normally I would prepare . . . my assignments – obviously before – but I try not to cram everything in together . . . I try to meet the assignment deadlines.*

She studied most nights of the week, sometimes doing 'some reading for a few hours'. Lam was at the computer 'most of the time', reading and 'extract[ing] out some of the words and put[ting] them into the computer' from 8.00pm to 11.30pm or midnight and at weekends '[m]ost of the time I spend the whole day for the study'.

Lam's work in community health assisted her studies:

> *. . . I'm certainly learning from them and trying my best to apply my learning experience to my work. It gives me a lot of help – just give[s] to me some [sense of] achievement of what I can learn and apply to society . . . I find it really useful and I got to know some people in the field. While I was working I was getting established . . . [in the] area – and I can prepare more for the future career.*

The resulting time commitment made it difficult to manage at times:

> *. . . sometimes I want to concentrate on my study but I still have to think about my work and all the commitments and how I can manage it due to the placement and my work.*

However, Lam was fortunate in that:

> ... luckily they've been quite considerate and offer ... [the] opportunity for me to ... work at home, rather than go into the office to work ... I can do a day's work without having to go into the office every day. So I can manage better.

Support

At the beginning of her course, Lam sought support from university language and learning services in an effort to improve her English:

> I tried to enrol in some of the courses they provide, try to enrich my knowledge ... to write a good essay, good report.

She did not find this helpful because she required proof-reading assistance, but 'they only have a very limited consultation time ... always the time I find it is not enough because they really ... have a lot of work':

> ... what I needed was for them to proof read my document. However, they said that's not their duty to proof read it. They said they'd be happy to ... [help with] the structure, the sentence structure.

Consequently, Lam felt let down by the support centre and she sought her friend's help. This was the only university-level support that Lam sought, although she attended some of the centre's short courses on topics such as paraphrasing and summarising. She found this a good experience because it involved group activity.

Lam did not require any other specific help from the university, but thought that the department in which she studied could do more 'small group gatherings' to build up class relationships. She thought that 'whole class activities, like a fun day together where we can learn from each other ... [and] we can know each other more' would have been helpful. She considered that this should occur throughout the course, not just at the beginning.

Her most difficult time was at the beginning of the course when she felt 'a bit lonely and lost ... [with] stress and the pressure of the course and all the things happening'. At that time Lam thought about giving up: 'it seemed like it was really hard work to start with'.

Her friends and her own determination helped Lam through this period:

> ... I think it was my friend encouraging me about not giving up and my determination to go and a lot of my experience in the past that actually ... [made me realise that] I've had that transitional period – it was normal. I also got some friends in uni, and we met each other here but we got the same problems in ... study[ing] – even though they are English-speaking people – so we are trying to encourage each other and support each other ... I find that other people like to help me – and one should really try to put [in] more effort.

Lam's boyfriend at that time was also 'a good supporter – encouraging me as well'. He subsequently left to work in Hong Kong, but they then communicated via the internet.

Lam knew that she could approach academic staff if she had difficulties and would do so if 'they're free'. However, her course peers and friends were her main sources of support: 'Sometimes we just try to brainstorm some of the questions. We share and discuss together.' Her friends outside the course provided 'mental support' that was not focused on her study. It was these friends who supported her through the difficult period at the beginning of her course. Lam's peer support network within the course continued to develop: 'We learn from each other and share things together.'

Summing up, Lam considered that the best forms of support she received during the course were from 'my parents, my partner and also friends [outside the university and] ... the classmates in the class'. Her parents provided her with '[v]ery spiritual and personal support':

> Basically they are not here, but they are still concerned about my learning progress, and sometimes we talk through some difficulties during the calls. They still want to know how it's going, how to fully support my learning.

Reflections and future plans

Lam completed her degree in the minimum time. Her parents and boyfriend came from Hong Kong to attend her graduation.

Reflecting on her development as a learner during the course, Lam considered that, at the beginning, she was 'a bit submissive and passive ... I would rather be a follower rather than a leader in the learning process', even though she had already studied in Australia for her first degree. However, she had the motivation to learn and was 'willing to seek further clarification if I'm not sure'.

As she progressed through the first year of the course, Lam became 'more proactive in learning':

> ... I have greater participation in the class, like questioning and also engaging in the group activities.

She felt that this was partly because of 'the dynamics of the class', as she was more comfortable learning in small classes. Lam became proactive gradually, because initially she was hesitant to ask questions:

> ... I'm not familiar with the environment at that time and I was new in the class and so was feeling that I was a bit unsure whether my questions were relevant and [I] fear to make any mistakes.

As she became more comfortable in learning Lam also noticed other changes:

> I do feel a bit more independent in learning. I have more ... self-esteem than before. I feel like I have ... increased in the knowledge.

This was because of 'the structure of the class' and also because of her interest in the subject matter, allowing her to feel knowledgeable and learn more. '[P]icking up the friendships ... with the classmates and our learning together' also assisted in this development. Lam had not experienced this much in her previous study. Feedback on her assignments also sometimes helped Lam to develop her confidence. As a consequence, her self-esteem, confidence, motivation, and knowledge increased during her first year.

This process continued in Lam's second year, as she developed a sense of 'gradually increasing my competency ... feel[ing] as if I'm learning the correct way' and consolidating her knowledge in what she considered to be 'a very pleasurable learning environment'.

On graduation, Lam saw herself as:

> Very open to learning. A very proactive learner. I seek ... clarifications and I also seek any criticism. I've also been a reflective learner. I think the whole process of my learning in the ... course is a reflection.

Lam considered that critical reflection had been 'quite important learning for me' during the course, helping her to know her personal beliefs and values.

In the future, Lam hoped to learn more about counselling skills, including assertiveness and confrontation skills, but her main aim was to 'start at my job and get more practice'. She planned to stay and work in Australia, hopefully in the aged care field in case management or counselling.

Zelin's story

Pathway to higher education

Zelin was in her early twenties when she commenced her present course and had come to Australia from mainland China the previous year. She had already completed an undergraduate degree in China and planned to undertake postgraduate study as an international student to prepare for a career in China. However, on enrolment she found that undergraduate study was necessary for professional recognition, so she transferred to her current course in order to achieve this. Like Lam, the initial advice about course selection that Zelin received meant that the course she initially enrolled in would not allow her to achieve her career goals.

Family background

China's one child policy meant that Zelin was an only child. Zelin considered that this policy is making a 'great difference' in China. Before her parents' generation, families consisted of several children and the economy then was 'not so good as now', with the result that:

> ... they can only afford maybe one or two children to go to ... school and only the boys go to school. The girls live at home and do some housework ... Even the girls that go to work ... have to take their salaries to their parents to support their brothers.

Now, because of the one child policy:

> ... the boys and the girls are the same. Now – even though I'm a girl – when I ... [have] my own family and I have my own job ...

> *I also have to support my parents ... but before it's only boys' responsibility.*

As a very young child, Zelin lived with her grandparents in the country, until her parents decided it was time for her to go to kindergarten in the city where her parents lived, in order to prepare for primary school. Zelin was five or six years old when she moved from her grandparents' home to live with her parents in a small city in the northeast of China. Zelin moved because of the limited educational facilities available in the country area where her grandparents lived.

Zelin's mother was a nurse, and one of Zelin's dreams when she was young was to become a doctor. In part, this was because she was impressed by the white clothes, but the profession is also well respected and well paid in China. Her father encouraged her to be ambitious and wanted her to study 'very, very hard' and to 'establish very high levels of education', although he did not have any particular future job in mind:

> *He just said that if you want to study and you have studied well, I can afford [it] ... even if you want to study a PhD.*

Her mother thought a Masters degree would be 'OK' for a girl, and was more interested in Zelin getting a well-paid job. She also hoped that Zelin's future partner would have a similar or better educational background, and that her education would improve her chances of this occurring. Her paternal grandparents, on the other hand, felt:

> *'Why should you let her ... go to other cities to do the so high level education? And you put a lot of money out for her and it will ... never come back because ... she will marry ...'*

Zelin noted that this is a common view held by her grandparents' generation, especially as they lived in a 'very small city'.

Reflecting the values of this earlier time, Zelin's parents' education was limited. Her mother finished 'secondary high school' (three years), but did not go to high school (a further three years). She gained her nursing qualification from 'kind of a short course' in a hospital. Her father was one of six children and, given the conditions of the time, her grandparents were only able to support the oldest child (Zelin's 'elder uncle') to go to college. Her father was the second boy in the family and, even though 'boys have the preference' for education, he 'had to stop his high school education and went to the factory and got a job'. Zelin's uncle became a teacher and then a manager in the local education department.

Educational experiences

The kindergarten that Zelin attended when she returned to live with her parents was not a formal educational institution. There was one kindergarten teacher for 20 or 30 children and the teacher's son, who was a high school student, taught Chinese characters and some simple maths.

Zelin considered that she was very lucky at the primary school where she commenced her formal education because 'there are a lot of people in China, so most... schools... have a lot of classes in the same grade' but in her 'comparatively expensive' primary school, there were only two classes in her grade. The students were also very good because they were selected on the basis of their ability. Her teachers supported her early ambition to become a doctor.

Zelin completed five years of primary and four years of secondary high school, commenting that 'in the Chinese education system, the primary school is six years and the secondary high school is three years.' Three years of high school follow that, making a total of 12 years. However, at her 'kind of special' school, primary and secondary high school were combined in the one school, with a shorter period of primary school education and a longer period of high school education, because 'they want us well-prepared for the test for the end of high school.'

Because Zelin stayed at the same school with the same classmates for nine years, she had 'very, very good relationships' with them. Some were 'just like my family and even now they are my best friends forever!' Consequently, when she changed schools in order to go to high school for the final three years, she felt very isolated. This school was 'very selective ... the most famous one in the whole province':

> [It was] [v]ery difficult to get into that high school and all the students from other secondary schools are the best from their classes, and they felt we are still the best in this class!

In this competitive environment it was 'difficult to be someone's true friend': '[Y]ou knew each other... and you used each other' to keep up-to-date with the work in different subject areas 'because we have to go to the college, and the university, and compared to the rest of the world, there's very few in China.'

Zelin found the academic work at high school 'extremely hard':

> *... from the first year, the teacher warned us it would be [a] very hard job and in fact ... we also have after class lessons from some private teacher.*

By the second year, students would work until 'one or two o'clock in the morning', and in the third year, 'I can't stand to remember that – it's terrible!':

> *Now when I think about that time I feel that all of my arms are so sore! I just got suddenly a feeling of exhaustion!*

She put on about ten kilograms in the third year of high school 'because at that time I didn't move – just stayed at the study desk, and my mother bring some food for me and I just eat it and continued studying'. She did not feel she had any other choice:

> *I have to do it because [of] my parents' high expectations. If I can't do it this year, I have to do the next year.*

Zelin finished high school when she was 18 or 19 and at that time had no ambitions for her future career. She was preoccupied with studying well and 'get[ting] into some good university'. Consequently, when she chose majors, she based her decisions on 'whether the requirements are suitable for university, not just my own interests'.

Zelin's mother had some friends whose daughters had been at the same high school and 'they went to some famous university and ... performed very well', and then went to another country. Consequently, Zelin's mother would say to her: 'You should set that as your course ... making new friends is just a waste of time.' Zelin did not make good friends at high school, but she kept in touch with her primary school friends, some of whom had entered the same high school with her.

Zelin did 'quite well' in her final high school exams and had several options open to her. One was to go to law school and aim for 'some job in the economy' but she was not interested in business. She enjoyed reading and literature and so she enrolled in a 'quite famous university in Peking [Beijing]' where she completed a four-year Bachelor of Arts degree, majoring in English linguistics and literature. Moving to this university meant that she was living 23 hours' travelling time from her parents' home.

She lived in student accommodation, but found that '[b]eing with your classmates [is] not good!' Although it was 'very difficult for you to enter the university ... once you're in there ... it's comparatively easy'; there was 'still some competition' and when 'you're living with your classmates ... they will always be looking at you [and saying] "Oh, you're still studying?" '

Zelin was also uncomfortable in her first year because, having come from a very small city, she sometimes felt 'not good enough in that university' and that 'all of my classmates are very good', particularly those who had come from schools with foreign teachers. These students had 'very good [English] speaking and listening skills', but Zelin was 'just good at academic reading and writing, but not so good at the speaking'. She lacked confidence at that time, so sometimes 'I just felt ... I should study more than them and use more hours at the study room'.

When she finished her degree, Zelin found that there were not many jobs that suited her major because 'English is a language – it's a kind of a tool.' She could have become 'someone's secretary, or something like that', but she did not want to do that. Another option was to 'continue my study in China, do the Masters of Linguistics' but she did not want to stay where she was and lacked confidence in enrolling in another university. She decided to talk to her parents to gain their agreement to go abroad.

She did some research and became aware of the university and department where she was now studying; she 'want[ed] to go overseas ... at my young age to widen my ideas'. She felt that people's expectations and dreams are related to their age and if she took the opportunity to go overseas 'when I am 30, or when I am 40 ... at that time it is a different experience, a different feeling'.

Hence, she decided to complete a Masters degree in Australia with a view to becoming eligible to gain work experience in Australia and later work in China. She began this degree, not realising that she would need to complete an undergraduate degree first for professional recognition in Australia. She then interrupted her postgraduate study and enrolled in her current undergraduate course to address this. She found undergraduate study much more difficult. As a postgraduate student, she had been in a small group of overseas students. She felt that these students were given special care and marked 'higher' because of this. She was doing well in that course, partly because her English may have been better than the other overseas students. Although she found undergraduate study 'much harder', she was learning 'a lot' and enjoying it 'very much'.

Zelin's experience in Australia changed her opinions about education. The postgraduate experience had been 'kind of similar' to education in China with some exceptions:

> ... the teachers are more patient and laugh – and they encourage me to ask questions ... but in China – **No**! You just shut up and they tell you to do the notes and never ask questions. No, they ask us to ask questions in fact! But there are so many students they can't answer.

She noticed a marked change when she commenced undergraduate study. Although she found it 'very difficult', she appreciated that 'in fact, I can learn some ... real things'. In addition to theories and concepts:

> ... [y]ou have the tutorial with individual study with your clients, and they have very small group discussions. And sometimes we did the role plays ...

She valued the two 70-day professional placements for their links to 'real practice', which were very different from her experience in China:

> ... because in China when people graduate from the university, it is quite difficult for them to find a job because employers think they only have maybe good results from the university, but they have no experience at all. And it's ... very difficult to get into the real career ... because the school didn't link their teaching with the workplace ... I can imagine in the future if I want to find a job in Australia it's much easier, because I know what I want to do, what I can do, I can't do. ...

This was in contrast to her experience when she finished her first degree in China.

Managing study

Planning

For her initial postgraduate enrolment, Zelin's planning was related to 'all the living stuff' involved in leaving China and coming to Australia. Prior to that, she had to sit for the international English language test, and choose the university and the course she was interested in. She then applied for enrolment in the course and received a conditional offer because she 'didn't do quite well enough' in the test, which meant she had to complete a language course upon arrival in Australia.

When she was accepted into the university course, she had to arrange a visa, which took 'ages . . . almost a half year'. Then she bought her ticket and other things she thought she might need in Australia. Her parents made contact with people they knew who were already in Australia. These Chinese family friends, who had been in Australia for eight years and ran their own business, met her at the airport, and she stayed with them for 'almost a half year'.

Zelin enjoyed this because the wife (whom she called 'aunty') was 'really nice' and was living alone while her husband travelled frequently back to China on business, so there were 'just the two of us [in a] very huge house'. She eventually moved out to reduce her travelling time to the campus at which she was studying.

Managing

For her first three months in Australia, Zelin was enrolled in the full-time language course. Although she had studied English for more than ten years, she found it difficult because, 'I just totally didn't get all the accents' as most of her foreign language teachers in China had come from America. In addition, 'I'm quite shy and just not kind of person to talk to people', so although her writing and reading were 'quite good', and her listening skills were 'all right', speaking was more difficult: 'it just took time for me to get used to everything.'

Later Zelin worked in her aunty's cafeteria, which gave her work experience as a waitress and was 'fun'. She worked '15 or 18 hours per week' but when she moved out she could not continue because she lived too far away. She then found a retail position, working two shifts, which usually amounted to ten hours per week. She kept this job, but also gained another position working as a carer for a 24-year-old girl with brain damage. Zelin helped her to shop and go to rehabilitation programs, completing two four-hour shifts per week, which brought her near to the maximum of 20 hours per week she was allowed to work under visa requirements, adding extra shifts to cover her colleagues when they went on holidays.

Zelin struggled 'a little bit' with study and two jobs, in addition to her personal life, so when she began her first professional placement, she left the first job and just kept the position as a carer. Although the placement was full-time, she was able to arrange this with her field work supervisor, who said, '. . . maybe you can leave two hours or three hours early on the day on your shift.' Zelin left early on Mondays but her other shift was on Saturday morning, which did not affect the placement.

To manage her personal life Zelin began to keep a diary to schedule her time with friends. She also needed to allow time for domestic chores, and filled her refrigerator 'with all kinds of food' to avoid shopping frequently. There were not many Chinese shops near her accommodation, so she had to travel to another suburb or into the city to buy Chinese food. This was particularly a problem in her first year when she did not have a car, but she bought one during her second year.

After she had been in her flat about six months, Zelin's boyfriend moved in with her. Coming from a one child family, Zelin was accustomed to being by herself:

> ... the reason I ... decide[d] to live by myself at first place is because I'm not sure whether I can get along with other people, sharing a house.

Consequently, her boyfriend's moving in involved some adjustment. He was two years older than Zelin and had completed two Masters degrees in Australia, the second one in the city where they now lived. She met him through her aunty as he had also stayed there before moving out to find a house. They were from the same city in China, and later found that they had friends in common and that their parents knew one another.

At first, Zelin's mother was 'not quite happy' with the relationship because her boyfriend had not graduated at that time, and her mother thought there would be 'a lot of changes in the future and it's not stable'. Her parents were afraid that she would get hurt. Later, when he got a job, and she told her mother 'a lot of good things about him', her mother felt, 'Oh, probably it's a good thing [having] someone to take care of you when you are overseas ...'

To manage her study with 'so many things going on in my life', Zelin had to 'squeeze time' and do things at specified times to try to 'do it all'. Sometimes she would rise early and go to the library when it opened at 8.00am to read before classes started. The library did not close until 'around midnight', which allowed her to spend more time there. Zelin studied mainly in the library because it was difficult to study at home when her boyfriend was there and might be cooking or watching television. If she had typing, research or reading that she could do late at night she would do that at home. She had a laptop at home but no internet access, so she used the computers in the library.

When she came to Australia, Zelin 'didn't know anything about cooking'. Her aunty cooked for her and they also ate at her aunty's cafeteria. She started to cook for herself when she moved out, but, as she was by herself and frequently busy or going out with friends, she did not cook often. When her boyfriend moved in, 'I started to ... feel quite interested in that, and so I did all the cooking', but later she became bored with it and, struggling with 'time and other things', they decided that they would 'just eat healthy, get some salad and toast'. Subsequently, she cooked about three times per week.

Another challenge for Zelin when she began to live independently was the need, for the first time, to 'pay all the bills'. She found this 'quite a challenge' and 'totally different' from China:

> ... when I talk to my Mum, I have to pay this bill, that bill, she says, 'What's that?' She's got no idea what I'm talking about.

Moving into her flat was also a challenge, because it was a 'totally empty room', and she had to buy items such as a television, refrigerator and microwave, and

> ... try to figure out how to get these things to my home and then call people to help or ask the shop to deliver and how much is the fee ...

At that time she 'couldn't think about my study' and 'just simply went to the class and took notes and read some things'.

Zelin found it hard to judge the impact on her study of her boyfriend moving in, but he was a positive influence in that he was always encouraging her to study more, saying to her:

> 'I know how important and how precious the time is when you study and [how hard it is] to find the time that you need, so you should ... enjoy that, and try to achieve more because once you start work ... [there is just so little time] to read and to think ...'

Despite these positive statements of support, Zelin continued to do the cooking, shopping, and bill paying because of the 'stereotype that woman tend to do all the things in charge of the family'. So, while she was struggling to do the domestic tasks as well as study, she would think, 'Oh, yeah, you say this and now I'm the one to do all those things.' Sometimes she discussed this with her boyfriend, but sometimes they would 'fight' and she felt the situation was not fair. They would resolve some issues and then 'other things come up', but she considered that 'that's ... life [and you] always have to learn how to balance everything'.

Zelin found the written English demands of the course a challenge and because there were no exams, only assignments, 'it requires a lot of writing skills and I don't think my grammar and expression of ideas is good enough to be competitive.' She felt that she 'lost some of my marks because of that'.

In other ways, Zelin had not found study particularly difficult, because 'I've been studying all my life so far'. She thought that it was just a matter of 'get[ting] used to the lecturers' teaching pattern and what he or she wants [and working out] the most important things I need to put down'. However, she sometimes worried about her future practice. She was 'good at all the theories' but was conscious that she came from a country with a 'whole different . . . system'. In Australia:

> . . . [there is] a totally different way of doing . . . things and the facilities and the structures . . . [are] different, and the language is another issue. When I talk to people about my major . . . I think I'm all right, but then we start the casual chatting about the footy [Australian Rules Football] so I say, 'Oh, OK.' I have no idea.

This led her to worry sometimes about who would employ her as a new graduate from a different background, without work experience. But the study itself 'never troubles me . . . much'.

Zelin considered that time was the major challenge she faced while studying, working out how to 'balance my study time with other things'. For example:

> . . . sometimes I find, well this assignment [will] take me two weeks to finalise, but when I actually do that and I look at the topic and see, well, it's just totally different from what I thought at first, and then now I have to change all the thinking and do all other research, and it . . . really take[s] time . . .

Zelin used a wall planner to help manage her time, writing down when an assignment was due and when she should start working on it. She found it difficult when 'sometimes two or three [were due] at one time'. She would start to feel 'rushed', and worried about failing an assignment because of completing work at the 'last minute'.

The course 'involve[d] a lot of tutorials and presentations' and discussion with classmates. Zelin found some of this 'quite interesting' but some less so and it was difficult taking part in discussion when:

> *... all these classmates just attempt to do all the talking, and they don't stop and, oh, I couldn't catch their signs of stop, and the other person just cuts in and they keep talking, talking, talking and ... I got this idea I want to say ...*

In contrast, in China:

> *... we tend to wait for people to finish, and pause for a while, and that period of time ... allow[s] people to think ...*

This thinking lends weight to what people say, and later they 'respond to this talking or we start another topic' but in the course Zelin felt she 'just never got this time'. In addition:

> *I'm quite shy and sometimes I got an idea I really want to say, and I couldn't, and I become more silent and then my tutor ... [has a] problem with this and decide[s] you need to participate, and I said, 'I really want to but you know ... for me, it's really rude to interrupt other people.'*

Support

Zelin used the university's language support services 'a couple of times' and found them 'quite helpful':

> *... I've done my assignment and not sure about some grammar and I just went to them and they correct that and they tell me what type of mistake I made and maybe I should pay more attention on this or that.*

The staff there also suggested books she should read to improve her English and writing. She could not think of any other ways in which the university could have helped her, although she acknowledged that assistance in meeting people at the beginning of a course could have been helpful, and a presentation, or the provision of brochures or information sheets by the department in which she studied, might have helped in understanding local systems and facilities.

Zelin regarded herself as the type of person who did 'all the things by myself', and sought support only when she needed to. In addition to the language support services, she talked to the information technology staff if she had computer problems, and the library staff if she had a problem borrowing books. Zelin also consulted the head of department when she failed an essay by two marks 'to talk through this and [ask] could he give me another chance to redo the assignment'. She used the university swimming pool ('I'm at the pool all the time') and the gym.

Zelin was in close contact with her family, receiving emotional support from her parents, as well as her boyfriend. Her parents also contributed financially to her studies and her living expenses, though she worked and saved money, perhaps to buy a house in the future. She phoned her family 'once or twice a week'. If everything was 'going all right' she called weekly, but if holidays were coming up or it was someone's birthday, she might call twice in one week. Her parents visited her and stayed for four months, which was demanding of her time while also studying.

Her friends from inside and outside her course provided a lot of support during her study. There were about 45 students in her course, but only three or four were Chinese:

> ... I don't know if it's a culture thing ... but ... the Chinese girls are actually closer ... it's easier to make friends with them or other girls from Asian backgrounds, like I have Japanese friends. Maybe because the international students ... share kind of similar feelings and go through similar things, so it's more topics to talk about, and always face kind of similar problems when it comes to the grammar or what [the] lecturer really want to see in [an] essay because we have discussed these things further.

Zelin found it difficult to bond with her local classmates because 'they have their own friends, families going on and we all kind of come to the lecture room and after that go back to [our] own place', but overseas students from [mainland] China and Hong Kong 'usually get together ... maybe ... because [of] the same cultural background'.

Zelin worried about the future and discussed the issues with a friend from the same international student background:

> ... we [are] quite worried about how to get [a] future job and settled in Australia. I mean really settled, not get financial support from family. Actually get a quite good job and ... earn money to support ourselves ... Because study, for us, is just a way to get qualification, but we really want to be able to find quite [a] good job.

Zelin thought the support available for new graduates was quite limited and 'basically we are by ourselves', though students could get assistance to update their curriculum vitae. As an international student 'the reality is, it's harder for us':

> ... language is an issue ... if there's two people there and they've got same qualification and one is local and of course the language is not problem for him or her, and also they know the culture better and the systems better ... And then there [are] visa condition[s]. As I came here as an overseas student ... I'm holding [a] student visa, so now I just have two months ... [until] my visa expire[s] ... but I don't worry about this because I'm applying for [a] permanent resident visa so I'm holding [a] bridging visa. But it's just difficult to explain the situation to people if now I'm going to interview for [a] full-time position and I have to say, 'Well, I'm holding a bridging visa and I'm waiting for the result from immigration,' then people may think, 'Well, they may grant it, they may refuse you. And if I give you this job and you didn't get the visa ... what's going on?'
>
> ... and also I feel my local classmate[s] have much more opportunities than us, either studying or working because we have the condition [that we] must do full-time study ... and they can do part-time, distance education, full-time, whatever they want. That means once they find a job, for example, during the holiday ... they can ... just go for that, and whenever they're going to come back ... they just change the course to distance education. Very sad that we couldn't do that. Take me, for example. During my final placement, there is a position came up and it's really good, in the agency I worked.

Zelin had just started her second placement when a part-time position became available. She spoke to her liaison person who said that 'you have to stick to the full-time ... you have to finish the placement and get your qualification first'. However, the placements were valuable for learning about local systems and facilities, and in starting to build 'social connections':

> ... during the placement we actually had networking with some people, and ask[ed] someone to be our referees in looking for a job.

Reflections and future plans

At the conclusion of her undergraduate course, Zelin resumed the Masters course that she commenced when she first came to Australia.

Thinking about her development as a learner, Zelin commented on how she approached her study when she started the undergraduate course:

> ... I was just totally new to everything in Australia, so basically I followed my old learning strategies and skills I learned from China, and later I found out it's not quite the same here, because in China we basically do what the lecturers say.

When she started her course in Australia she 'really read a lot, but I didn't know a lot', particularly about local facilities, until her first professional placement. Reading also had limited benefit compared with the practical experience, because some of the texts were British and some American 'and they're not quite local'.

In her first year she noticed the following changes in herself:

> ... I was brought up in the kind of environment where you would listen to your teachers' opinions and you normally don't give your opinions, because you are young and you are a student and you are learning from others ... All your opinions are built on others telling you what to do, and here I think the tutors and the lecturers actually encourage us to give your opinions, even [if] sometimes it's immature, sometimes it's not right ... I think most of the people I meet in Australia, they encourage you to say your opinion. I think this [is a] good thing, and it actually encourage[d] me to speak out my ideas and that give[s] me some confidence and sometimes I think ... 'I'm really glad I say that because it inspired other people in some way,' because we [are] all from different cultur[al] ... [and] education[al] backgrounds, so I think it's [a] good thing and it make[s] me feel good about myself and it helps to ... [develop] self-esteem and ... confidence.

Zelin reflected on the first time she gave her opinion to her placement supervisor:

> ... I was her first student and she's my first supervisor, and she's just three years older than me, so it makes us more like friends than ... supervisor/student, so I kind of talked to her about things during the supervision and also during the interviews with the clients. At first, we start[ed to] kind of co-interview with clients, so after the interview ... she give me some feedback and I give her some things

I felt or I think about during the interview, so it help[ed] give me confidence.

In terms of the timing of these changes in herself, Zelin could see a 'big change' before the placement and then after the placement. Before the placement she had not done 'a lot of my own thinking'. During the placement, her supervisor, who was 'very experiment-orientated . . . [and] also doing her PhD at that time', engaged her in discussion about theories and they 'debate[d] the case study together', so applying theory helped her to make sense of the case. Consequently, in her second semester, when she worked on case studies or applied theories, 'I can think about the case I did during the placement so . . . it's easier.'

In her second year, 'everything was very intense' because of all the things that were 'going on in my life'. She felt pressured because she was 'thinking about in the future, where I'm going to work' and how she was going to develop job interview skills: 'a lot of people say [a good] . . . placement is really important and you [will] probably work there if they need someone.'

The placements also affected her own development. She was going to be a case manager during her second placement and felt 'I can do that.' The placement was a success. When she thought about the future after this placement, she felt, 'I'm fully qualified . . . so I take myself as [an] employee in that agency, not just a student anymore.'

After completing the course and resuming her Masters degree, Zelin felt, at 22, 'like a researcher' and was thinking that she may apply to do a PhD in the future. When she began the Masters degree (prior to the undergraduate course), she 'didn't think about any of this'.

In short, Zelin thought that the most important learning for her during the undergraduate course came from the placements, because they gave her opportunities to 'practise' and provided work experience in Australia. She also thought that the course tutorials were 'quite good'. The lectures were good 'but you go there [and] you basically just listen' whereas 'the tutorials actually give you opportunity to share and practise and . . . discuss things when you choose to'.

Zelin's immediate plans after completing her Masters degree were to take a break and spend 'probably two or three months travelling around China and come back and start . . . finding [a] job'. She was not sure yet what her 'true interest' was, so she hoped to try different fields before possibly going back to university. Zelin hoped to work in Australia for several years and after that 'probably go back to China' to work there.

Implications for managing and supporting student diversity: international students

Lam's and Zelin's stories illustrate issues that are unique to international students and also issues that are experienced by local and international students alike. Among those particular to international students are the academic and cultural challenges of studying in a different education system with different teaching conventions and practices and in a second (or sometimes third or fourth) language. Both Lam and Zelin were capable students, having demonstrated their success in the highly competitive and demanding Hong Kong and Chinese school systems, and in their studies since arriving in Australia. Yet both reported on the importance of *time* in supporting their learning in this course. While courses have timetables, semester patterns, and cycles, often students from diverse backgrounds require more time to fully comprehend course material, to integrate new knowledge into their existing frameworks and make sense of it. With time, it becomes possible to succeed.

Associated with this is the time students need to learn how to live in a new city and look after themselves. This involves learning how to shop, cook, clean, and do the washing; learning the public transport system and roads, where to shop for what goods, finding part-time work to help support themselves, and so on. For Zelin, living with her boyfriend also involved negotiating in her daily life a gendered work order where she was expected to do most of the domestic labour alongside her studies. These are features of everyday life that many women experience, each requiring new skills and knowledge, and involving complex negotiation and management. However, developing life skills quickly in an unfamiliar country is important for the successful transition of international students to university and has implications for all staff associated with them, particularly those in support roles. It re-emphasises the idea of all staff being involved in assisting students so that the most effective channels for getting advice to students can be explored.

An especially important aspect of the advice that international students require before they embark on overseas study is course information, including requirements for professional recognition and professional registration. Inadequate information affected the progress of both Lam and Zelin. This has implications for advice provided in recruitment information for overseas students before they arrive and also at the commencement of their course.

Once enrolled, central to the success of each woman was the importance of a group of peers or friends. Friendship networks among fellow students offer emotional and moral support in reassuring students that they are not alone and that others are going through similar experiences. Lam's comment on the value of more 'small group gatherings' to build up relationships between class members points to a practical step teachers and professional staff can take to enhance interpersonal relationships among students through social activities, which could also be used early in a course to encourage networks for advice and information about living arrangements. While Zelin commented on the difficulties of bonding with 'local classmates', strategies for 'facilitating meaningful interaction between students from different cultural and linguistic backgrounds in and out of the classroom' (Leask, 2009: 205; Teoh, 2008) have the potential to provide avenues of social and academic support and information for international students. Campbell (2012) provides an example of a 'buddy project' used to support the transition of international students. However, students also feel a natural affinity with others of the same culture, such as Zelin's group of Chinese and Hong Kong students. This enables group members to empathise with each other's positions, and these groups should be supported by university staff. A critical aspect of peer and group support, which is not limited to international students, is their role in learning, for example, in discussing the assignment questions and helping to improve their understanding of the course material.

However, what is often difficult for international students is the difference in teaching styles and expectations, as illustrated particularly by Zelin's comments, which reflect different cultural expectations relating to teaching and learning. McLean and Ransom (2005) consider a number of ways for increasing the intercultural competencies of students and staff, noting the importance of becoming aware of your own cultural pre-programming, and learning about the cultural encoding of others, while Carroll (2005) focuses on the importance of being explicit with all students, but especially international students coming from different learning and social cultures. As Edwards et al. (2003) noted, the recent focus on internationalisation of the curriculum, which aims to prepare students for the globalised world, has in some ways assisted the adjustment of international students to their new education systems. By teachers 'providing course content that reflects diverse perspectives' (p. 188) and citing examples from a range of countries to explain the disciplinary principles, international students can feel that their backgrounds and experiences, which probably differ from those of the host country, are authenticated. It is important to ensure that internationalisation at this level exists for the students that you work with.

A key change for many international students, which Zelin's comments illustrate, is the expectation of more participation and discussion, which may be very different from the passive role in learning to which students are accustomed. While both Lam and Zelin valued the small group work in their course, Zelin's comments ('it's really rude to interrupt other people') illustrate the initial difficulties students may face in participating. This suggests the importance of early scaffolded participatory tasks which provide a comfortable and defined space for students to contribute. Reflective tasks that ask students to relate their past experiences to their current learning are potentially valuable here, as they are for students from other non-traditional backgrounds. Promoting this kind of discussion of difference in experience and background can be related to the course subject matter, for example, by drawing attention to the culturally bound nature of much knowledge, whether it is education knowledge or professional and workplace knowledge. Both McLean and Ransom (2005) and Ryan (2005) suggest a range of strategies for encouraging participation in tutorials and seminars.

These women's stories illustrate the enormous challenges of studying in a language other than your first. Most university teachers and support staff have not faced this challenge and cannot imagine what it feels like. This includes the demands of becoming proficient in academic English, and the challenge of learning the day-to-day language of the context, and other aspects of cultural life. Many international students report on the extra time required to study in a second (or third) language, as they translate course ideas or discussion points into their own language before returning to English to make their response.

Zelin correctly pointed out that while essay writing is difficult in a language other than your first, many local students also struggle with writing essays, and in particular with constructing an argument in their essays. This has profound implications for teaching, as the capacity to absorb and integrate reading and develop an authorial voice and argument is at the heart of many teaching programs. It highlights the importance of investing class time and effort in teaching students how to develop and set out an argument in their written work and recognise the role of critical thinking (McLean and Ransom, 2005). Both the issue of assistance with language in academic writing, and that of assistance with academic literacy more generally, have important implications for the way support services are provided. There are similarities between Sesh's comments (in Chapter 3) on services which did not really assist her and the comments made by Lam in this chapter. Both suggest that these services needed to be more student-centred, focusing on students' perceptions of the help that they needed. You may wish to review your response to the discussion topic at the end of Chapter 3 regarding academic skills such as essay writing to see if considering Lam's and Zelin's stories changes your views in any way.

Lam's and Zelin's stories point not only to the importance of planning in their success, but to the need to review and revise study plans and approaches at intervals during the course. For example, Zelin changed her study pattern in her second year to build in her part-time jobs. Much can happen in a student's life over a period of study, so university staff can create opportunities for students to consider how their needs may have changed and how new strategies may be needed to achieve their goals. This could be part of social support group activities but it could also be embedded in class work. Teaching staff could, for example, create a small group exercise for use in tutorials where students discuss the forthcoming semester's key ideas, the semester's demands, and consider their goals and the factors that will support or hinder them to achieve those goals. Students could be supported to draft a plan as the outcome of this activity, setting out also what they need to do, and the forms of support they need to seek from others, including university staff.

Like the students in earlier chapters, Lam and Zelin valued the professional orientation of the course and the opportunities their professional work placements provided for them to test out what they had learnt and develop their skills. Work-based professional placements have an additional advantage for international students by helping them to develop their understanding of the local social and cultural context. This understanding is necessary for them to practise effectively as professionals with clients and to help them find jobs in the field when they graduate. These women's stories also emphasise the importance of providing – through the curriculum – a comprehensive introduction to the field of professional practice as a way to anchor teaching and learning in the course, and the value of linking study to the workplace (Bamber, 2008).

For these students on student visas, anxiety about their future status and their ability to work in their profession following completion of their study is an important consideration. If you are working with international students you should familiarise yourself with the relevant information to increase your ability to support them. Conditions for students can fluctuate depending on government policy. The Australian Government (2011) changed the conditions of student visas so that on graduation from undergraduate and coursework postgraduate programs, international students have the right to work in Australia for two years.

Summary

In this chapter we introduced Lam and Zelin, two Chinese-speaking women studying and living in Australia. Their stories illustrate the range of practical and emotional issues that must be addressed to live and study in another country, as well as the educational challenges. Both grappled with issues related to language, particularly the writing demands of study. Lam found that university language support services did not provide the support she needed, while Zelin's comments highlight the challenges associated with different approaches to learning. However, their stories echo those of Sesh and Shannon in Chapter 3 in their recognition of the need for self-reliance and responsibility for their own learning and success. They also felt a strong sense of responsibility to their parents overseas who supported their study. For both Lam and Zelin, the moral and practical support of fellow international students was critical.

Lam's and Zelin's stories demonstrate the kinds of social and cultural factors that affect students from international backgrounds and we have suggested some implications for improving learning, teaching, and support with these students in mind. Strategies which you could implement (or influence) will depend on your role and your institution. Use the following discussion topics to think about ways that you could improve the experience of international students that you are involved with.

Chapter 4: discussion topics

1. How is the basic survival information (such as the climate, food and shopping facilities near the campus, the cost of living, how to rent a flat, use public transport, get a job) imparted to international students in your institution? What could you do to improve the information that students receive and the way they receive it?
2. In addition to providing information, what are three things that you could do as an individual teacher or professional staff member to assist students with the social and cultural transition issues involved in moving to another country to study? What are three things your department or unit could do as a group?
3. Course information, including professional recognition requirements, is an important aspect of the advice that international students require. How is this information provided to students at your institution (a) before they leave home and (b) when they commence their course? What could you do to improve the course information that students receive and the way they receive it?
4. If you have a teaching role, how could you use the curriculum and your classroom contact with students to support wider and stronger peer relationships, involving both local and international students?
5. What work-based components of courses that local and international students undertake are you familiar with? If you have a teaching role, what could you do to improve the relationship of these components with classroom learning to enhance the relevance, support, and learning of (a) all students and (b) international students in particular?

5

Coming to education later in life: Alex Carole and Virginia

Abstract: Alex Carole and Virginia are two women who commenced university study in their forties, when their life circumstances, including the support of their husbands, made it possible. Both grew up under apartheid in South Africa, though on different sides of the colour bar. Alex Carole is of Indian origin while Virginia is white. Both demonstrate a determined and organised approach to their study, valuing the opportunity to pursue it, and showing resilience in overcoming obstacles they faced. Their graduation had a powerful impact on them. Their stories provide an opportunity to consider ways of teaching and supporting adult learners to take advantage of their maturity and experience while responding to their particular needs.

Key words: adult learning, feedback, gender, off-campus study, mature age students, social justice.

Introduction

Alex Carole and Virginia were in their forties when they enrolled in the studies which they successfully completed. For both women, study became possible because their children were growing up. Each of them was also supported and encouraged by a university-educated husband. Their gender was one of the factors that had limited their opportunities to access higher education earlier in their lives. Coincidentally, both were born in South Africa and grew up under apartheid, though on different sides of the colour bar. Alex Carole is of Indian origin while Virginia is white. Both subsequently migrated to Australia, Alex Carole as a teenager and Virginia much later with her husband and children.

Their return to study was triggered by different factors: for Alex Carole it was a serious health crisis and a serendipitous encounter, while for Virginia it was grasping an opportunity that circumstances made possible ('it's now or never'). Both valued the experience of higher education and it had a major impact on the self-concept of each woman. Students like Alex Carole and Virginia have life experience and determination to assist them to overcome obstacles they face, and their stories provide an opportunity to consider management and support strategies for older mature age students entering higher education.

Alex Carole's story

Pathway to higher education

Alex Carole was in her late forties when she enrolled in her course. Following the death of her much loved grandfather, she migrated to Australia as a teenager in the 1970s with her mother and sister. As a 'coloured' person in South Africa, the educational opportunities available to her under apartheid were limited. Alex Carole was the first in her family to attend university.

Family background

Alex Carole grew up in Durban. Her parents separated when she was young but she stayed in touch with her father. She was also in contact with her paternal grandparents, aunties, and uncles. The house she grew up in contained four generations from her mother's side of the family: her great-grandmother, her grandfather (who was 'my whole world'), her mother (who was an only child), and Alex Carole and her younger sister.

Alex Carole always wanted to be a nurse:

> *. . . that idea came from my grandfather whom I was very close to. In my first year of primary school he got very sick . . . he used to wait for me every morning at eight o'clock . . . by the gate, just so he could say hello to me . . . and the same in the afternoon . . . That's what gave me the inclination [for nursing] – and besides . . . [for the] the non-whites, coloureds, the Indians, the Malays or Africans, the opportunities to do anything more than a few professional jobs [were few] . . . there weren't a lot of [girls]. . .*

> when I was growing up who wanted to be anything other than . . . a receptionist or a secretary or a nurse or a teacher . . . they weren't encouraged to have higher aspirations, to becom[e] doctors and lawyers.

Alex Carole described growing up under apartheid:

> . . . from the time I was little and from the time I could speak English, I was told, 'You can't do this and you can't do that. And this is the way life is' . . . as I grew older, I thought, 'Oh, hang on a minute. Is it the same in Cape Town? Is it the same in Johannesburg?' And I was told, 'Yes. Because [of] the law of the land.' And I thought, 'Oh, OK.' So you grew up accepting and doing what you were supposed to do, and . . . not mak[ing] any waves.

When she finished high school Alex Carole enrolled in nursing at a teaching hospital in Cape Town, despite her grandfather's resistance ('my baby's not going away from me'), and then six weeks later he died. He had encouraged her mother to leave South Africa with her children to escape apartheid and after his death the family migrated to Australia. Alex Carole enquired about a nursing career in Australia but was told that she needed to 'go back' and complete the final year of high school:

> But I'd finished high school! You know? I've got my certificate with me! But it's not acceptable in Australia. I said, 'Oh, OK' and I couldn't . . . how would my Mum support me?

Alex Carole felt that she had to continue to work and help her mother support her younger sister who was still at school. She then worked at a department store for three and a half years, obtaining her driver's licence, marrying, and having a baby: '[going] back to work in the retail sector' when her son was 18 months old. She did not consider further education over that period:

> . . . my then husband would have been most against it! You know, he was . . . a very typical South African man . . . your place is at home, you look after the house and the children and you made sure there is dinner on the table every night. Don't try and get too smart by wanting to go back and get a higher education.

Later, Alex Carole married again: 'I have a very good husband now.' Her husband is an engineer, with a university degree. She has two sons, one in his thirties and the other of school age.

Educational experiences

Alex Carole completed secondary school but regarded herself as 'an average student':

> *I don't think I was ... overly zealous at being ... a student – I excelled in some subjects more than others, of course ... maths wasn't ... a very good subject for me. English, biology, geography, home economics – I loved cooking. Still love cooking! Typing. I did all the girlie things ...*

The most important event in Alex Carole's decision to return to study resulted from managing a significant health problem 25 years after migrating to Australia:

> *I got really, really sick. I was losing a lot of blood on a fortnightly basis. And a friend of mine said that I should speak to the [hospital], and they helped me there and put me in for ... a hysterectomy ... I parked the car in the car park across the road ... And on my way to pick up the car, found I had no money on me.*

Alex Carole was helped by hospital social workers, not only with money for parking, but also in clarifying how she would cope after her surgery. Following this experience:

> *... when I was sick, and thinking, 'Why me?' ... I thought, 'Why you? Why don't you do something about it?' And while I was recuperating after having the hysterectomy, I [thought] ... 'hang on a minute; I can do ... something different. I can do something better. I can do something good. But why not?'*

She applied to enter university and was offered a place in a social science degree. This was not her main area of interest but 'I just saw it as an opportunity to turn my life around and here I am!' Alex Carole completed two years of social science at a major metropolitan university, gaining admission with her South African high school certificate, an essay, and personal references from two people who could vouch that she was who she said she was.

She commented on commencing the social science degree:

> ... I know when I first went back ... I thought, '**Oohh** – oh, my goodness, what am I doing here? With all these babies.' It was a big challenge to sit in a class with so many young people and see myself as a dinosaur! And then halfway through the first semester, to look back and think, 'Oh, I've stuck it out' ... it actually made me feel very good in the sense that I could actually stick at it.

Despite the discomfort of sitting among 'all these students [who] are old enough to be my kids', her ability to 'stick at it' was particularly evident because:

> ... there were so many kids when I started the first year ... that I didn't even see after the Easter break. [I thought], 'What's going on? Where have they gone to?'

After two years Alex Carole applied for and was accepted into her current undergraduate course at another university, studying in off-campus mode because she moved to Malaysia with her husband while he worked there. In Malaysia, Alex Carole worked as a volunteer at an orphanage where she experienced a strong sense of wanting to help the orphaned children to achieve their potential. She felt passionate about her new course and ready to make a difference in the lives of others.

Managing study

Planning

Alex Carole described herself as 'a big planner': 'I like to know what I'm doing, when I'm doing it and how I'm going to do it.' Consequently, when she received her course materials, her response was to 'get up and go through my book and I highlighted all my assignment dates so that I knew when they were due'. She then planned which parts of the course requirements she was going to address first.

Managing

Alex Carole allowed a number of hours 'per subject per week' and then tried to 'stick to it'. She was unable to work in Malaysia and so studied most days, relying on access to broadband internet:

> ... I actually broke up the day for the subjects that I was doing and [would] spend about two hours on each subject.

When she returned to Australia, Alex Carole did not have a separate room for study in her home, but used a corner of the lounge. When her husband and younger son were at home on weekends, she would take her laptop computer and books and study in the local library.

Alex Carole completed the first field placement for her course after she returned to Australia. She found organising the placement challenging, both in terms of practicalities (getting there) and the emotionally challenging work she was required to undertake. One of her clients, an elderly man, died and Alex Carole attended the funeral. She questioned whether she could have intervened differently, but was supported by her field teacher:

> ... one of the nicest comments that the field teacher and my supervisor have made is that they found that on placement I have accepted every situation as a new experience, and not judged any of our clients, because of who they are or where they come from ...

Alex Carole found her field placement to be an important aspect of her learning. At the completion of the placement she was offered employment for two days a week at the agency and continued to work there.

She felt satisfied with how she had managed the demands of moving to Malaysia and back while studying and then completing the field placement:

> ... it had been a challenging year all around. Re-settling back into life in Australia and coping with the many demands of family, work and study. I am amazed that I have come this far. I have also learnt many things about myself along the way. If at first you don't succeed, try, try again ...

However, Alex Carole did not complete the course without difficulty. She failed a compulsory research subject twice, and she struggled to understand why this had occurred. She then investigated alternative ways of completing the subject, and found a similar subject at another, regional university:

> ... [b]efore I would have just accepted that I had to wait and do the subject again. But the drive as a mature age student is more intense.

> *I was committed to getting this degree. I'd come this far. I needed to do it for myself – [it] wasn't going to beat me . . .*

During this time Alex Carole had to manage a number of family issues. There was a court order from her ex-husband opposing her intention to travel overseas with her younger son. At the same time her father died in South Africa. By this time, though, she had learnt enough about how universities work to know there were alternative ways she might meet the research unit requirements of her degree. Her proposal to complete an alternative subject was accepted and she allocated a full day once a week to travel to the university to attend and complete it.

Support

Alex Carole's husband and older son supported her decision to study. Her husband worked with her in sharing responsibilities, including the household chores:

> *About the only thing I really do if I study is . . . I stick to the house and I do the cooking. [My husband] cleans up after dinner. He washes up the dishes. I put the washing on the line, he brings it in, he irons it. He puts everybody's clothes on their bed. So . . . we work well together . . . it has to be if one person's trying to do something that's going to benefit everybody later on, then everybody needs to share.*

Alex Carole did not use any of the support services provided by the university but she was supported by the online group that she belonged to as a requirement for one subject. In this space, she discussed issues that came up in relation to study and assignments:

> *. . . if I'm stuck on a particular topic, I just put my idea out there and ask someone to comment back on it. I like to make sure I'm on the right track and I tend to use my group more . . . than anything else . . . I tend to utilise all my friends more . . . than anybody else.*

She did telephone the university's online help desk a few times 'because there were some technical problems with the [subject] site'.

For Alex Carole, the friends she made among her fellow students, her husband who would proof read her work, and the flexibility provided by her work (obtained via her first placement) were the best supports of her learning.

Reflections and future plans

Alex Carole completed her degree part-time in three years. Reflecting on herself as a learner she was '[s]urprised that I'm so persistent' and described persistence as her main quality.

She noticed changes in herself in the first year of her course:

> The role plays ... [were critical for] building my confidence ... Gave me the confidence to believe in myself. In first year I started to look at things from different perspectives. Before that I had a social conscience but went about my business. Things didn't worry me – as a family we would give to the Red Cross or Salvation Army but I started to feel more strongly about issues. Like affordable housing – that everyone should have access to a decent home. I've grown in more than one way, not just self-esteem and confidence but in my sense of social justice.

Alex Carole's fieldwork placement at the end of her first year contributed significantly to her learning, along with her experience in Malaysia:

> First placement was so significant – it was everything, the people, the clients – older people and so many different groups. Living in Malaysia for 18 months as well, I became more aware of disadvantage and society and I am so grateful to live in this country, but we still don't look after our disadvantaged groups enough.

During her second year Alex Carole noticed subtle changes in her development as a learner. She commented that her ability to keep going rather than dropping out when she failed a subject was evidence of her growing maturity and confidence:

> I was aware of my abilities and limitations. Even today I know and accept that I am a good worker and can accept criticism as a learning process and not take it too personal or too serious ... I'd grown as a person. Had high expectations of myself that I didn't have to that degree at the start. It was failing [a subject] – and all the self-talk – I disappointed me ... The self-talk: 'I didn't pass it, get over it, and move on.' If my confidence hadn't grown over the first 12 months I would have thought, 'Just drop out.' But I wasn't going to. Work was really great. I worked Monday to Thursday and had Friday off. When I said I had to go to [the regional university each week] ...

> *they let me change the day. I enjoyed it – the drive was time for reflection. I'd think about what we learnt and then come home and sit at the computer and write it down. I could have applied myself more at [that university] but in the last couple of weeks, I didn't need to – I just needed to pass the subject.*

Alex Carole gained employment on graduation, describing herself, at the end of the course, as '[s]till learning. Still a sponge of sorts.' She thought that in the future she would like to learn more about psychology or counselling. She 'was happy with the whole course' but would have liked '[m]aybe [the] opportunity to resubmit that particular assignment':

> *Doing the course has given me the skills to advocate on behalf of myself. I couldn't do that before . . . [I] look back now and think, 'Wow, you have come a long way, Alex Carole.'*

Virginia's story

Pathway to higher education

Virginia is a white woman from South Africa. She now lives in an Australian city with her husband and three children. She met her husband at 22, married at 23 and, at the commencement of her course, had been married for 17 years.

Family and personal background

Virginia grew up with her parents, a brother who is '[a] year and a bit' older, and a sister who is five years younger. She did not see the context of her upbringing as a white person in South Africa as 'advantageous', but as 'terribly ordinary'. Her parents were just 'bringing up children, earning a living'.

While she was at high school she became aware of her father's alcoholism:

> *. . . we had a lot of family dramas going on throughout my high school years . . . And my parents eventually divorced in my final year of school. So neither my brother nor I achieved as well as we probably could have, had we had a more stable family home.*

Virginia's mother was one of seven children, none of whom went to university. Her mother married again but no one in the family of her second husband had been to university either. Virginia felt that going to university was seen as 'what other people do' because '[w]e're not smart enough', although meeting people who were taking degrees led her to recognise that 'if they can do it, I know I can, too'.

Virginia did not think that her father had any expectations of her when she was young ('he was too wrapped up in his own things I suppose'). She considered that her parents' expectations of her were different from their expectations of her brother:

> ... you know your place! ... I don't think my mother intended it. Certainly, she's extremely supportive of what I'm doing now ... [but] I can remember her saying to me – although she denies it – that I didn't need to go to university because I'd get married! ... I think she always wanted to get married because that's what you did, and bring up the children ...

Virginia's brother 'went on to become a chartered accountant – he's had a very successful career', while her younger sister was 'very much like my mother' and became a housewife. Although Virginia did not have any particular support when she was young to encourage her in the direction of higher education, her brother was '[a]bsolutely' a role model. He completed a correspondence degree after leaving school: 'I often think I should have been more like him ... a little bit more focused possibly.'

Virginia's husband became a role model and key source of support. He came from a 'traditional' nuclear family and was university educated. Reflecting on this, she commented:

> Had I married somebody equally as nice, but someone from a slightly more dysfunctional family, he wouldn't have been as supportive. Somebody who maybe didn't have a university degree themselves.

Virginia's mother-in-law is an occupational therapist and her father-in-law, an engineer. Virginia did not think that they went to university in England ('it was that sort of technical education') but her husband's sister had been to university, as had various other family members: 'I've got cousins who are lawyers – one's a doctor – spread all over the world', so university education 'certainly wasn't out of my consciousness'.

However, as she was growing up, Virginia's most influential role models were people who had not entered higher education through traditional pathways, from a position of middle class comfort:

> *I think living in South Africa ... there were a lot of people – the most obvious example is Nelson Mandela ... who [demonstrate that] you don't have to do it traditionally.*

Virginia regarded these people as probably more successful because 'you know more about life – and you know more about who you are and what you want.'

Virginia had had a sense of social justice from an early age, though she did not think of this in terms of a potential profession when she was a child:

> *I remember when I was about six, and saying to my mother, 'I wish we could pick up all the black people at the side of the road' – they were actually just waiting for a bus to go home – but that was me thinking, 'Oh, I should take them home and feed them ...'*

This sense of social justice continued as she grew up, partly because of the South African context, but also because of her own emerging social consciousness. In the mid-eighties, when apartheid 'was just coming apart at the seams, and everybody had an opinion', Virginia, then aged 17 or 18, became very involved in left-wing politics, 'which caused a lot of friction with family and friends'. She was never afraid to express her feelings, in contrast to her brother who would 'just keep quiet about it'. As she grew older she became increasingly aware of the barriers that black people faced.

Virginia wanted to go to university when she finished high school, and was accepted, '[b]ut there was no money':

> *... in South Africa, there's no welfare system. User pays. And my Mum didn't even own property where she could find a bank surety ... She was a single mother with three children.*

Consequently, she started work, '[a]lways intending to study'. She did not know what she wanted to study, although her social justice leanings continued to influence her and she considered political studies. She worked for a blood transfusion service that 'trained us as medical technologists':

> *This was an opportunity to get some training. You're getting them to pay for it and you're earning a salary. So I understand that . . . but if it taught me anything, it was what I didn't want to do.*

Virginia then 'backpacked around the world for a year and a half' before she married.

Educational experiences

Virginia 'wasn't a great achiever' in primary school ('[m]ost of my school teachers would be amazed that I'm here'). She 'didn't make the most of' primary school but she had a lot of fun. She was not aware of barriers to her achievement at the time, although problems relating to her father's alcoholism 'would have been there'. Virginia was happy at school and had good friends.

Although she recognised that the education system was 'for the most part . . . superior for white children', Virginia considered that it was 'no more so than in an average Australian government school' and that '[y]ou work hard at school . . . you get what you pay for'. She did not feel that being a white person provided advantages 'for the most part'.

Virginia compared the maturity of her children with her own level of maturity as a child. Noting the maturity of her older daughter, she thought 'if only I could have been like that at your age', but her experiences had taught her that her son, who is less mature, will 'find his way . . . and probably do well at the end of it'. Virginia saw her son as being similar to her when she was young:

> *. . . I don't think he's naughty or anything, but he has a good time at school and he's so smart! But I see his homework and I think, 'It doesn't matter. The penny will drop with him one day.'*

Virginia's immaturity at school, in contrast to her brother, who 'was the model student', continued for the first few years of high school. She changed when her mother told her that unless she took her schooling seriously she would fail and then her friends would be a year above her; they would be 'going to their formals before you'. Virginia reluctantly complied thinking, 'What on earth is the point of this?' However, her mother had picked on the one point that had an effect on her: 'I could just think of them all getting dressed up . . . these were girls I'd grown up with and it was a real shame to stay down.' As a consequence of this intervention, Virginia came second in the class: 'the light switched on and the penny dropped' and she realised, 'Oh, I can do this!' People's expectations of her then changed, and Virginia 'moved up' to meet their new expectations.

Nevertheless, Virginia 'hated' high school, probably because 'a lot of stuff was going on at home, as well'. In addition, she was not encouraged by her teachers. Virginia remembered asking her final year English teacher whether she thought she could do English at university. The teacher said, 'No . . . you're not up there.' Virginia's mental response was 'Stuff you!' Virginia remained conscious of the influence teachers have through labelling students, relating this to the harm that can be done by prematurely dividing children into 'the university ones' and the others, when the children who are 'talking in the back are OK but they're bored or naughty'. However, she also felt that:

> . . . sometimes we're not ready for certain things at certain times in our life. Maybe I would have been a really crap [professional person] at 21. That it wasn't meant to be then.

She also noted that South African education was 'very much "this is what you must learn"', with 'no questions asked'. Virginia studied history in her final year at school, including apartheid, but the students were 'not allowed to question it'. Thus, the approach to education did not support her understanding of what was happening in South Africa. It was a revelation when she first read about the 1957 Group Areas Act on the separation of black people from white people and she thought:

> What was the Group Areas Act? I just knew . . . [i]f you drove up the road and went left, black people lived there. Nobody had ever discussed the fact that there was [a] Group Areas Act. Actually [white people] weren't allowed to live there! . . . if you were black, you could not go higher than middle management! If you were black, you could not go there. If you were black, you could not – and that was my first sort of – 'Ooohh' . . . Most people just said, 'Oh, OK, turn the page.' I remember thinking, 'This is wrong!' . . . but there was no way to express that.

Despite her mother's encouragement to improve at high school, she 'really just wanted me to get a job'. This was partly because her mother did not have the funds to support her at university.

As she was unable to go to university when she finished school, Virginia began to study after her first child was born. She enrolled in a correspondence course at the University of South Africa, on the basis of her school qualifications: 'I think I just always knew that I wanted to do it.' At that time, Virginia's brother was undertaking his degree, and circumstances in her own life made studying achievable.

Virginia did not quite finish this course: 'I got two credits short' and then 'life [got] in the way of it'. She studied criminology, English, and psychology, before discovering she could study social work off-campus. She completed Social Work I and II, and did well. She changed to social work because she felt that 'when you go to university, you really should train to be something' based on her experience of working in recruitment for some years, and recognising the disadvantage of entering the workforce without a practical, vocational qualification. Looking back, Virginia presumed that she also realised that studying social work would help her to fulfil her social justice aspirations.

She was unable to continue due to the need to complete a practical component. Virginia had had a second child by this time, and 'really needed to earn a living':

> I thought, well, 'I'll put it off for a year and I'll go back to it,' but by then we were building a house! And my income was very necessary. And ... in South Africa, you lose credit for Social Work I and II, for degree purposes, if you don't do it within one year of finishing the course ...

Consequently, 'it almost became too hard again' and although she had a good media job she would sometimes think:

> 'This is not where I want to be.' I'd meet social workers and think, 'Oh, you're so lucky! I wish I was doing that!'

During this time the family emigrated to Ireland and then to Australia. When Virginia's husband (an architect) was setting up a business in Australia, she was able to consider higher education again as her youngest child had started school. She thought:

> The kids are settled. It's time! It's like it's now or never. We haven't bought a home, even. We're still renting a house. Once you get on to that wheel you can't get off. And I said [to my husband] ... 'while you're ... setting up a business – maybe this is the time ... If I'm going to have to work for the rest of my life, which I accept that I will, and I don't mind doing it, I want to do it for me.'

Virginia was accepted into her current course on the basis of her studies in South Africa. She had previously investigated finishing her degree while in Ireland, but was deterred by red tape, and because 'they wanted you to have done your majors at that university'. As she embarked on the course, Virginia commented that, financially, it would be 'a bit of a struggle', but she was 'glad to be here'. However, she recognised that:

> *. . . when you're doing it off-campus, and older, you do need support. You don't need somebody saying to you, 'Do you really have to be doing this? I wish you were earning some money . . .'*

Virginia commented on the advantages of off-campus study in her situation, 'because you're not restricted by time' and 'you can fit it around things so much better!' If a child is sick and unable to go to school, or needs to be taken to a doctor, study can take place 'at two o'clock in the morning', if necessary. Virginia also valued the Australian system of deferred fee payment because it means that anybody can go to university if they want to, which is not possible in South Africa.

Managing study

Planning

For Virginia, ceasing paid employment was an important aspect of planning for study. She knew that she 'could have a few months of not working and I didn't know how that was going to go', so she had a 'little contingency' plan whereby she could reduce her study to part-time if she had to return to work. However, Virginia's husband won a big contract, which provided her with the financial freedom to focus on her studies. Although he worked a 60-hour week, which 'gets a bit stressful', this allowed Virginia to continue.

Managing

Virginia studied, on average, for about 30 hours per week. When she returned from taking the children to school, she made some coffee and then went to the computer: 'I take a break at half past ten, read the paper for 20 minutes, go back' to study until about 2.00pm. Hence, Virginia's study day 'pretty much' replaced her work day. Once the children came home from school, she could devote time to them and to the household chores.

Virginia was flexible enough to accommodate variable demands on her study time. In busier weeks, she studied at nights as well, once the children were in bed. She did this a 'fair bit', starting at about 9.00pm:

> ... I tend to be a night person ... sometimes I think, 'Oh, I'm a bit tired,' and then I think, 'I'll just go and have a look' – and then I'd sit down – and once I've got past that time ... the quietness again took me through to one o'clock in the morning.

Virginia tried not to study at weekends but this depended on 'where I was in terms of assignment dates'. There were times when she and her husband were 'like ships passing in the night', and also times when her plans to study were disrupted. Her flexibility and commitment to her study allowed Virginia to accommodate those times, and other major interruptions, including a six-week visit from her South African in-laws: 'I had to, without being rude, say, "I'm going into the study".' She commented that, 'It sounds like I was ... organised, but I wasn't all the time.' Nevertheless, she handled time management 'quite well', because she 'had to do it'.

Virginia found her first field placement to be 'fantastic', which helped her deal with the small doubt she had had about it: 'What if I'm doing all this and I get there and I think, "'I don't want to do this?"' This placement was a valuable source of support and a change from the isolation of study. It was different from her previous corporate work environments, and contributed to her successful study experience:

> Luckily I was in a place where no one really cared when you had lunch ... people would stop and chat for ages about things. In the private sector you're not supposed to do that ... because time is money.

There were other differences in this community development work environment:

> ... people did a lot of weekend work ... a lot of stuff happens after hours ... 'time in lieu of' was very much a big thing ... once a week one of the support groups would do lunch to thank the organisation ... So you'd have Sudanese women doing lunch and there was enough food to feed half of Africa ... they'd bring it in and they'd want you to eat and they'd do some dancing for you ... So to be working in an environment like that was just so inspiring ...

Virginia's previous work experience and 'dormant' organisational skills contributed to her successful placement:

> ... in my final evaluation my supervisor on placement said one of the Somalian guys that I'd worked with had said to her that I'd helped him a lot in terms of organisation, which I hadn't realised ...

Virginia benefited from communication with her student peer group, but commented on one of the limitations of distance education:

> You get this mark back that says 75 per cent – so that's good. But how good? ... maybe that was the bottom of [the lecturer's] grades.

Virginia was offered a place in the Honours program, which was a high point at the end of her first year, but owing to the lack of opportunity to measure her achievement against her peers, she wasn't prepared for it:

> ... when [the lecturer] phoned me at home and offered me Honours he said, 'You sound surprised.' I said, 'Well, I am.' He said, 'You've got very good marks.' I said, 'I know they've been quite good. But I didn't really know that they were that good.'

It would have been difficult for Virginia to continue her paid work, given the placement requirements. Not having to do paid work offered other benefits in that her husband and she could share responsibilities, and 'it actually works for both of us'. They were able to work around the 'odd occasions' when rearrangements needed to be made, for example, to allow Virginia's attendance at residential workshops. These arrangements were supported by her husband, which Virginia illustrated with reference to his response to 'a few jobs that came up in placement':

> ... I said, 'Oh, I'd really like to apply for those,' and he said 'But this is working right now! ... You have to finish what you're doing ...'

Virginia managed the demands on her time from her husband, his business, their three children, her mother, and other family and friends, by putting 'some things on hold' and making sure that people understood the new demands on her time. Other things that Virginia put on hold included sewing, which she loved, but she knew she could 'come back to that'. Virginia's mother was on her own and asked Virginia to come around 'fairly frequently', but she also provided support. Although people told Virginia, 'You need to take care of yourself. You need to do things for yourself,' which made her think, 'I really don't have a very balanced life,' she realised that she was 'doing this for me'.

Study involved constant juggling but 'life carries on'. Virginia and her husband bought a house during her first year of study. They 'moved at a fairly inopportune moment but you just work around it'. She recognised that she must be a good manager and others acknowledged this, even though 'it doesn't feel like it at the time'. As Virginia had 'always worked ... even when it's been in a part-time role', she was 'quite organised' about managing household tasks and meeting the children's needs, so her aim was to continue this while studying:

> ... when I left the house to take my youngest to school, the beds were made, the washing was hung on the line and the dishes were done, and the kitchen was as I would have left it for work. So when I get home at quarter past nine, I'm not thinking, 'Oh, there's washing to do'. . .

Virginia found managing these responsibilities easier than when she was working. Although she and her husband had always done whatever was necessary to attend school plays and functions, now, when parents were asked to 'come to school at nine o'clock for five minutes worth of a song that they've practised', she could do it easily, because she was just 'up the road', whereas 'when you're working maybe half an hour away, it's a huge commitment to make, just for that five minutes.'

For Virginia, personal commitment was a major factor in successful study:

> ... when you're older and you make a commitment to do it ... then you really want to do it ... Knowing all the time that things could change tomorrow. Your child can be sick. And you go, 'OK! That'll have to wait.'

Occasionally, Virginia went to lunch with friends, but the things she gave up did not bother her, even though there were times when she thought, 'Oh! It'd be nice to get out of my study' because '[h]ome and study just becomes your world totally'.

Virginia emphasised the importance of a stable life context as a factor in successful study, compared to:

> ... when my kids were small and small kids are a lot more unpredictable ... they suddenly get sick at the drop of a hat, and they're really sick. Now if they get sick I can just say, 'Now lie on the couch or sit and watch TV or lie in your bed – I'm here' ...

Although Virginia managed her study successfully, '[t]here were times that I thought, "What am I studying family therapy for? We need a bit of it ourselves!"' There was a 'little bit of clashing of stress levels' and an attitude of 'you think your study is more important than mine' from her elder daughter, who was studying for her school exams: 'There were some nights where we were queued up at the computer.'

Competition for the computer extended to children wanting to check their emails, with the result that a management strategy was needed:

> I literally had to say, 'OK, well, I'll go on at half past eight; [Sally], you can have it at half past seven; [Carl], you can have it now!'

In addition to the children's demands, 'my husband would come home from work and want to do his business accounts on the computer.' Competition escalated when Virginia's five-year-old daughter also wanted her turn: 'she's over-reacting – she says "I want to use the internet!" And she doesn't even know what it is!'

The problem occurred because Virginia used the home computer when she was studying:

> And my stuff is around it. And I've got a little bit maybe – territorial. And then, of course, my son's friends would come home and they want to play this game ... the kids come home and they close all ... the things you had open to go back to later ... you kind of manage that I suppose eventually and you start saving things properly ... It's still a work in progress.

The week the family moved house was when all the 'big' assignments were due:

> Somehow most of them got in on time. One I asked for an extension for, because it was the last one. And I just thought, 'I can't' ... I was not going to have the internet for a week. And I was at placement, so I thought, 'Everyone else asks for an extension, so stop being a martyr ...'

Virginia dismissed the challenges to her study, as just the 'usual life things', explaining there were no major hindrances to her study. She never thought seriously about discontinuing:

> *There was one silly little assignment that I failed in . . . And that threw me . . . but I still didn't think of stopping. It gave me a jolt.*

She was particularly upset because this was an 'opinion piece', but she learnt from the experience, placing it into a broader perspective:

> *. . . it made me realise that: (a) if I did fail it doesn't matter; (b) read the question very, very, very carefully . . .*

This experience had an important impact on her subsequent study:

> *. . . ever since then, every assignment I write, I get my daughter or my husband to read the question, and now read my answer . . . Because they're reading it fresh, you know. Because it doesn't matter if they understand it, but, 'Have I addressed what they say [in the question]?'*

Support

Virginia's husband and children were her main sources of support, despite the impact of her studies on the household. As she embarked on her final year, she commented that she thought her husband was 'taking a deep breath . . . and so are my children!', but she added that:

> *. . . it's the last year, so there's that sense of it being an easier year – there's light at the end of the tunnel.*

At the end of the course she contrasted her husband's support with the experience of a fellow student:

> *. . . her husband's . . . a great guy, but he's not educated and there's been this little bit of not wanting to celebrate her success, which I can understand. Whereas my husband's not threatened by it at all . . . he's wanted me to do it. Even though we had lots of fights along the way about who was cooking dinner and what not . . . when you feel like you're not getting support, but underneath it he has, completely and utterly.*

Virginia's mother was also a source of support, even though Virginia felt her mother could not relate to what she was doing:

> ... she's fantastic in that ... she'll sort out the kids occasionally for me when I'm on placement ... so it's nice ... she's very sweet and very supportive. She's always saying, 'Is there anything I can do to help you?'

Having seen her brother as a role model, Virginia noted that 'interestingly, he's probably the least interested in what I'm doing.' This did not bother her because 'we're past that', but she would have appreciated recognition from him. When she was offered a place in the Honours program, 'it didn't even register on his radar ... But it was Wow!' for Virginia.

One of the aspects of studying that she found '*hugely* supportive', was being part of a student group and being able to email other students because '[a]s much as your partner and children may be supportive and praise you – you can't really discuss this with them':

> ... just knowing that other people are going through what you're going through ... That you're not sitting alone at home thinking, 'Do I not get this? Or is it that simple?' Or you're sitting at home thinking, 'This should take 20 minutes, and I'm the only one' ... you find a range of people do a range of different things. You somewhere sit in the middle of all that. Some people do it in 20 minutes, some people do it in two days. I did it in one day – so I'm OK.

Virginia did not feel the need to access any university student support services, but she contacted course staff when necessary. When she failed the assignment, she contacted the relevant staff member, who said, 'Virginia, you'll be OK!' She contacted staff members by email and 'most of them email you straight back ... most of the time the lecturers have been very good.' She thought that 'the one thing' that could have been improved, to provide better support, was feedback:

> ... you get an assignment back with a mark and four lines written on it and you think, 'OK, there's got to be more ...'

She appreciated the general feedback a lecturer sent out to everyone in one of her first research assignments but 'I think she was the only one that did it.' Just as lecturers' approaches to feedback varied, so did the timeline within which the feedback was returned to students:

> Some lecturers were fabulous. Three or four weeks afterwards you would get the feedback and get an assignment back, others two and a half months and in the meantime you're having to write a second assignment.

She referred again to the assignment that she failed, to emphasise the importance of feedback:

> ... when I got the feedback I was able to can the assignment I'd written, the second one, because I knew I had to get that right.

Virginia saw this as particularly important for off-campus students, who do not have the opportunity to talk easily to the lecturer, and who 'don't want to be a pain' by constantly phoning or emailing for assistance.

A key form of support, which made study possible, was the university funding system in Australia:

> We've only been in Australia five years and by being citizens I've been able to access university through the [funding] system because I was stopping work and so we were losing an income and then having to pay out university fees.

This allowed her to say to her husband, 'this is how I can do it', in contrast to South Africa where:

> ... you can take a student loan but your parents have to underwrite with their mortgage or, not everyone has mortgages. So . . . to me it was a really important aspect of being able to study.

Reflections and future plans

Virginia completed the course in the minimum time. At graduation, reflecting on her development as a learner, she considered that, prior to commencing the course, she 'probably wasn't a very good learner, in that I wasn't motivated to stick with it'. This time:

> ... possibly knowing that this was what I wanted to do and I had the opportunity to do it so I knew that if I didn't finish it – this was a case of age happening and life circumstances . . . there wouldn't be

> *a second chance to do it . . . if I don't do this now, I'm never going to finish it and then I'm going to be disappointed with myself.*

Virginia also thought that the 'style of learning' in the course helped her, in contrast to the prescriptive approach to study she had experienced at school, as did the opportunity to study off-campus:

> *I'm not very good at sitting and listening to lectures. The style of learning helped me I think . . . I'm better off with a book and doing it my way.*

Her lack of confidence as a learner during the first year of the course was related to a sense of, 'how am I doing?', and, as an off-campus student, the lack of feedback about 'where you're at' compared with other students, as she had mentioned previously. But, by the second year, 'there was a sense of, "OK, I know what to do and I know I'm doing something right."'

Failing the assignment in the first semester of her first year shook her confidence. She commented that 20 years ago if that had happened, she would have 'walked away from it' from 'fear of failure'. Overcoming that fear was important in building her confidence.

Another experience that changed Virginia was her first placement:

> *. . . there was . . . a sense of, 'I hope I'm going to enjoy this because if I don't then I'm doing the wrong thing.' And I had the most fantastic placement and that for me was . . . 'Yeah, this is where I'm supposed to be.'*

Being offered a place in the Honours program was also a defining moment for Virginia. It was:

> *. . . an affirmation that you are doing the right thing . . . particularly for someone older who decided to study again, and you don't know if you're doing the right thing, because you're putting your family through things, a lot of things, so it's got to be worth it for them and getting the Honours was sort of, 'Well I can do this' . . . that kept me going throughout the year.*

In her final year, Virginia demonstrated her resilience when she encountered a problem with her thesis, after she had been working on it for four or five months. The organisation that was going to support it 'suddenly' indicated that they wanted ownership of copyright and began making other demands. They wanted her to 'do their topic' using a quantitative research methodology, whereas she had been preparing for a topic using a qualitative approach: 'I can remember having floods of tears and thinking, "I've put [in] all this work and it's all just gone out the window".' She was ready to 'ditch the whole thing', feeling 'particularly exhausted' and that her 'thesis idea was a bit stupid'.

At this time, she found it very motivating to talk to the Honours program coordinator at a residential workshop, and to other students who encouraged her. She was given the opportunity of completing the thesis over two years but 'had this thing in my head' that she needed to finish by the end of the year, so she began again with a new topic. She was also encouraged by a visiting professor who was present at the workshop and thought her thesis idea was 'fabulous'. This was particularly important to her in the context of being an off-campus student:

> . . . you've only got yourself and the people around you and you're trying to think, 'Hang on, was I doing something really dumb? Really, really dumb. Was it that pathetic an idea?' So . . . it was like getting back on a horse again and saying, 'Oh, yeah, I can do this.'

Her determination increased through this experience, as reflected in her internal dialogue:

> . . . I finished something that I didn't think I was going to be able to, which is extremely motivating . . . I remember one particular morning, about four weeks before handing in the thesis, hanging out the washing and thinking, 'I don't actually have to do this . . . I could just chuck it in now, but no, keep going, you're nearly there, just keep going. It's only four weeks. In five weeks' time you'll regret this if you [pull out]' . . . it was almost myself saying to myself that, 'you're doing this out of choice, still you have to do it. It's something you have to do in life' and it was sort of, 'Do you really want to do this?' 'Yes.'

Having older children was also a motivating factor 'because you don't want to set the example of . . . giving up'; by overcoming negative experiences during the course, 'it was motivating to keep going'. By the end of the course, Virginia was aware of 'knowing how much I don't know' and of the need to keep on learning. Her self-confidence had grown 'in terms of my ability to learn and . . . you don't know how much you've learnt'. She illustrated this from a conversation she had during her second placement about doing a research Masters degree:

> ... they all said, 'Oh we wouldn't touch research, that scares us,' and I thought, 'Oh, OK.' You don't realise you've absorbed information and got some knowledge base that you just assume everybody else has ... So all those sorts of things are quite empowering.

This confidence was a marked change from her feelings about research at the start of the course:

> ... they talked about this research subject and I thought, 'Oh, my God, [in] my psychology degree that was my worst, the statistics' ... I thought this was going to be my downfall. And yet it was something I mastered, so that is again empowering.

In the future, Virginia wanted to learn 'so many things'. She found it difficult to identify one direction because the course 'open[ed] up so many more doors as to what one can do'. On completing the course, she was about to start a job at a crisis centre and was 'looking forward to learning a lot about that and about all the issues surrounding it'. However, she was already thinking about a PhD: 'I don't want the learning to stop':

> The seed has been planted ... I'm open enough and maybe it's an age thing, I'm not prescriptive about what I want to do ... I'm passionate about social justice issues but there's not much paid employment in social justice issues ...

Virginia's volunteer work with Sudanese people had made her interested in working in sexual assault with a refugee population:

> A lot of refugee girls and guys have been sexually assaulted. So there's lots of possibilities and ... at the moment, just starting my career ... I'm not very specific about where I want to go because I think doors will open and I'll go to [some]where that I'm not expecting, probably because that tends to be what has happened so far.

Virginia's graduation made her think, 'you've got your Honours degree but there's all these people with six PhDs ... Oh, I'm nowhere yet.'

Echoing the feelings she had about the need for a qualification to have practical value when she first began to study in South Africa, Virginia considered that if she undertook a PhD in the future she would like it to be supported by an organisation and offer real benefit 'arising out of a need to know something', and with some funding involved:

> ... there's many things one could research but if you're not within an organisation, it would probably get quite difficult to get it published and for it to have any real impact ... I don't know what the future holds but certainly that's what I would like to do ... and then it would be nice to get paid to do it as well.

In the short term she was interested in doing 'a few smallish things', exploring issues she had 'touched on' in the course which she would like to investigate further, but she would not be able to do that immediately while coming to grips with her new job. Virginia thought further study might be possible 'in a couple of years', although her 15-year-old son had suggested waiting until 'maybe ... after I finish school'. Virginia was also aware of supporting her elder daughter, who was now in her final year of high school. She was glad that she had finished her own course, because it would have been 'pretty stressful' to have been studying at the same time as her daughter.

Virginia thought she had been a good role model for her children, using her experience of failing an assignment as an example:

> ... mothers come from the dark ages as far as they are concerned ... 'You did school a hundred years ago and what do you know? It's all so much harder now.' They can't run it by me anymore ... '[I can tell them] I know how hard it is and you have to read the question and you have to read it properly' and I think they listen to me.

Her own study gave Virginia 'a bit of credibility' with her children. She recognised that she 'must stop being so harsh' when her daughter had an exam on and she asked her to 'bring the washing in', and that she should avoid asking, '"Why don't you cook dinner and clean up after three children and then go and sit and study?"'

On her own success, Virginia commented that:

> ... it's something I always wanted to do and so having done it, it's like a nice big tick next to something ... And then when you do

achieve something there's that whole thing about more things become possible.

To Virginia, completing the course signalled a major step in personal development, which was very empowering. That she was able to overcome 'the different hiccups along the way, which is part and parcel of life', was a significant achievement:

I've never given up, but I could've walked away from it and I chose not to, which has been good ... but I did absolutely love every minute, well most minutes of it. And ... I sort of feel like I took my own future into my own hands.

Her study nurtured her enjoyment of learning, providing Virginia with freedom to 'explore areas of interest in terms of assignments'. Both her placements allowed her 'to use that knowledge and my interest in social justice in assignments where it wasn't prescriptive: I found [that] fantastic.'

Her study also exposed her 'to other areas that I didn't realise I would be interested in', providing an extraordinary move forward personally, in a very short time:

It's incredible. Sometimes when I think back, it's only just over two years ago that I started and being new to Australia, I didn't know much about the welfare industry in this country at all ... all those things that you absorb through osmosis ... when I think to what I know now ... [it has been a huge learning curve]. Huge, but it's great.

Virginia illustrated the empowerment and opening of doors that had come from her completion of the course through her recent experience of voluntary work with Darfuris (an ethnic group from Darfur in Sudan):

And they all think I'm fantastic [professionally] and I think, 'Wow, two years ago I would've just been a volunteer.' That's been empowering too ... So just a little bit of experience I gained in my placements ... [it] opened so many doors.

Virginia valued 'the opportunity to say how I got here' and noted that 'every single person in the university has got a story to tell.' She thought this was particularly important because 'you tend to look at other people and think they've got it all together and this is all OK for them and it's not':

> ... I think undertaking a university degree ... when you come from a background where ... people have not gone to university and it's something that is outside of their scope of knowledge and they're really stepping outside the square by undertaking this ... people appear to be confident all the time and they appear to be knowing what they're doing but I don't think most people are ... I know a lot of people said to me, '... you've always got it together, how do you do all this?' You don't see me at two o'clock in the morning. But I think that we don't see other people in the same light and everyone is just doing their best I suppose.

Implications for managing and supporting student diversity: mature age students

Alex Carole's and Virginia's stories illustrate the tremendous social and psychological hurdles that many mature age students experience in undertaking higher education studies. Their life experiences and sense of social justice, combined with previous positive experiences with professionals, stimulated both of them to study in the field. What comes through strongly in both stories is the passion with which they undertook their study, as it was something that they previously saw as not possible for them, and the resilience they showed in overcoming obstacles. Their studies also had a powerful impact on their self-perception and sense of personal fulfilment. The stories illustrate how the need to manage a range of responsibilities led to them exercising strong management skills so that they used the time and resources available to them as effectively as possible, but they also highlight the important role of family support and favourable family circumstances in making study possible. Virginia's story illustrates that these circumstances may include being able to manage on one income and negotiating with their partner to achieve this.

The commitment to study that these mature age students demonstrate may suggest that their own determination to learn is sufficient, without the need for additional assistance or support from university staff. However, research on the first year experience in Australian universities has indicated that mature age students are generally highly satisfied, have clarity of purpose, and are more likely to seek assistance from staff than younger students, working consistently and enjoying the educational process and its associated challenges (Krause et al., 2005). An Australian study on attrition (Long et al., 2006) also found that mature age students have clarity of purpose and are less likely than their younger peers to drop out of university because they have chosen the wrong course but that students with children are more likely to discontinue because of conflict between study and their family commitments. Staff can minimise this risk by including family-related reasons (e.g. sick children) in the terms under which extensions on handing in assignments are granted. Staff can also ensure assignments are spaced out through the semester so they do not clash with placements and avoid school holidays when children are at home. Policies and practices that offer flexibility, particularly relating to assignment submission dates, may provide a valuable safety net for students under pressure.

Alex Carole's and Virginia's focused approach to study illustrates key assumptions about adult learning (andragogy) developed by American adult eductor Malcolm Knowles in the 1970s, and 'probably the best known set of principles or assumptions to guide adult learning practice' (Merriam et al., 2007: 79). Among these are the assumptions that an adult's self-concept develops from dependence to self-direction; that experience becomes an increasing resource for learning; that adult students' readiness to learn is closely associated with moving from one developmental stage to the next; and that adult students have a life-centred orientation to learning that focuses on immediacy of application (Knowles et al., 2011). These characteristics have important implications, especially for teaching staff. They demonstrate the value of drawing on the experience of adult learners, and providing practical, relevant learning experiences. The appreciation of the practical components of learning by Alex Carole and Virginia, and students in other chapters, clearly illustrates the importance of these aspects. Similarly, the value Virginia placed on freedom to explore areas of interest (echoing Sesh's comments on freedom to choose in Chapter 3) reflects the importance of self-direction to adult learners.

Despite the maturity and experience that Alex Carole and Virginia bring to their study, their comments also indicate ways in which mature students can demonstrate a degree of vulnerability as they adjust to the new sense of self and new boundaries to their experience which becoming a university student involves. This is evident when Alex Carole needed to overcome feelings of not really belonging at university while studying with students who were much younger than her. It is also evident in

Virginia's uncertainty about her progress and need for feedback, and her reluctance to approach staff because she did not want to be 'a pain' by constantly phoning or emailing for assistance. An issue for both professional and teaching staff is how to provide new adult learners with the support they need while treating them in an 'adult' way.

Alex Carole's and Virginia's stories reveal the impact of student assessment results on self-confidence, and how a failure in one assignment can almost tip the scales for them to consider dropping out, though the stories also demonstrate their resilience as mature age students in overcoming the obstacles they faced. Alex Carole's story highlights the importance of learning the ropes, and knowing how the university system works. This enabled her to work the system to meet her needs, at a time when she needed to repeat a subject. However, Virginia's comments about the value of supportive comments made by staff (as well as other students) when she was under stress, and the affirmation she received by being offered the opportunity to study at Honours level, further emphasise the need for all staff associated with students to provide positive reinforcement and clear avenues for contact, whenever possible. This is particularly important as, like others in previous chapters, these students did not seek out assistance from university support services.

Virginia's comments illustrate the importance of feedback, particularly when off-campus study limits the communication channels for receiving feedback that are more easily available for on-campus students. For teaching staff, this highlights the need for prompt, regular, and comprehensive feedback that provides a way forward and for improvement if assignment grades are poor.

Despite the limitations of off-campus study, both women's stories also point to the value of the flexibility it provides and to the critical role of online communication in supporting distance students, in particular. Both stress the academic and personal support they derived from being in touch with their peers in the course via email and discussion forums. This breaks the isolation and normalises the intense challenges that are integral to higher education study, providing further implications for the important role of the teacher in facilitating the establishment of student groups that has been mentioned in previous chapters.

The impact of study on both these students, and Virginia's use of the word 'empowerment' to describe its effect on her, highlights the role of critical social theory in informing the design of adult learning, with its links to Freire (1972) and the concept of the teacher being a partner with the student in the act of knowing. Recent developments in awareness of the social context of learning have further emphasised the importance of recognising the 'power dynamics' involved in learning, as Merriam et al. (2007: 430–1) note:

> We are beginning to realise that it is important to know the backgrounds and experiences of our learners not only as individual learners but also as members of social and culturally constructed groups such as women and men; poor, middle-class and rich; black, white and brown.

They comment on the importance of this issue to teaching, learning, planning, and administration, which has implications for all staff in the ways they interact with the adult students that they encounter.

Summary

In this chapter, we introduced Alex Carole and Virginia, two mature age students who were passionate about their study and their reasons for engaging in it. Both women implemented a range of strategies to manage their study effectively, as busy, older women adjusting to higher education. Each woman overcame obstacles to enrol and then successfully complete her course.

A key factor that emerges from Alex Carole's and Virginia's stories is the role of favourable life circumstances in making study possible, particularly the critical role of practical support by their partners and families to release them from some of the chores and activities that would otherwise consume much of their time and divert them from their studies. We have noted some of the implications for teaching and support by university staff suggested by their stories which are relevant to their characteristics as adult learners.

Chapter 5: discussion topics

1. How do you currently support adult learners while respecting their 'adultness'? What changes could you make to improve this support?
2. What changes could you make to your current practice to assist mature age students to cope with study and the demands on their time and energy from other life responsibilities and situations?
3. If you have a teaching role, how can the passion, experience, and life skills that mature age students bring to their studies be harnessed in your classroom or program to enrich the program for all students?
4. What policies and protocols are in place in your institution, faculty or department to provide for flexible assessment practices? How are these policies and practices publicised and how are they applied? What improvements in flexibility can you suggest to better support student progress?
5. What measures could be put in place in your setting to improve opportunities for students to receive prompt, regular, and comprehensive feedback and ensure that they have sufficient support and guidance in their studies?

6

Finding my voice at last: Lillian, Marie, and Harriet

Abstract: In this chapter we focus on the experiences of three women, Lillian, Marie and Harriet, to consider the transformative impact of higher education on their life directions and sense of identity. All were in their forties when they commenced the study that changed them. Marie and Harriet are from migrant families that valued education. Both had completed degrees previously but experienced a number of disruptive events in their lives, and considerable anxiety during their study. The study that led to Lillian's successful enrolment was her first experience of university education. From their accounts of their study experiences, we consider some of the ways that teaching and professional staff can provide a climate for transformative learning in higher education.

Key words: ethnicity, gender, identity, mature age students, perspective transformation, racism, transformative learning, social class.

Introduction

Like Alex Carole and Virginia, Lillian, Marie and Harriet were in their forties when they enrolled in their current course. We present their stories together because of the powerful impact of their study experiences, which resulted in significant personal transformation.

Higher education was not part of Lillian's background but emerged as a desirable option during her working life, becoming feasible after her second marriage and the birth of her child. Marie and Harriet are both from migrant families where education was valued. While both had completed degrees previously, they had experienced a number of disruptive life events and considerable anxiety during their study, which were finally resolved by successful completion of their current degrees. For all three, the study experience had a significant impact on their lives and identities.

While there is evidence of perspective transformation in other students' stories, the intensity of the changes reported by Lillian, Marie and Harriet provides opportunities for staff to consider the implications of their experiences for managing and supporting student diversity in ways that promote transformative learning.

Lillian's story

Pathway to higher education

When she enrolled in her course, Lillian was living with her second husband and young daughter. Lillian had worked since she was 15 and was the first in her family to go to university. The study that led to her current enrolment was her first experience of higher education.

Family background

Lillian described her parents as 'working class': 'My Dad was a builder and my Mum was very much a worker – she worked often three jobs at a time.' Neither her parents nor her two brothers had any experience of higher education:

> . . . university wasn't an option . . . it was never discussed. University, I suppose, was for more middle class, upper class people which we weren't. So I can't even remember anyone in our street going to university . . . They were all plumbers, builders, electricians . . . They were all tradespeople in our street growing up.

Lillian's father was an alcoholic and did not provide any parental guidance:

> I think Mum was surviving in that relationship and we were surviving along with her, so there was no extra time for putting in for development of the kids . . .

Lillian felt her family's values were centred on going out to work and being financially independent:

> ... working was very much my culture. And I had part-time jobs since I was 15. I was financially independent fairly early on. So I felt going out to the workforce was the way to go ...

As a teenager, her ambitions were more focused on relationships – 'a male relationship and getting married and all that type of stuff'. She married at 21 and divorced at 27, working in secretarial jobs that suited what she called the 'needy' side of her personality. She married again at 40 and her daughter was born two years later.

Educational experiences

Of her primary school years, Lillian said: 'I don't remember anything being challenging, but I do very much in high school.' High school 'was a very lonely time for me . . . it was a time of really learning about how hard it was'. This was related to:

> ... friendships, about being part of a group, of peer groups, and about what you needed to be to be popular ... it was tough for me. I didn't have a close relationship with my parents, really to talk about it so I don't know how I coped with it really. I just did. I sort of flip-flopped in and out of groups, but I do remember feeling very, very lonely and hurt ... I just got through. I survived, I suppose. There were some parts which were good, but the friendship part was hard and the boy thing was hard. I remember the boys used to run around and run their finger down the back of you to see whether you were wearing a bra ...

During this period, Lillian struggled with identity issues:

> Most of my identity, I think, was created through other people ... I wasn't able to grow an identity from within myself. I didn't have that base to come from. It was very much formed from the outside. And that's hard work when you're trying to form an identity from what other people think of you.

However, Lillian recalled some happier times at high school. She was quite athletic and spent a lot of time doing gymnastics and dancing.

Organising social events such as school dances was also a positive experience for Lillian as group activities were important to her.

At that time, Lillian wanted to be a model when she left school: 'I think I had the looks and I had the body but I didn't have the confidence.' The only person who suggested she should think about further study was her sports teacher, who was 'one of my mentors'. He wanted her to go to teachers' college to become a physical education teacher, but this did not appeal to Lillian. She discussed her sports teacher's advice with her mother: 'And I think she would have said, "No, don't – just go out and work".' Lillian felt that office work was the only option. She studied shorthand and typing at school and left in the penultimate year of high school.

Although Lillian identified lack of parental support as one of the major obstacles to her succeeding at school and beyond, her mother wanted her to go to an elite private girls' school, 'which is surprising as we don't come from private school backgrounds'. Lillian refused to go because she did not want to leave her friends.

She did not recall any career guidance at school, and wondered whether it would have been offered if she had completed the final high school year. Her gender influenced both Lillian's academic and career expectations and over time she became less ambitious:

> . . . high school to me was hard emotionally. I don't think I had any ambitions, except just to work.

When she was about 30, her feelings began to change:

> I needed to do a lot of . . . identity work and I started doing that at 30. And I was uncomfortable in the secretarial field. There was no autonomy in it. You were always doing something for somebody and I think I always wanted to think for myself and have direction for myself.

She recognised that workplace autonomy requires an education. She had a break from secretarial work at 42 when her daughter was born and realised she could 'either go back into that type of work or do something else'. She knew that it was 'now or never . . . that I wanted to go to university'. Lillian's university-educated husband was able to provide her with a secure emotional base. She did not think she would have had the 'mental fortitude' to go to university if 'I didn't have that safety net'.

About this time, she joined a mothers' group where she met a 'well-educated mother' who supported her and 'pushed me gently' into thinking about university. Lillian completed three university subjects online through an open access provider and then was accepted into an arts degree. She commented on her experience as a student:

> *[It's] just having the confidence I suppose and being in the right frame of mind to be able to do it because . . . it's damned hard . . . this is the hardest thing I've ever done in my life . . . trying to write an essay, it really is hard. I'm getting old. I'm getting too old to be up until 2.00am and 3.00am in the morning writing essays!*

Lillian's love of learning became obvious to her once she commenced her studies but she reiterated: 'I don't think I probably would have done it if I hadn't . . . had that secure base . . .'

She was very enthusiastic about the open access pathway she took into higher education:

> *I thought it was great. A great way of getting into uni and a great way of studying if you've got a small child . . . so I used to study when [she] would sleep . . . it was fantastic and I love to read anyway, so for me . . . it was like, Wow! . . . I think it's fantastic they offer lots of interesting subjects. I found the tutors very helpful.*

Lillian's mentor from the mothers' group continued to be an influence and support:

> *. . . [she] sat me down and we talked about it – about actually studying a bit more about being a social worker, because that's what I really want to do . . . she convinced me, I suppose, to even go full-time . . . and not to give up my arts [course], just to defer it . . .*

That is what Lillian did. She deferred from her arts degree and enrolled to study social work.

Managing study

Planning

Lillian was not in paid employment when she began her university studies but she had to work around the needs of her then two-year-old daughter.

Thus, her planning involved choosing courses around this commitment and studying in off-campus mode. During her daughter's pre-school year she was able to enrol part-time and moved to full-time, on-campus mode when her child went to school.

When she began her course, planning was also important to the way Lillian worked:

> I don't leave assignments to the last minute. I just can't work like that. So it's self-awareness, I suppose . . . I can't knock an assignment out in two days – I can't.

Managing

Finances were not a barrier to Lillian's enrolment in higher education, although the fees for her open access course were 'not cheap . . . and then the books on top of it'.

Unlike many mature age students, Lillian was computer literate and that made it easier for her:

> I'm computer literate so . . . that's a big plus . . . That was second nature to me, so I imagine that would be an inability to many people.

Persistence and resilience were very important in the way she managed her studies:

> . . . you just need a bit of self-determination, really. You've got to be able to hang in there. And people just say, 'I just don't know how you do it,' and it's not because I'm bright by any stretch of the imagination. I'm probably used to hard work, I think.

Lillian drew on the resilience she had developed during the challenging times she experienced when she was younger:

> . . . because I come from a very anxious-ridden family, I can certainly survive a bit more in tougher times . . . I see that as normal, whereas some people lead their life a bit more wrapped up in cottonwool and everything needs to be fluffy and happy. And that's fine, but my life hasn't been like that . . . So perhaps my background has helped me – I certainly haven't come from a precious background.

Timing was important in allowing Lillian to manage her study. Having 'finally found my secure base' with her husband and child she felt that the time was right:

> ... *for me it was the right time, because I didn't want to get to 50 and say, 'I wish I had've done that.' And I also see so many regrets in my life, about a life that's been wasted. And I don't want to do that, so that keeps me going as well.*

Lillian's main challenge was balancing her parenting role with her study commitment. For example, organising child care around 'split' lectures (such as a 9.00am lecture followed by a 4.00pm one) was difficult for her. She had to accept offers of help from her friends, particularly regarding child care. She considered that it was easier for her than for some other mothers because she only had one child to look after, and she studied while her daughter slept.

Studying at weekends was another strategy that Lillian used to manage her studies. She employed a cleaner so that she could study all day on Saturdays while her husband minded their daughter:

> ... *so how I manage my time now is I say to [my husband], 'I need to study all day Saturday from 7.00am till 7.00pm to manage the workload' ... And I study for an hour at night time ... A consequence of that [is] the shopping never gets done.*

Lillian was very focused and single-minded about her studies:

> *If I have an assignment to do, I can work nine hours straight on that. And so I don't go for a walk, I don't do the shopping and I don't buy birthday presents ... I suppose ... a desire to learn, a desire to do well, helps me cope with the workload.*

Although she did not do any paid work during her time at university, Lillian did do canteen duty and help in the classroom at her daughter's school.

The illness and death of Lillian's mother was very difficult for her as she dealt with the pressures of looking after both her child and her mother. She was offered the opportunity to complete her degree at Honours level but she declined because of the pressures and the grief following her mother's death.

Lillian also felt that her studies had impacted on her social life ('I can't study straight for eight hours and then go . . . and socialise'). At times she felt she had been studying for too long, with her previous study and then her current course, which led to 'burn out'. She felt impatient to get into the workforce and start practising as a social worker.

Despite these feelings, Lillian was clear that she had to finish the course:

> *I just know I have to finish it. I'm so close I can sniff it . . . I've studied now I think for six or seven years and I'm not going to walk away not having a degree.*

Reflecting on what drove her to continue with her studies, Lillian spoke of determination ('you know, "finish what you start" type of thing'), although she found it hard to foresee how completion of her degree would change her life:

> *I've got some friends who . . . have degrees and . . . [are] doctors and I suppose they know how hard it is, but they also know . . . the reward is at the end. But I don't know what the reward is going to be . . . I've got a piece of paper and I think . . . I would be a different person, but I don't see that changing. So I think I'm exactly the same. Except . . . I'm going to have this piece of paper.*

However, she also felt that: 'I would disappoint lots of people if I didn't finish it. And I would disappoint myself.'

The work placements in her course created a challenge for Lillian. At the time of her first placement, she felt her daughter was too young to go into after-school care. This meant that 'I had to compromise . . . my placement . . . but I think it truly affected my confidence.'

Lillian felt under pressure to perform better in her next placement:

> *. . . and that concerns me, especially coming into a placement where I think they . . . expect quite a bit from you. And especially being mature age I think I might be [expected] to perform a little bit better than what I can. The expectations of me I think might be a little bit higher. But I'm actually . . . feeling quite under-skilled to fulfil my placement.*

In summary, Lillian identified planning, determination, and resilience as key elements in managing her studies and continuing with her course.

Support

Lillian's husband contributed significantly to her studies by providing practical and emotional support. Having access to formal and informal child care was also an important form of support. It meant that Lillian could complete her studies in a shorter period of time:

> *So I suppose that means child care has impacted on the amount of hours that I was able to study and that means that I can finish my degree more quickly. Otherwise it would be dragging out over more years.*

Although she went to essay-writing classes when she first started to study, and she talked to one of the lecturers about applying for special consideration following her mother's death, Lillian did not use any of the university's support services, nor did she rely on her peers during the final year of her course:

> *I just knew I had to do it myself . . . I didn't ask for any help. I didn't have any buddies or colleagues to bounce ideas around or to meet at lunchtime . . . which was disappointing but I guess that might be a mature age thing . . .*

Reflections and future plans

Lillian completed her social work course in the minimum time. Reflecting on her university experience, she realised that as she progressed, her confidence and self-esteem increased, 'but not 100 per cent'. For example, she found it difficult to maintain her confidence in her final year, although she was part of a student group:

> *It was a very quiet group and I went quieter as well so that surprised me. I was hoping when I came out of the degree that I'd have the confidence to mount an argument and have stronger opinions but that didn't happen . . .*

Her mother's death played a part in her diminishing confidence: 'I didn't really have any buddies in fourth year. I didn't cement with anybody really.'

Looking back over her course, Lillian realised that she was an independent learner who loved learning; this was an essential part of who she was:

Yes, my self-esteem did go up. I always got good marks so I surprised myself ... so my self-esteem did increase. I enjoyed it ... loved learning.

She did not know how she learnt or what her learning style was before she came to university, except that she learned by watching other people. At university, Lillian's engagement with the subjects and topics motivated her to become a successful learner:

[Previously] I did my work but don't think I actually learnt about anything that I was interested in. So I guess through learning I discovered I had interests which actually gave me more of a definition about who I was. So, yes, I learnt something about myself through my learning.

Lillian explained these changes in terms of her values and interests, which had not been engaged in her working life:

I didn't have a chance in my corporate job to think about sociology or think about the impact of homelessness or those social issues that don't get really talked about in a patriarchal corporate scenario, I guess.

From her earliest classes, Lillian felt a deep connection with her subjects, that they were relevant, and that they provided her with information about issues of great interest to her.

Lillian remembered feeling overwhelmed when she first entered a university campus, and also a strong sense of achievement at having finally got to university:

I was crying as I drove into uni because I was just so overwhelmed and proud that I got there ... I'd talked about it for so many years because it was a pretty big deal for me to go to uni and, yes, it was an overwhelming feeling that I'd done it, that I was actually going to learn something. I guess I had a thirst for learning that I hadn't really tapped into until I went to uni.

During her arts degree, Lillian began planning her next step:

> *I started to learn and then I'm thinking about, 'What am I going to do with this learning once I leave uni?' . . . Then I suppose I looked at my courses and the outcome that they would bring me in terms of paid work and that's when I decided to go to social work, knowing that an arts degree would stop unless I went down the academic field which I don't think was going to suit me . . . but I knew a social work degree would get me a job and it dovetails into social issues and working with people . . . I started thinking like a uni student I suppose, 'What are my opportunities once I get my degree?'*

Lillian was exhausted by the time she finished the course, but gained employment as a social worker. Her mother's death had impacted heavily on her last year of study and this affected her plans:

> *I would have liked to have done [Honours] because I am a bit research-based in terms of getting [into] an issue . . . what I don't like about the social work [course] is that you never got to explore one subject totally. It was all bits and pieces which is what a degree is. It gives you a little bit of everything, doesn't it? So I was looking forward to actually getting one issue and really exploring that in terms of Honours, but anyway I knew I couldn't do it because losing my Mum really rocked my world . . . I had to knuckle down last year and just focus, whereas I'm in a different phase of my life now . . .*

This meant that, on graduation, further study was not an attractive proposition ('I don't want to see the back end of a uni now'). Nonetheless, Lillian missed the sort of learning she experienced at university, and recognised how her appetite for academic learning had been stimulated by her experiences:

> *I miss the learning. I miss the writing of essays and things because I think that's where you get a little bit of depth in your knowledge, so I miss that. I miss forming those arguments . . . I suppose paid work overrides that spare time to be able to study . . . But then there are some opportunities sometimes that come through like for PhDs and things and I think that would be good, so there's still a desire there but I think I've missed the boat. I don't know, who knows?*

Looking back over her time as a student, Lillian felt that the offer to study at Honours level was the highlight because it challenged her perception of herself:

> ... that was a recognition that I could actually study. I still think deep down I have this feeling that I'm not very bright so it always buffers up against that. That was a recognition that ... my hard work I suppose had paid off ... perhaps who I am is different to how I perceive myself.

She was proud of her achievements:

> I'm proud of myself that I've been able to change my career at such a late stage in life and I guess I've learnt how determined I can be if I need to be and if I say I'm going to do something, I'll do it.

Marie's story

Pathway to higher education

When Marie commenced her course she was living in a capital city with her husband and two children, then aged 18 and 14 respectively. She had suffered from a serious illness (lupus) for 12 years. Prompted by her experience of voluntary community work, and taking a drug that controlled her symptoms, she enrolled at the age of 49 to pursue a long-standing interest in social work.

Family and personal background

Marie has a European background:

> My mother is Italian and French and my father was Polish but he lived in France for a number of years so he could speak French and my parents met at a French Club and so we only spoke French at home.

Her mother:

> ... hates Australia and everything Australia stands for – always has – and really went out of her way to make us different.

However, Marie's mother's views were progressive in a 'whole lot of ways':

> *I knew from a very early age that I was expected to go to university and that was it! Education was, from my mother's point of view, freedom for a woman.*

Nevertheless, as a child, Marie's ambitions did not include university:

> *I wanted to be an athlete. I was very good at running. Or a basketball player, because I loved to play basketball. I wanted to be an actress, because I loved watching movies.*

As she grew up, Marie's behaviour and the family dynamics were influenced by her older sister, 'who was very rebellious and caused a lot of problems within the home':

> *. . . my main concern was not to be like her. And she took drugs and she caused a lot of heartache in my family. So we – my two brothers and I – were sort of very much sidelined, because a lot of focus was put on her.*

Her mother had 'desperately wanted' her sister to go to university:

> *But she just didn't want to. She just rebelled against everything that my mother represented . . .*

Another major impact on her was her mother's return to work when Marie was 14. This occurred because her father 'kept getting retrenched', although he was an engineer ('an educated man'). Her mother did not arrive home until 6.30pm, leaving Marie to look after her brothers, cook dinner and do the washing, as well as her schoolwork. By this time, Marie's sister had left the family home.

Marie began a commerce degree when she finished school because she did not know what to study and was influenced by a boyfriend who was studying in this area. She 'hated every living, breathing minute' of her course and got 'very poor marks', but enjoyed her social life:

> *I loved dancing. I went to a lot of discos. I discovered that it was fine to be 'ethnic' because the disco scene at that time was full of ethnic people. So it was suddenly OK to be a 'wog' . . . my brown eyes, and*

> *I tan in the summer quite dark, and I had long brown hair, and I looked very Italian, it was OK to look like that . . . And suddenly when I went out and actually boys looked at me and found me attractive, I thought, 'That's a shock!' because boys at school had just called me a 'hairy greaso' and suddenly when I went out, I wasn't like that . . . I finally found a peer group . . . like other ethnic children.*

This was a circle of friends that extended beyond university:

> *I met one girl at uni, but I knew another girl [studying elsewhere] and she knew somebody else and we all . . . got together . . . one was Italian, one was Egyptian, one was Greek . . . and we'd all meet every Saturday . . . and a lot of these girls weren't allowed to go out. And we'd all meet at my house . . .*

The other girls shared Marie's feeling of alienation from ' "surfie" type boys . . . Aussie [Australian] type boys' who thought 'a beautiful girl is a girl with long blonde hair and blue eyes . . . and I just didn't fit into that mould.'

Marie continued her family support role while at university:

> *. . . my sister had two children and she suffered post-natal depression. And she didn't want her two children . . . And so she took the baby and I had to take the three-year-old, and it was really difficult . . . And I'd often take him to lectures. And he would sit with me . . . sometimes when I had tutorials I'd make him sit outside the [tutorial] room and say, 'I won't be very long,' and he was only three. And that was terrible.*

When Marie completed her degree, her parents were '**so pleased**':

> *I thought, 'Well, my father's happy. My mother's happy. It doesn't matter.' I hadn't quite made the connection at that stage that I had to be happy too . . . I think at that stage I had no concept of myself because I was always seen as the nurturer, the carer – and I'd been sidelined too often. So I had no real concept of my own needs or my own desires and my own life . . . I thought, 'That's OK. Everyone's happy. Whether I like it or not is irrelevant' . . . And I **hated** it.*

In pursuing something she hated, Marie had taken on the attitudes of her mother and grandmother:

> ... my mother had this ... strange notion that women were born to suffer. [When] I was young ... my grandmother used to say ... [t]hat was sort of partially our role.

At this stage, '[e]njoying what I was doing' would have meant success for Marie ('I needed something that was just me') but this was precluded by 'my own lack of confidence in myself', which was, in turn, affected by her role in the family. She felt that her mother was an obstacle to her freedom. Marie had a brief taste of liberty travelling overseas after finishing her degree, but when she was 24 her father died 'and I just felt that I had to be there for [my mother]. I never felt free.'

Prior to her father's death:

> ... he became a violent alcoholic and my mother was constantly confiding in me ... And I said, 'Oh, well leave him!' In the end, I left home. And it was the first bit of freedom I'd tasted. And then he got sick. And I was away from home for like six weeks. And then she said, 'You've got to come home. Your father's sick. He's got cancer. And he's dying. So you've got to come home and help me look after him.' And he only lasted six weeks ...

In the following years Marie married and had children. She 'did some work that I enjoyed and some that I hated'. She worked in a government department for four years and ran a business with her husband for eleven and a half years, which she hated. Then, at 37, she became ill with lupus.

It developed into a very severe form of the disease:

> ... I could only really work in a call centre because I was too tired ... it affected my brain and became systemic ... And at that point I had a massive seizure at work and then a year later I had a pulmonary embolism. And it was actually galloping through my body. And ... I just stopped work ... I had a year off work and my doctor put me on a trial drug because I was losing the capacity to think – I had lost my short term memory ...

Marie started on the drug a year before enrolling in her current degree. It stopped the progress of the disease, and enabled her to complete a community centre volunteer course. She 'really enjoy[ed] this type of work' and the experience brought her back to university. She was determined to make the most of this opportunity, 'wish[ing] the penny had dropped earlier':

> I feel all my life that I've been led along by the nose and given in to what other people wanted. And this is the first time that I've said, 'No, this is what I want to do! And this is what I'm going to do. And no one's going to stop me from doing it. And this is who I am.'

She had 'a fair bit of opposition' to her enrolment from people she knew because of her age and her health problems:

> 'Why on earth would you want to do this at your age?' and 'You're too sick to do something like this' ... but I've just said, 'Well, this is what I want to do ... this is the first time in my life I can say, "This is what I want to do!" ... let me be!' ... I think they've seen me very sick ... I think it's genuine concern for me. And I think also there's a part of them that doesn't see me as a successful person ... 'You're not that kind of person that can be successful.' I think it's a subconscious thing. I don't think they would really say that.

However, her husband was very supportive, and although her mother was worried about Marie's health, 'she's very happy that I'm doing it'.

Attending university was usual for the men in her family, with her father, brothers, and husband all university-educated. Marie was motivated to study because she wanted 'a career that I'm proud of', fulfilling a desire that had 'been there forever!' She also thought it important for her two children 'to be proud of what I'm doing'. She tried to convey to her children the value of pride in what one does:

> ... my son pointed out to me the other day, 'Social workers don't get paid very much!' I [said], 'They may not be paid very much ... it's not what it's all about. It's more about what I do. I value what I will be doing' ... And I said, 'It's taken me a very long time. I'm 49 now and I've found it ... it doesn't matter if when you turn 18 you don't know what you want to do because you've got plenty of time in life to decide ... So just enjoy ... you don't want to be in a situation like me at 49 starting off my career path.'

Marie acknowledged that her illness had reinforced this point of view:

> ... when you have an illness like this, it really knocks your self-esteem around ... you feel a bit worthless, because ... you become a burden ... you try not to be, but you are! Because you're always needing something, you're always putting somebody out ... you're always worrying somebody ... it's a terrible thing, you know? And no matter how much you try not to complain [it becomes a part of you] ... And I said, 'No, I just have to keep on with my life,' and I kept on going to the gym. Sometimes I couldn't go to the gym and I'd do water aerobics ... Just trying to get some normality in my life because you can become possessed by it ... it can totally own you. And I just did not want that to happen to me.

Her enrolment removed some of the stress on her family ('[a]nd now, seeing me well, they're all thrilled. And it's great'):

> ... when I had the embolism ... everyone was pacing backwards and forwards – 'Is she going to live? Is she going to die?' ... So all this makes you feel very bad about yourself ... this is a great opportunity to give a little bit back ... I've sucked everybody dry. Now maybe I can give a bit back ... it's a good profession to give something back.

Educational experiences

Marie started primary school (in Australia) at a Catholic school. She couldn't speak English and found it very difficult:

> I hated the Catholic school. Classes were very large and I didn't have any friends, and I was very unhappy there. And then my parents moved me across to the local state school in Grade 3 [aged about nine] and I was very happy there. My English had improved. And the kids were nicer. And I enjoyed sports and made friends. And although I was very different, it didn't seem to matter as much.

Marie had 'a real need to fit in'. She had 'learnt some socialisation skills' and 'had this sort of outgoing personality' with the result that 'I was very happy at [this particular] primary school.'

However, she did not enjoy secondary school:

> Unfortunately ... [it] was very Anglo-Saxon ... and both my sister and I and my younger brothers experienced an extreme amount of

> racism. We got very isolated by it ... And the other ethnic children that were there left very quickly ... I hated high school. [It was a] very negative experience. I pretty much made very few friends and friends that I did have were not very loyal. And I didn't have the teachers – it was not a good school. And my learning experiences were very negative ...

Marie's secondary school experiences were also influenced by the pressures she was under at home:

> I got all right marks in [my final exams]. They weren't brilliant, but I didn't know what to do. And I think I didn't know what to do because the anxiety level in my home was too high ... My parents expected me to go to university and that ... remained a constant. But I thought, 'Well, I don't know what to do at university' ... And I didn't want to be a teacher because I **hated** the teachers at school. And I went to a school which was really rough and the kids gave the teachers such a hard time ... And I didn't get good enough marks to get into social work ... the mark for social work was very high ... I thought, 'There's no way I'll get into social work' ... there was nothing that really appealed to me.

It was at this point that Marie enrolled to study commerce, influenced by her boyfriend. Although she had the support of her friends, Marie had no role models to give her direction while she was at university.

Now, many years later, with the drugs controlling her disease and motivated by working at the community centre, she found the direction that was missing earlier:

> I just think that in life sometimes you get a second chance. And it feels like this is that ... I thought I initially wanted to be a social worker and I wondered whether it was not too late to try and do it now ... And so I did all the various things and wrote all the essays and [a staff member] interviewed me. And I got a little message on my answering machine, saying that he'd 'take a punt' on me and let me do the course and I nearly died – **What?**

Marie was accepted on the basis of her commerce degree, her voluntary work, and the selection interview ('I begged him!').

Managing study

Planning

To prepare for study Marie needed to:

> ... organise a computer for myself ... a desk for myself. I had to organise a space of my own. And that was very difficult in that house because I never had a space of my own. And that was something that I insisted on having ...

Managing

Marie was initially challenged, but was glad that she had enrolled:

> I can't say I've found the course easy because the workload is immense but I'm enjoying it. And I'm getting through the work ... I've only got three pieces of work back. My marks haven't been great, but I'm getting through it. And I'm understanding the work. And I hope that I'll be successful ...

Coping with the computer was a major challenge:

> I'm very computer illiterate ... and I was totally daunted by the fact that I had to use this computer ... I had ... the study and an additional layer of computer illiteracy ... And I've got no dexterity in my fingers ... even now typing is just such a chore ... And I think that what lecturers and the whole university culture fails to understand [is] that ... they really want the presentation of the essay to be ... well structured, well presented, and it's all to do with how good you are at the computer. And some people can go in there and they can do an essay in a week, because they know where to search. They know the search engines on the computer. And if you're good at that, then you can do an assignment like that, but if you are not ... you struggle ... you struggle to find everything.

This impacted considerably on her study:

> I had to do a lot of things manually ... at the library, searching for journals, rummaging through cases, whereas kids just got it on the computer and they would do things in a quarter the time. I had to

> *write an essay by hand and then type it on the computer. So everything, for me, took three times the amount of time that it would have taken another student. So it was just like you couldn't compete . . . I would get . . . a Credit for an essay, where I would have worked maybe four times as hard as someone whose essay got a High Distinction because my skills were just nowhere near as good.*

Marie also had problems with the demands of academic writing:

> *. . . there would be little things like . . . I had not punctuated properly, I had not referenced properly . . . they were just technical things.*

She felt that academic expectations had changed since she completed her first degree. In one of her recent essays she 'just got a pass' and the comment was 'A really good essay' but she felt aggrieved that she was penalised for grammatical errors and incorrect referencing.

Marie had other academic problems as well:

> *I tend to read things but I don't absorb them . . . when I have an essay I'm trying now – very hard – to do a lot more reading for it . . . if there's something relevant, first of all I'll just read – I'll look at the essay question and I'll try and figure out what the essay question wants because sometimes I can't even understand what they want . . . So what I've got to do now is learn to not panic. And give myself time to process what the lecturers are saying in the class.*

To assist her, Marie bought materials prepared for the off-campus students, and found these to be 'full of really good tips' and 'excellent sources of reading material'. They included journal articles which saved her from having to 'go and find them' and the materials provided a source for checking if she missed something in the lectures.

Having established her study space (in a room shared with her children), Marie then had to manage the shared use of the computer ('I allowed my son to play his games on my computer and then my computer crashed'). She resolved the issue by putting a password on the computer, removing the games, and 'turn[ing] it off at the end of every night'. Her son was 'very upset':

> *Because he would just come in . . . [and] just push my stuff aside . . . he's [now] understood, that this is my space . . . and that area has to be respected.*

Marie also had to cope with her daughter's needs:

> ... she's reaching puberty and she wanted a lot of my time ... to go shopping ... to watch her play tennis, and ... watch her go dancing ... and I didn't have time! And she was constantly feeling let down.

Marie did not resolve this during the first year of her study: 'I think that there's a great deal of bitterness that she feels towards me.' Meanwhile her husband was retrenched and 'spent six months at home'. While this challenged the family, it also meant he could provide some support for their daughter.

However, additional stress followed:

> ... after six months he had to go to the Middle East for work ... and I got ill in June – I couldn't do my placement in June because I think that I'd pushed myself so hard that I got ill.

Marie's ageing mother, who lived in a unit behind her house, was another demand on her time:

> ... although she helps me a lot in terms of washing and ironing and things like that ... she has to be driven here, she has to be driven there, and [as] ... she hasn't assimilated very well into Australian society ... a lot of the responsibility is on me to take her out ... she likes to see Italian movies and French movies ... I didn't do any of that last year and she felt very lonely, isolated and a bit betrayed ... And I don't like that, because she does do a lot for me ...

Marie also had to manage running a home and family:

> ... there's the shopping, the paying of the bills, because I've got to do all that on my own – there's the budgeting, there's the demands of getting my son to cooperate ... there's a dog that's always sick ... all those little things that ... sometimes I just can't be bothered with! Sometimes I just think to myself, 'Should I get the dog put down?' And then I think, 'No, no, no ... that's just not family' ... the moment you just sit down, something happens ... my daughter ... wants me to help her with her homework all the time ...

While studying, Marie continued her voluntary work, once a week, which involved 'giving out food vouchers and food and also support materials and doing some advocacy work'. However, she allowed some time for herself: 'I go to the gym four times a week. I try very hard to keep Saturday free.'

Marie's husband's retrenchment and departure to work overseas was a significant challenge during her first year, along with the re-emergence of her illness:

> *I remember a little voice saying to me, 'It might be under control, but you've still got it.' And I just went off and did this course . . . and then in June, I had this terrible form of tinnitus . . . And it just nearly drove me insane. I've got this all the time now . . . I've learnt to sort of put it in the back of my mind. And it started up again and I thought, 'I feel as though I could kill myself.' It's a terrible thing to say, but I did.*

When this happened, just before her first placement, it was one of only two occasions when Marie thought about giving up:

> *I'm trying to write all these essays with this noise in my head and I was hysterical, literally hysterical . . .*

Marie decided to defer her placement because she thought, 'I will go insane.' Fortunately, her husband was still at home 'so he was driving me round to all these different doctors'. She wanted to try and finish her assignments:

> *I had done two essays . . . and I had got reasonable marks for them. And I thought I could still work with that noise . . . I just wanted to do it . . .*

She continued with the course but, to add to her difficulties, a few months later she had a 'massive internal bleed':

> *. . . just out of the blue . . . and I ended up in hospital, and that was when I really thought, 'This is it, I'm really going to cark it [die].' And my husband was not here. And that was very bad.*

Marie was hospitalised for about five days and returned home 'exhausted'. She had been in the midst of preparing three assignments, all of which she completed on time. She was amused that, by mistake, she handed in a draft of one assignment, rather than the final version:

> *I got it back and I got a Pass and I thought, 'That's a bit odd' and then I thought, 'Oh . . . that's my draft' . . . And it was really funny because . . . I was really, literally exhausted . . . and I didn't know what I was doing.*

Marie received Distinctions for the other two assignments but only a Credit overall: 'I thought I must have done badly on that last assignment. I couldn't figure it out.' When she worked out what had happened, 'I was just shocked. But I laughed. At least I'd passed. I was very, very lucky.'

Marie completed her deferred placement at the end of the year. This was the second time she thought she was 'close to giving up':

> *. . . the first seven weeks I had an absolutely awful, awful supervisor . . . And I thought, 'This woman is just so mean.' And then they all went on holidays . . . and then I had a really lovely supervisor. So I was lucky to have . . . seven weeks of a really good experience . . .*

While on her placement, Marie decided to change from full-time to part-time study, feeling 'physically, totally exhausted'. She thought:

> *'I will have a week off, and then to go straight back into full-time study would just be so detrimental to my health and to my family.' And my daughter was saying, 'You can't have a year like you did last year . . . I won't have a father and I won't have a mother.'*

Marie also thought that this would help her change her approach to her study:

> *I study whenever I can . . . I don't think I came up for air last year. And I said to myself, 'I'm not doing that this year . . . that's just not good' . . . I think I suffer from over anxiety. And I think my problem is that I lack self-esteem . . . and I think that I compare myself to other students too much . . . I've got to stop doing that and see myself as being able to accomplish things in my own right . . . and say, 'Look, you're OK . . . and just because somebody else is getting a HD [High Distinction], a Credit is just fine for you; do your best at what you can do.'*

She would sometimes panic about the work to be done, but began to feel the benefit of part-time study.

Despite the challenges of her first year, Marie also highlighted the positive aspects:

> ... just the whole ... enlightenment process. I mean, I just loved being in my [tutorials] – I just have such a good time. And I loved most of my subjects ... I really enjoyed meeting a lot of the students. I've made some really good friends.

She thought she was able to rise above the difficulties because:

> I believe it's just part of who I am ... It's what you have to do to get things done ... My mother just taught me that you just don't give up ... In fact, my mother ... has this dogged determination ... and you just fight on. That's that real migrant determination ... that I think both my parents had. You keep at it.

Marie felt that she had 'flown by the seat of my pants a lot of the time', but also felt a sense of accomplishment:

> I feel like I'm sort of halfway there ... like the worst is over and I feel that I can almost pat myself on the back, saying, 'You did that and you accomplished it and that's great.'

She was also pleased that, since her last medical emergency:

> I've been very well for a long period of time now. I thought that my placement would make me quite ill, but it didn't ...

Support

Marie's best forms of support during her study were her lecturers, one in particular, but especially her family. Initially her husband had been 'very supportive', helping her with the computer, 'because I've always looked at a computer as an enemy'.

She lost this support when her husband moved overseas for work, and later their marriage broke down. These challenges helped her to develop her own inner strength:

> You use survival techniques – you have to find some other way ... And really at the end of the day I feel I have to learn myself. So it forces you to learn ...

Although she lost the support of her husband, her mother played a major role:

> ... my mother used to say, 'You're in this for a reason, so stick it out because if you don't you'll end up doing call centre work ... and you don't want to do that ...' She was a great source of support. She used to type out my essays because she's a great typist ...

Marie was also supported by her children and her girlfriend:

> I use my children when they're cooperative. And I have a girlfriend that's really good ... [she] said to me the other day that it's part of my personality that I'm a little bit driven. And she said, 'but you can't be like that ... you will drive yourself to the grave. You have to learn to relax and ... take time out. And you don't know how to do that. It's just a skill.' And it's true ...

As well as being a major impetus for enrolling in the course, Marie's volunteer work also supported her:

> ... [it] has really been an enormous support because it's just opened up a whole new world for me in terms of dealing with people who are in crisis, so it's just given me a lot of skills.

At university Marie was particularly grateful for the help of one staff member who 'was really supportive when I was having problems with my essays':

> ... she helped me so much with my research essays – I think she probably gave me more help than she had given other students. I think she obviously recognised that I was struggling ...

Although she suffered from a severe illness, Marie did not seek or receive support from the university's services such as the Disability Liaison Unit. However, she did seek counselling outside the university to help her after her negative experiences on her first placement. She thought that more university support should be available, both generally, and at departmental level:

> I think that the university doesn't provide enough support for its students ... I think that there aren't enough tutorials. There's not

> enough help given to students who are struggling with their work and a lot of the students do struggle . . . I think the workload is too heavy . . . I think the course is . . . very, very demanding and I can't see how that learning is constructive for any student . . .

Consequently, Marie felt that the course should be reviewed. Although she acknowledged that there may not be funding for more tutorials, she thought that this assistance would help, for example, to provide for discussion on assignments and better engagement with students:

> . . . some lecturers won't even look at a draft of your assignment and that makes it really difficult because you don't know whether you're on the right track or not and some of the assignments are so badly worded so you don't even know where to go with an assignment and if you don't know where to go who do you ask? . . . the lecturers are so busy and they're very abrupt in their manner. One lecturer in particular, she was a dragon and a lot of kids had so many problems with her . . .

She also felt that more tutorials would improve preparation for the workplace:

> . . . you're just sort of thrown in and I don't think it's particularly well run because I think there should be more role-playing. The kids should be more prepared to go out into the workplace . . .

In addition, Marie suggested the provision of 'modules where you can specialise', because the course was 'a little bit too generic'. This would need to be on an elective basis given the heavy course requirements.

Reflections and future plans

Marie completed the course part-time over the following two years. Reflecting on her development as a learner, Marie thought that she would have been '[a] very poor learner' prior to starting the course, given the cognitive deficits associated with lupus. Before becoming ill:

> . . . I already had a degree but I never really enjoyed essays or learning or anything like that. I was always lazy. I did the minimum . . .

Partly, this was because she was not interested in her study: 'I did it just to do something to please my parents, I think. I wasn't a great learner.' She regarded learning as a 'pain':

> [It was] just something that I had to do to get by, to get through ... I didn't have the inquisitive mind. I just wanted to go out and have fun ... I just thought ... [learning] was something other people told me that I had to learn just to get by, to get a job. It wasn't something that I initiated myself ...

Her approach to learning was different when she began her current course:

> It was because I really wanted to do the course that I was very motivated to do it and I think it was such a shock to my system. I was so overwhelmed by the workload ... it was just like, 'I have to get through this because this is my aim', so I was very directed ...

Despite the stress, she was aware of her development as a learner during this time:

> I noticed that my learning curve just went through the roof ... and I remember thinking, 'There's so much to learn in this topic area' and I had a lot to contribute in class ... and everything I said made sense. I remember thinking ... 'I'm a person of value.'

Marie noticed her development as a learner particularly toward the end of the first year:

> I think it was gradual. I think I started to understand the referencing system ... how to write an essay. I started to understand what was required to be a university student. Before I didn't understand, I was just groping in the dark. By the end of the first year I knew what was required and I felt like I was on top of everything ... I was actually pretty vocal all the time because I had a really good tutor. It was more towards the end of the year I became more succinct and more eloquent in what I had to say and more aware. I remember I started to read the papers a lot more and I was more aware of what was going on ... so it was a real consciousness raising.

She enjoyed study more when she became a part-time student, recognising that 'my health wouldn't allow me to do it again over one year':

> *I was able to reflect more on subject matter. I was able to enjoy the learning a lot more and I was able to motivate myself to research the topic a lot more rather than just quickly [studying it] ... it was a better year because I was doing fewer subjects so I got much better marks and so I was able to spend a lot longer on each unit so my research skills became a lot better and I think that I was a lot more relaxed about learning ... I think that that made a big difference to my life. I could incorporate family and life a lot better ...*

Consequently, Marie felt that she developed more as a learner during this time:

> *I was able to use my skills in my volunteer work, which I thought was really good ... Some of my counselling skills I experimented with on some of my clients in my volunteer work. I was integrating my knowledge with practice a little bit more. That became a lot more useful. What I was learning took on some relevancy rather than just being theoretical and also I started to think about where I wanted to go as a career and where my passions were.*

This period was difficult for her at a personal level, because of her marriage breakdown:

> *... and I think that uni just took a second place. I think that it was just hand in the assignments and attend to what was happening on the marriage front and that was really hard ... I think that what kept me going was the fact that I was at uni and it was ... a positive distraction and the fact that I had a placement and it gave me direction ... it sounds weird to say that because a lot of people would have just chucked the whole thing in but I thought, 'No, this is something that's going to give me ... a career and it's going to give me something to go towards otherwise I will end up in a heap.' So it was a good thing to actually persevere with the course because there were times when I thought, 'I just can't do this, it's all too traumatic.'*

In addition:

> *My son dropped out of uni ... he had half a semester left of his music degree and he's just kind of doing nothing and my daughter is*

> *pretty shattered by the whole thing, so there's a lot of grief and loss issues there for her as well as me.*

Having finished her degree, Marie felt more confident and independent as a learner:

> *I was a very anxious learner. I'm not such an anxious learner [now] and I don't underrate myself so much. I used to really underrate myself terribly, which was a real problem. I used to think I was very inadequate. I don't feel I'm so inadequate anymore. That was a really good thing.*

Partly this came from her experience at her second placement:

> *I was just thrown in at the deep end . . . and I didn't have much supervision at all . . . and I thought, 'Well it's like sink or swim. I had a really crappy placement the first one . . . I really need this one to be good . . . I just have to grit my teeth and do what is required,' and . . . I did a really good job, so I said to myself, 'Pat yourself on the back' . . . Can you use the word, 'cathartic'? . . . because I recognised in myself I can do things without panicking and I can be regarded as a competent person and that's how I really want to be regarded . . . I've always thought of myself as incompetent.*

Marie felt that the most important learning for her, from the course, was that:

> *I learnt that I'm OK . . . I'm not a fool. I'm not the brightest person in the universe but I have a lot to share with the world.*

On graduation, Marie commenced work in a government service where she assisted long-term unemployed people. Focusing on her work helped her to cope with the problems at home. She recognised that she had become 'a lot more assertive' with so much having happened in her life.

Given the difficulties in her family life, she was unable to spend too much time contemplating the future:

> *I can't think about that. For me it's one step at a time. My future is just stability and work, making sure that my children . . . especially my youngest child, feels loved and safe . . . and making sure that I*

> create a stable environment and a happy environment and just
> making sure that I take care of myself and that I enjoy my life.

If she were to study again, Marie thought she might undertake a training course to qualify her to teach welfare at further education level. Apart from that, she was not motivated to study:

> I didn't enjoy all the study and the essay writing. I found it difficult and I'm glad it's over and I'm glad I can pick up a book and read it and enjoy it. I'm not really a person that likes to study all that much. It hasn't really spurred me on to further study, only if it's easy. I don't want to do anything really hard ... I'm tired. The steps have been big enough ... I just hope that in a year's time I can look back and say ... 'Oh well, I'm enjoying my life and I feel safe and happy' ... I'm not looking for anything else.

Marie no longer felt 'driven' and once the details of her divorce had been dealt with, she thought that she would be 'OK'.

Harriet's story

Pathway to higher education

When she enrolled in her course, Harriet was living with her partner and daughter in a regional city. Harriet's socio-economic status as an adult was lower than that of her parents. Although she had previously studied at university, some of her experiences as a young woman in the secondary and higher education sectors had derailed her first attempts at higher education.

Family background

Harriet grew up in a migrant family in a 'very working-class ... netball-playing, football-playing kind of town'. Her mother was a nurse and her father a truck driver. Her brother is two years older than her. Her mother migrated from Scotland when she was a child and her father from England when he was 21: 'we were Anglos but migrants, and experiencing racism.'

Harriet was not the first person in her family to go to university. Her brother completed a business degree, but his experiences as a student did not influence her. She had educational support during her childhood: her parents paid for her to attend a private secondary school. However, she felt she lacked guidance and encouragement:

> ... *nothing specific was ever requested of me. Or suggested. And I think I really missed having some sort of direction or guidance, because I really didn't get that from anywhere.*

Her brother had a learning difficulty, so her parents spent a lot of time on him. The only expectation was that she would complete high school, including mathematics. Her father's feelings of inferiority about educational matters contributed to this expectation:

> ... *he told me in confidence once that he'd actually gone to ... uni one day – probably just as lost as I was ... [a] truck driver going off to ... uni to see if he could enrol there. And, you know, he must have been in his sixties when he told me that. And had tears in his eyes.*

Educational experiences

Harriet was a good student. Her years at primary school were happy – almost idyllic:

> *I remember my primary school days as being wonderful ... I remember feeling very unfettered. ... And it was a bit like a wonderland where adults were only incidental ... it was the seventies and was all very relaxed. And a lot of it was very avant-garde – particularly for the time; it was all student-driven, pretty much. It was very unstructured and ... we might just come in from playing at playtime or recess and want to put on an ABBA concert or put on some other sort of play, and the teacher would say, 'Yeah, fine.'*

Harriet thrived in this environment:

> *I always did really well, and had absolutely no problems academically, so I was able to focus on the social and I was very adventurous and mischievous and just had a wonderful time really.*

Her parents were supportive to some extent: 'I did very well through primary school and they did acknowledge that.' However, their responses to her successes were limited:

> ... [there was] an award that I won where I think I was in about Grade 5 or 6 [the last two years of primary school] and ... it was for the whole region and I think the [local] council were running it – and we had to write basically a futuristic kind of response to how we would create our shire if we were able to do whatever we wanted ... and I think the prize was meant to be actually going and being a junior councillor ... the most significant thing about that was that I don't really remember my parents acknowledging it. Or celebrating it.

During primary school Harriet showed talent for art and drama, but this, too, was not remarked upon or encouraged by her parents. She felt that they were disengaged in some way, perhaps because she was doing well academically or because her brother's learning difficulty was the focus of concern. Her brother had a very hard time at primary school where he was bullied by other boys and also by teachers. Harriet took on the role of his support person, standing by him when things were difficult. Class was a factor, too – her brother did not like the working-class, sports-loving environment they grew up in. With her parents' attention focused on her brother and his learning difficulty, Harriet was left to her own devices.

The first thing she can remember wanting to be was a hairdresser:

> I've always seen the artistic connection, because I actually did a fine arts degree before this, and I've worked as an artist. So I see that as my five- or six-year-old self looking around and seeing what I was interested in, and of course in the environment I was in, I wouldn't see an artist or any of those sorts of professions. I saw the hairdresser being creative, and the other day I was thinking that they're also very talkative and so I've ended up in social work!

Harriet's other early ambition was to be a housewife, which she thought was a reaction to her mother working full-time as a nurse. This made her unusual among her peers:

> ... all of the children I went to school with, their mothers didn't work and they were involved in the mothers' club – you know, very heavily involved in the mothers' club and all the school sorts of things ... that was a norm for the seventies I think.

Harriet's educational experiences changed when she moved to secondary school. She chose to go to a secondary school in her local area because her friends were going there:

> *... it was completely unsuitable. It was a technical high school ... it was extremely rough. And I found myself doing sheet metal and woodwork and stuff like that!*

The teaching of subjects in which Harriet performed well was not of a high standard. One of the teachers told her mother that Harriet was 'real good at English'. This prompted her mother to move her to a private school in a more affluent area.

Harriet's feelings about school changed when she moved to her new school. She felt 'some sort of class difference and financial status difference between myself and the other kids'. She had gone from 'being a big fish in a small pond to what I perceived as being a small fish'.

Connecting with friends in her local area was important to Harriet and this stopped when she 'got into quite a bit of trouble' at the end of her first year of private secondary school and her parents 'decided to cut me off from all of my friends in my local area'. She had become withdrawn at the new school because she felt 'really intimidated' about where she came from and after this her feelings of withdrawal continued for the rest of her time at high school.

Locally, Harriet suffered from being called a 'snob' because she was enrolled at a private school. However, she did make some good school friends and enjoyed the academic work at which she did very well, but she 'didn't get as much out of it as I could have'. Although she was still receiving A's and B's for her schoolwork, Harriet felt she should have taken advantage of the music lessons and drama productions that the school offered, but she was too afraid to become involved.

Harriet's fear extended to feeling uncomfortable with success:

> *... there was ... something about not wanting to be noticed ... there was something that was holding me back from really doing as well as I think I might have. You know, I didn't want to be number one.*

Attending a 20-year school reunion and meeting other women who had been in the second year of high school with her caused Harriet to reflect on the way gender issues affected her and her female classmates:

> *... we had our 20th year reunion last year and all of the girls said ... that [in that year] the boys started putting the girls down in class ...*

This had a dramatic effect – she lost her voice:

> *I remember the day I stopped contributing to class and never, never did again. And when we got together last year, we all remembered it . . . one of the girls was saying, 'Why weren't the teachers doing something about it?'*

One of the 'very bright' female students did stand up to the boys and appeared to do so successfully, but she developed anorexia. Harriet connected the two things: 'they managed to get to her too'.

Other negative factors played a part in Harriet's secondary school experiences. When she was in the penultimate year of high school:

> *I failed something for the first time in my life. I got an E or an F or something like that. And it was absolutely devastating.*

Then, in her final year, she made some poor subject choices, and at about that time she overheard her parents talking about divorce:

> *. . . it was a complete shock . . . it was sort of seen as a very unusual, very exotic thing . . . And I think [there were] only two or three of the people in my class or in my school group . . . whose parents were divorced.*

As a result, Harriet did not do as well as she might have in her final year. She was very disappointed, particularly with her English results.

At this time Harriet was not sure what she wanted to do when she left school. Looking back she felt she lacked good careers advice at home and from teachers at school, and good role models. Although her final year English teacher 'ended up being a role model':

> *. . . my parents didn't really model for me very well, and they didn't really have any . . . close family friends. There were no other significant adults really that I looked to. And I think that's probably why I missed out on some guidance and advice . . .*

Because she loved writing, Harriet thought of becoming a journalist, but her English teacher did not support this idea. She also had thoughts of becoming a doctor, which were not realistic because of the subjects she had chosen. In hindsight, she thought that she was interested in social work even then.

Harriet's first awareness of social work came when her mother, who worked as a nurse in the community, had social workers in her team:

> *And I can remember the first time I considered being a social worker was when she was telling me what one of the social workers ... on her team had been wearing when she came to a meeting ... and I was very interested in fashion at the time ... to be able to go to a meeting and ... look creative and interesting sounded good!*

After she completed high school Harriet went overseas for a year on a work exchange scheme. But she found it difficult that her friends had moved on to university while she was away – '[s]o I kind of missed the boat with all of that'.

Although her brother had been to university Harriet had no knowledge of its practices or its language. She found applying for a place very confusing:

> *I can picture myself there ... trying to fill out the application form, and trying to choose a course and having absolutely no idea what a BA was, what Masters was, what Honours was ... what arts was, what humanities was ... So – I knew I was meant to go! But I had no idea where or how!*

Harriet enrolled because she felt it was expected ('I think probably the expectations of the school really'). She enrolled in an arts degree and began studying philosophy, art history, English and Italian. She dropped out early and began to work as a picture framer, which she enjoyed much more.

It was Harriet's father who finally set her on the path to a degree that she completed. He found an advertisement for a fine arts course offered in part-time mode. She enrolled and then converted to full-time. She did well in first year and again felt uncomfortable with the notice that success brought. She decided to accept a part-time job, which took her away from the course and the time she needed to spend on course tasks.

At the time that it appeared she might fail, she was sexually harassed by one of the lecturers. When Harriet was called in to discuss her academic progress, the head of department suggested she take a summer course with that lecturer. She was distressed that she was not able to do anything about the lecturer's behaviour. She did finish the course but felt the injustice of this situation very keenly and regretted that she had not reported him. Its impact continued to have an effect on her:

> *I was completely lost in my early twenties. And I thought, 'Yes, I want to look after people, but I can't look after other people if I haven't done some living and I don't know how to look after myself yet.'*

Some time later Harriet enrolled in a Graduate Diploma in Psychology but that was interrupted by crises in her family. She deferred the course when her mother had an accident but, in retrospect, realised that she 'had already started to feel like it wasn't what I really wanted to do'. She was 'looking for a framework that I felt fitted me' and '[d]idn't find it there, but have very much found it in social work'.

Managing study

Planning

Harriet did not need to make many changes in her life to engage in the course. She had adjusted to study when she had started her previous course, and was not in the paid workforce:

> *... after I'd had my child I didn't go back to work for some time ... I was living on one wage anyway.*

While there was little effect on her daily routine, enrolment involved some psychological preparation:

> *... it probably took me 20 years to feel like I could handle studying social work ... I realised, yes, I'm ready to actually begin study and not feel overly responsible for changing the world.*

Harriet made a plan (on the back of an envelope) for the next couple of years. This involved working out what she wanted, and where she wanted the course to take her.

Managing

Previous jobs had satisfied the artistic side of Harriet's nature. However, the practical nature of social work became important to her as the course progressed and motivated her to continue with her studies even in difficult times:

> *I was never going to give up right from the start, because I wanted a good solid qualification that would get me a job.*

Harriet was successful in her first year, was offered a job by the organisation at which she had completed her first professional placement, and was asked to interview for a second position. Her academic success also provided her with a pathway into studying at Honours level. While this was motivating, it presented a challenge in terms of making sure she was not taking on too much. She changed from a full-time load to part-time to accommodate the increased workload. Having a room of her own, a space where she could lock herself away and concentrate on her studies was very important:

> *... the physical space, albeit tiny and all the rest of it, that was really helpful to have a door to close.*

She was happy with her choice of course and looked forward to using her writing skills in the required research component.

Support

Except for attending some library workshops on how to use EndNote [bibliography software], Harriet did not use any of the university's student support services. She was supported by an equity bursary in her Honours year. She had not known these existed until one of her lecturers suggested she apply. In this way she received the financial support she needed to continue with the course. Just as important in Harriet's estimation was the sense of validation the bursary brought with it:

> *... when I got the letter in the mail saying that I'd gotten it [the bursary], it was just amazing. Because again that was validation.*

Being supported to push herself was very important for Harriet who commented that, in the past, she did not know what it was like to push herself: 'I had no interest in competition, even with myself, I suppose.' She was very supported by the mentoring and career advice her supervisor provided and by 'the support of all of the lecturers'. In addition:

> *... my partner has been extraordinarily helpful, and my daughter as well, and I think they have put up with an awful lot of doors*

> *being shut in their face [and me] saying, 'I've just got to get this done . . . it's another deadline.'*

Once she became immersed in her studies, Harriet found she did not receive much support from friends among the mothers at her daughter's school, but she met new friends with similar interests during her placements.

Harriet identified the way the course was designed and taught as a key source of academic and social support. Early online subjects were broken down into what she called 'small achievable chunks' and the students received feedback on their work very early in the course. Getting marks early helped to build her confidence:

> *. . . we got a few marks fairly quickly and I remember clicking on . . . and it was a HD [High Distinction] and then the next one was HD and then the next one was HD and then the next one was HD . . . and I thought, 'My goodness!'*

This motivated her to succeed even more:

> *So then it was HD, HD, HD, and I remember getting half way through and thinking . . . 'I want them all to be HDs.' And I hadn't felt that way before. I just didn't care, I [just] wanted to pass. And I guess that was a pivotal moment . . .*

Harriet considered that the way the on-campus learning component of her course was conducted in small group settings was crucial in allowing her to find her voice, to have enough confidence to speak out and offer an opinion:

> *I'm going to put myself out there, I'm going to use my voice and that has been the theme throughout . . . what I have found has been really powerful, is that I was brave enough to be myself . . . And then I found myself in small group settings where I couldn't keep my mouth shut. And I'd find myself starting to talk because I'd found I had something to contribute . . .*

The curriculum design facilitated social connections too:

> *. . . there was a group of six of us who worked online together and then met up at the workshops. We had a really strong social connection there . . . there was a real strength in that . . .*

Reflections and future plans

Having successfully completed her course, Harriet regarded herself as 'very much a lifelong learner', but that was not always the case. She believed she came to this position through her various educational experiences prior to the course and informally through reading and discussion with her partner. Early in her studies she was a 'semi-self-motivated and self-directed learner' and studying psychology for eighteen months gave her learning skills in the off-campus (distance education) mode.

An increase in confidence and an associated reduction in anxiety was something else Harriet experienced along the way. This showed itself in better organisation of her learning tasks. Reflecting on her early days in the course she came to realise that:

> *. . . part of what has helped me to be more organised is a lack of anxiety . . . the calm and confidence to sort of think, 'It's going to be OK. I'll be fine.'*

Although her confidence grew throughout her course, achieving good grades in her early assessment tasks did not necessarily alleviate her anxiety: 'as I became successful in the course my anxiety level actually increased', continuing the fear of the attention that success brings that had been evident during her high school years when she made sure that she was never the winner, but always second best.

Harriet completed her Honours degree, receiving the top mark in her year, and was awarded a prestigious academic prize. As well as the validation that this brought her, she also felt that being supported to do her best and pushing herself 'as hard as I could for the first time ever' increased her confidence to a point where she felt 'I've got no anxiety about anything, about study or anything.' At the end of her course Harriet was told she could go straight on and enrol in a PhD ('that was just beyond imagining for me'). She decided that as 'money has been an issue for us', she would not do her PhD unless she won a scholarship:

> *. . . we've made huge sacrifices, we've scraped through on nothing financially for the last four years, we've always been poor but we've gotten really close to the bone in the last four years . . .*

Harriet got the scholarship and began her doctoral studies. Looking back, she was very aware of the way education had transformed her life:

> ... the other thing that's been incredibly powerful about this course is that I have found my path in a huge way. The whole course has just been transforming for me, astonishing and transforming ... My voice was taken away in so many settings through so many experiences in my life.

During her study Harriet had begun to realise how 'it was impacting on ... my identity' with the result that 'really what I feel now is ... a sense of wholeness and integration.'

Having completed the course, she reflected:

> ... it's a really lovely thing that the course has done for me, so many things, I've gained so much. Even if ... I wasn't to have a qualification out of this, if I wasn't to have new opportunities opening for me in research and academia, it would have just been a wonderful self-development course, a wonderful experience, because it's just brought me to a place in my life where I feel like I can do anything really ... And I have a lot of people to thank for that journey.

Implications for managing and supporting student diversity: encouraging transformative learning

Lillian's, Marie's and Harriet's stories illustrate the way that higher education can provide a life focus and a pathway for forging a new sense of self-worth, and a new identity, in addition to new career opportunities. All three stories powerfully illustrate how gendered experiences impacted on their pathways to higher education. Lillian left school early and became a secretary, Harriet became silent and Marie, who had to undertake a nurturing role in her family, was influenced in her initial course selection, not by her own interests but by those of her then boyfriend. Each of these students overcame huge social and emotional barriers to succeed (and in Harriet's case, to excel) in their studies. This success provided them with a great deal of self-fulfilment and confidence, changing the way they perceived themselves, releasing Marie and Harriet from anxiety and allowing Lillian to transcend the limiting influences of her 'anxious-ridden family'. A strong sense of commitment and direction was evident as they faced and overcame barriers, placing them well to make a strong contribution among their peers while at university and in their careers on completion of their studies. This was in spite of the effects of the death of her mother on Lillian's journey, and the breakdown of Marie's marriage, both in their final year of study. Lillian's and Marie's muted responses at the end of the course (Lillian was 'exhausted' and Marie 'tired') illustrate the fact that transformation is not always accompanied by elation, but occurs in the context of, and is influenced by, other life experiences.

In Lillian's story we see a young person who 'wasn't able to grow an identity from within myself' and are reminded of the importance of good friendship groups among adolescent girls at school, and the impact that negative experiences can have on girls' self-confidence and educational choices. Although she began to envisage another version of herself when she was about 30, Lillian's story again draws attention to the value of serendipitous contact with another encouraging adult, in this case an educated woman who later encouraged Lillian to see herself as capable and deserving of higher education. Once this door opened for her, Lillian was on a path that was of fundamental importance to her, illustrated by the impact of her first arrival at a university campus: 'I was crying as I drove into uni because I was just so overwhelmed and proud that I got there.'

The story of Marie is inspiring. Her determination to study and succeed despite her debilitating illness, and her difficulties with academic and computer literacy, and then to embark on her career to contribute positively to improving the lot of others, is motivating. Like Lillian, as a young person she 'had no concept of myself', in her case because 'I was always seen as the nurturer, the carer', so when the opportunity came to say 'this is who I am', she embraced it. Just as Marie gave much to her studies, she also gained much herself and in many ways the study was cathartic for her, helping her to cope with her illness and her life in a more positive way.

For Harriet, the impact of poor socio-economic circumstances, limited opportunities at secondary school level, and the sexual harassment she experienced at her first attempt at higher education led to the silencing of her 'voice'. Harriet's story demonstrates how these circumstances can resonate throughout one's life course. Her story highlights the importance of the support of partners and children, peers and academic staff in addressing obstacles to study. Successful experience of higher education enabled Harriet to find her voice and develop the self-confidence and awareness to continue onto further study. As she says, '[t]he whole course has just been transforming for me, astonishing and transforming', and she notes some of the teaching strategies (small 'chunks' of work, early feedback, and grades) that helped in this transformation.

The changes that Lillian, Marie and Harriet underwent as they evolved as learners illustrate the personal transformation that adult students often experience through study and raise the question of what university staff can do to guide and support such transformation. Like those in previous stories, these students succeeded for the most part without the assistance of university support services, although Harriet's story shows the value of financial assistance through an equity bursary. Lack of early course and career guidance was evident in each of their stories. In her current course, Marie's story in particular highlights how well-targeted services could have assisted her with managing her illnesses, counselling and with problems associated with computer literacy and academic literacy. For example, Marie did not appreciate the importance of strong professional writing skills, which in her case would be needed later in producing court reports and other documents on behalf of clients. Although these students showed sufficient resilience to succeed without additional university assistance, it is likely that they could have been helped on their transformative pathways by further assistance from university staff.

Mezirow (1978) introduced the concept of perspective transformation to explain the fundamental changes that adults may experience through learning. This idea was based on critical social theory but Mezirow's focus was on empowerment and emancipation through personal (rather than social) change. His theory suggests that the emancipatory aspect of transformative learning occurs when individuals change their frames of reference by critically reflecting on their assumptions and beliefs, engaging in discourse and consciously making and implementing plans that bring about new ways of defining their worlds. Cranton (2002: 64) explained the 'elegantly simple' nature of Mezirow's central idea: if through some event an individual becomes aware of holding a limited or distorted view and 'critically examines this view, opens herself to alternatives, and consequently changes the way she sees things, she has transformed some part of how she makes meaning of the world'.

Mezirow's theory has evolved over the years, both through his own refinements to it and the contributions of others (see, for example, Kitchenham, 2008; Mezirow et al., 2009). While Mezirow saw perspective transformation as a rational process, these other contributions include acknowledging the roles of emotion and imagination in constructing meaning, the importance of context, the varying nature of the catalyst of perspective transformation, and the role of relationships. In considering both Mezirow's rational approach and the 'extrarational' approach of others who regard transformation as extending beyond cognitive ways of knowing, Cranton (2006: 77) discussed whether rational and extrarational transformation can occur suddenly and dramatically, gradually over time, or as a developmental process. She concluded that 'from the perspective of the person experiencing transformation, it is more often a gradual accumulation of ordinary experiences that leads to a deep shift in thinking, a shift that may only become clear when it is over'. She suggests ways of supporting transformative learning based on these concepts. While her suggestions are for teaching staff, if your role is to support students in other ways, it is likely that you are also working with students in ways that can encourage transformative learning.

Cranton (2006: 122–9) includes the following suggestions for empowering learners:

- Exercise power responsibly (e.g. reduce the trappings of formal authority; avoid being in the position of providing all the answers; be open and explicit about all strategies that you use).
- Encourage empowerment through discourse (e.g. stimulate dialogue from different perspectives; avoid dismissive statements or definitive summaries; be conscious of non-verbal communication).
- Support learner decision-making (e.g. encourage learners to contribute to planning of educational activities, suggest topics or resources and lead discussions; provide choices of methods; encourage students' self-assessment, and regularly ask them for their perceptions of the learning experience).

Cranton's suggestions for fostering critical self-reflection and self-knowledge include:

- questioning (e.g. being specific and conversational, using open-ended questions, and drawing on learners' experiences and interests);
- using consciousness-raising experiences (e.g. reversing roles and presenting ideas from another person's point of view);
- using journals to encourage students to record thoughts and experiment with different styles and content;
- implementing experiential learning activities and setting aside time for critical discourse; and
- asking students to think back over a period and record critical incidents, and then encourage critical questioning (pp. 135–55).

Another recent idea that has gained acceptance in higher education for explaining the transformative nature of learning is the notion of threshold concepts where mastery of a subject

> ... can be considered as akin to a portal, opening up a new and previously inaccessible way of thinking about something ... representing a transformed way of understanding, or interpreting, or viewing something without which the learner cannot progress ...

and which results in an irreversible shift in perception (Meyer and Land, 2006: 3). Much of the work on threshold concepts has differed from Mezirow's approach because of its emphasis on how students acquire knowledge in the disciplines (Land et al., 2008; Meyer and Land, 2006), though it is now extending beyond this focus. If you have a teaching role, this is nevertheless a useful concept to help you think about learning activities that, for example, would help these students transform into thinking of themselves as social workers.

You can see how the various ideas about transformative learning can provide guidance for supporting and extending some of the strategies we have considered in previous chapters, such as encouraging group work and communication, facilitating experiential learning through role plays or professional placements, and providing flexibility for students. They can be used to respond to the adult learning characteristics we addressed in Chapter 5.

Summary

This chapter has presented the stories of Lillian, Marie and Harriet, who demonstrated a passion for and strong engagement with their studies and a love of learning. They reported on the ways their lives and identities were transformed through their higher education studies, with each woman experiencing a new and more positive sense of her own identity and ability to contribute to the world through her studies. This is a goal aspired to by all educators, where students can reach their potential and achieve fulfilment through the educational program. What is most inspiring about these stories is the hardships and difficulties these students faced, and the sense of self-confidence and self-efficacy they developed through their ability to manage and cope with these challenges. As with the other students whose stories we have considered, family support in various forms was vital in making their success possible. The chapter concluded by focusing on the important role of university staff in facilitating success by fostering and supporting transformative learning.

Chapter 6: discussion topics

1. Think about the stories of Lillian, Marie and Harriet in turn. In each case identify how and when their perspectives shifted. What were the elements that drove these changes? For each student, consider what you would have done in your role to support perspective transformation.
2. If you have a teaching role, what strategies do you currently use to support transformative learning? What are three or four other strategies you could try?
3. If you have a professional role, what approaches do you use now to support students' positive perceptions of themselves as learners? What are three or four other strategies you could try?
4. Is perspective transformation always a good thing? Why or why not? How would you support a student whose higher education experience is contributing to the loss of former friends or the failure of a marriage?
5. Experiences such as sexual harassment can create major barriers to transformation. What are the sexual harassment policies in your institution? How, in your role, could you support a student who has experienced sexual harassment?

7

Helping students to succeed

Abstract: In this chapter, we review the stories of how students from diverse backgrounds succeeded in higher education to identify the main factors that contributed to their success. We consider these factors in the context of recent literature on how students succeed and then discuss the overall implications of the stories for managing and supporting student diversity. We summarise the key implications for university staff, noting the value of thinking about these in terms of strategies to assist the transition and retention of students from diverse backgrounds who enter higher education, with a particular focus on supporting international and mature age students, and encouraging transformative learning. These are the topics we focused on in our discussion of the implications of students' stories in Chapters 2–6. The key implications suggest the importance of: supporting peer interaction and practical learning; offering feedback and encouragement; being flexible in response to student needs and circumstances; and facilitating student-centred access to information and services.

Key words: feedback, flexibility, student diversity, student success, student support, study modes.

Introduction

This concluding chapter aims to:

- summarise how students from diverse backgrounds succeed in higher education, drawing on the cases in this book, and on some of the directions provided by recent literature on this topic; and
- prompt you to consider the overall implications of the cases for your management and support of students from diverse backgrounds.

Our focus is on your role as a practitioner either directly involved in teaching or supporting students, or involved with students as part of your work – for example, in recruitment, enrolment or administrative tasks relating to their study at university.

Implicit in the students' stories and our discussion in the preceding chapters is an account of higher education that presently does not cater well for students who enter from diverse or non-traditional pathways. This is supported by evidence from a range of countries that we presented in Chapter 1, suggesting that universities are still largely oriented towards young people of middle class background with a strong and coherent, and usually urban, high school education. As the literature on students' first year at university illustrates, some young school leavers may face challenges entering higher education, but those students who enter *without* this background face particular challenges (e.g. Klinger and Murray, 2012; Yorke, 2008). The students' stories illustrate how some of them succeed in the face of these challenges.

What makes success possible for these students includes a mix of individual students' personal characteristics and circumstances, forms of support and assistance offered by others, and structural factors, which can be broadly divided into individual and institutional factors, as we noted in Chapter 1. As a practitioner, you will primarily be concerned with institutional factors by improving the structures and supports that make success possible. In their stories, the students identified the factors that were key to their success. We summarise these below as a basis for addressing the overall implications that they suggest for university staff.

How the students from diverse backgrounds succeeded in higher education

We begin this section by reviewing the key factors that contributed to the success of each of the students in Chapters 2–6. We then consider these in the context of the literature on how students succeed in higher education that we outlined in Chapter 1.

In Chapter 2, *Miranda's* story suggests that the key contributors to her success were her personal qualities, including the skills she developed in organising her study and circumstances, and the support she received, primarily from people outside the university. Despite her unsettled background, the stability and sense of direction she developed because of factors such as the needs of her mother and sister, the female role models in her life, the perception that she was smart, and the 'pluck' resulting from her mother's influence, all appeared to contribute to successful study. As a student, her organisation of her study ('[I]t's a priority. It's like work') and her related determination ('I'm extremely stubborn') contributed to her success, along with support, particularly from her mother and partner, and also from university staff and her employer. Other structural factors included the flexibility of distance education, which made her study possible, along with the earlier educational opportunities she had grasped; and the guidance of the Salvation Army Officer, which led to a 'government job' and subsequently to further study. These factors gave her directions that she might not have otherwise taken. The specific learning opportunities provided by the course, and their application in the workplace, contributed to Miranda's success as well.

Also in Chapter 2, *Rochelle's* story reveals a similar pattern of how successful study occurs, despite the fact that she lacked confidence as a learner. She failed in her first two attempts to enrol in a further education course and took a long time to find the direction that she needed (perhaps as a consequence of her earlier schooling in a remote regional town, where 'everyone's a tradesman'). Along the way she received continuous practical support from her parents, which included funding a final year of education at boarding school, and providing accommodation for her while at university. Rochelle also developed confidence and direction from a number of serendipitous encounters that led to her enrolment in her course. Tenacity ('[when you] start something you should finish it') and the desire to 'use my brain' positioned her well, and once in the course, like Miranda, she developed a routine where she treated her study as work. A number of structural and course-related factors contributed to her growing confidence during the course. These include her professional placements, her collaboration with peers in the course, and with friends, and the motivational impact of passing her subjects. Rochelle, too, benefited from the availability of distance education and also support from the study centre of another university in her town.

In Chapter 3, *Sesh's* story demonstrates how the development of critical skills in time-management and a systematic approach prioritising study, combined with various forms of support, were key factors in success. Although Sesh had successful experiences at school, the disruption in her family life, and her education in a rural area – which reinforced gendered expectations and offered inadequate preparation for higher education – did not provide for early success at university. After various work experiences and the influence of an employer who recognised her abilities, she developed the capacity to move forward irrespective of her family's influence ('It's pure determination now') with a focus that meant 'there's nothing else in my life. I've made uni such a central process.' Sesh benefited from accommodation and financial support (such as funding to attend a conference) provided by her family, as well as peer support available through online contact with her fellow students, the feedback provided by teaching staff on her work, and the experience of her professional placements, which increased her motivation.

Also in Chapter 3, *Shannon's* story is notable for the sophisticated use he makes of the organisational tools on his computer to manage his study. This use, combined with a study approach that demonstrates both rigidity and flexibility, are important factors in his success. Shannon's story also highlights the important role of personal circumstances in success. It was the birth of Shannon's son when he was young that disrupted his first attempt at university study. His subsequent work history, combined with his family situation, then drove the need to 'set myself up', which led to his enrolment at university several years later. Also influential in providing direction for his second attempt at study was the example of his mother, who returned to study and completed a teacher education qualification as a mature age student, as well as a significant encounter with a social work student and the influence of others at a training course he attended. This training opportunity enabled him to mix with university-educated staff in his field and reaffirmed for him the possibilities of higher education. Like Sesh, Shannon experienced considerable personal development in the years prior to enrolment, pursuing opportunities offered in his workplace. His continuing development as a learner was evident from the way he engaged with his study, particularly through the application of theory to practice during his professional placements. Shannon demonstrated his persistence and determination by tailoring his study times to suit his work and family responsibilities, getting up early to study before his family was awake. He also demonstrated careful financial management to deal with forgoing income from his job to undertake the professional placement requirements of the course. In addition to his own commitment, the support of his family and workplace, and the availability of off-campus study contributed significantly to Shannon's success.

In Chapter 4, the stories of international students *Lam* and *Zelin* show a different study trajectory from the students in previous chapters, with successful study an expectation, as held by their fathers in particular. Nevertheless, their stories show many similarities with the students' stories we have considered so far, demonstrating initial difficulties in finding the course that was right for them, the importance of support from others, and the role of their own motivation and determination in their success.

Lam showed early initiative and independence, resisting the direction her father suggested for her and becoming an international student in Australia. She was, however, disadvantaged by lack of knowledge about the career opportunities in the field she chose. It was her subsequent experience in the workforce that led to her successful experience of study. Once enrolled in the social work course, Lam, like the other successful students, demonstrated determination and strong organisational skills (using a year planner to guide her study), receiving assistance from others (peers in the course, other friends, her family, and boyfriend). Her comments illustrate the importance of curriculum design in contributing to success, in this case through the inclusion of small classes and group activities that provided a supportive environment for questioning and participation.

Zelin's enrolment followed school and university study in her home country ('I've been studying all my life so far'), but her misunderstanding of the career opportunities associated with the postgraduate course that she originally undertook led to a change of direction a few months later. Once enrolled in the undergraduate course, she used similar organisational skills to Lam, and benefited from support from her friends and peers in the course, financial assistance provided by her parents, and the emotional support of her parents and boyfriend. Like Lam, she referred to aspects of the design of the course which contributed to her success, including its practical focus such as role plays in class and learning from professional placements. She also valued the encouragement from lecturers to express her opinions.

In Chapter 5, *Alex Carole's* story demonstrates a personal commitment to study resulting from a health crisis, a serendipitous encounter, and awareness of an 'opportunity to turn my life around'. These contributed to her persistence in achieving success, even when she failed a compulsory subject twice. The support of her spouse and the voluntary work she undertook in Malaysia were factors contributing to her success. Like Zelin, Alex Carole noted the value of the practical focus of the course, including role plays and professional placements. Being able to study in distance education mode was also important to her success, as was the support of her peers in the course through online communication.

Virginia's successful study experience presented in Chapter 5 was underpinned by a long-held desire to study combined with circumstances that made it possible. Contributing factors were the support of her husband, her mother and her children, and the availability of off-campus study. Like others, she formed strong skills in managing her time and her study, combining organisation with flexibility and treating study as work. She demonstrated resilience by overcoming setbacks, taking 'my own future into my own hands'. She also benefited from the 'style of learning' offered by off-campus study, the non-prescriptive nature of the course, and the support provided by her student group. The experience gained in her professional placements and the motivational impact of being offered the opportunity to study at Honours level were also major contributors to her success.

Lillian's story in Chapter 6 highlights the combination of personal characteristics, favourable circumstances, and support in successful study. While her desire to study had emerged relatively recently compared with Virginia, it was characterised by persistence and resilience and nourished by the 'secure base' provided by her husband and child and by the friend at her mothers' group who encouraged her initial enrolment. Favourable circumstances included a secure financial position, and access to child care and a cleaner. Like others, she benefited from the option to study in distance mode, and was willing to sacrifice other aspects of her life, particularly her social life with friends, to manage and prioritise her study, although she needed to make compromises to care for her daughter, and for her mother before she died. Her mother's illness and death precluded her acceptance of an offer to study at Honours level, an offer she, like Virginia, found motivating. Despite the difficulties, her desire not to let herself and others down drove her success.

Although *Marie* came from a background where education was valued, her story in Chapter 6 initially illustrates the multitude of factors that can adversely affect capacity to study. Much later a major event in the form of a serious illness, complemented by a direction-giving experience (her voluntary work) triggered a personal commitment and a set of circumstances that made successful study possible ('I just think that in life sometimes you get a second chance. And it feels like this is that'). Marie's 'migrant determination' ('you just don't give up') was evident in the way she overcame difficulties to succeed. These difficulties included study problems, further episodes of illness, her husband's departure to work overseas, and the breakdown of their marriage. She was supported by her mother, her children, her girlfriend, one lecturer in particular, and initially by her husband. Other factors included her skills in managing her anxiety in order to study, while at institutional level, the option to transfer from full-time to part-time study, and the experience of being 'thrown in at the deep end' during her second placement, also contributed to her success.

Finally, *Harriet's* story in Chapter 6 illustrates the role of motivation and tenacity in success ('I was never going to give up right from the start, because I wanted a good solid qualification that would get me a job'), which was validated by her early academic success in the course. Like Virginia (Chapter 5) and Lillian, Harriet found being offered a place in the Honours program affirming. She recognised that the way the course was designed and taught helped her to succeed. Her appreciation of early online subjects that were broken down into 'small achievable chunks' with feedback offered early, echoes Shannon's preference for 'lots of little assignments' (Chapter 3), while small group work developed Harriet's self-confidence and facilitated social connections. She also benefited, as Marie did, from being able to change from full-time to part-time study. Her success was assisted by the mentoring and career advice her Honours supervisor provided, along with 'the support of all the lecturers' and her partner and daughter. As well as providing financial assistance necessary for her to continue her studies, an equity bursary from the university gave her further affirmation of her worth and supported her ultimate success.

The students' accounts of how they succeeded in their studies support the evidence of what makes success possible, outlined in Chapter 1. The experiences provided by the students' stories vividly convey the impact of individual factors such as age, gender, ethnicity, location, and financial status, plus institutional factors such as flexible study modes, inclusive curricula, integrated support, and scholarships on their capacity to succeed. Read together, these stories offer a mature age perspective on success compared with research that focuses on students entering university directly from school.

Among the individual factors, the stories confirm the important role of family and friends in success noted by others (e.g. Devlin and O'Shea, 2012; Kinnear et al., 2008; Kuh et al., 2006), even when those who supported them had limited understanding of what university study involved, a factor that characterises the experiences of students who are first in their family to enter higher education (Ferrier and Heagney, 2000). The central role of students' motivation, personal goals, and career aspirations in shaping success similarly affirms these other findings (e.g. Devlin and O'Shea, 2012; Kinnear et al., 2008).

For many of the students, the decision to come to university was the outcome of a long process of self-awareness formed through often painful life experiences, favourable circumstances that made study possible, and a realisation that 'the time was right'. Favourable circumstances included having children who were at school and a stable financial situation. For others it was a case of 'seizing the moment' and realising that the circumstances were favourable – the 'second chance' in life that Marie (Chapter 6) identifies. For some time before she enrolled in her course, Harriet (Chapter 6) knew she wanted to work in a 'caring' profession in her twenties but she was aware that she was not yet ready to take that step:

> Yes, I want to look after people, but I can't look after other people if I haven't done some living and I don't know how to look after myself yet.

Among the institutional factors supporting the students' success, the important roles of teaching staff in relation to personal support, teaching strategies, and curriculum design were apparent, reflecting factors identified by others (e.g. Crosling et al., 2008; Devlin et al., 2012; Hockings, 2010), with the value of group work, feedback, practical learning, and use of the online environment highlighted in particular. At a broader institutional level, the availability of flexible study modes made successful study possible for a number of students. Some students' comments also reinforce the importance of financial support for success (e.g. Devlin et al., 2012; Kinnear et al., 2008; Kuh et al., 2006; Long et al., 2006) and, in terms of support beyond the university, the experiences of Miranda (Chapter 2), Shannon (Chapter 3), Zelin (Chapter 4) and Alex Carole (Chapter 5) indicate the relevance of flexibility on the part of employers as a factor for students who are working as well as studying (Kinnear et al., 2008; McInnis, 2001).

Overall implications of the cases for managing and supporting student diversity

In a context of universal participation in higher education, the questions facing practitioners include: What can you do to assist students from non-traditional backgrounds to succeed? And how can the life skills and experience of talented students, who have taken non-traditional pathways into university or who come from non-traditional backgrounds, be respected and harnessed in ways that support their success in higher education? In this section we consider the implications of the students' stories for ways that you, as a teaching or professional staff member, can reconsider your role, as an individual and as a member of a department or team.

We do this in two stages: first, by focusing on comments made in students' stories about strategies by academic or professional staff which assisted them, or which could have assisted them; and secondly, by summarising some key implications for managing and supporting student diversity in higher education which emerge from the students' comments. We relate these to strategies for transition, retention, supporting international students, supporting mature age students, and encouraging transformative learning that we addressed in Chapters 2–6.

Implications from students' comments

The importance of support from family and friends was evident in all the students' stories but particular mention of support from peers in the course was made by Sesh (Chapter 3), Lam and Zelin (Chapter 4), Alex Carole and Virginia (Chapter 5), and Harriet (Chapter 6). This suggests an important role for teaching staff in facilitating peer interaction from the beginning of a course, through both informal activities and the use of group work as a pedagogical approach. It is notable that the two international students made particular mention of the value of peer interaction and of small classes. Lam suggested the inclusion of more group work as well as whole class activities, and Zelin commented that assistance in meeting people at the beginning of a course could have been helpful. The availability of online forms of interaction provides opportunities for exploring creative use of the virtual environment to assist students to engage with their fellow students and teachers. For professional staff, the importance of peer interaction indicates the value of alerting students to the range of group activities available at the university (bearing in mind that non-traditional students may be time limited and therefore restricted in their participation in such groups, or they may lack confidence and be reluctant to join in). In this situation, professional staff could advocate through committee participation for increased online and physical participation in activities and groups and they could develop strategies to invite students to participate in activities that may be relevant to them.

Another important factor in supporting students' success was the practical focus of their study, including authentic activities such as role plays in class and, in particular, professional placements. This aspect of study was mentioned by Miranda and Rochelle (Chapter 2), Sesh and

Shannon (Chapter 3), Zelin (Chapter 4), Alex Carole and Virginia (Chapter 5), and Marie (Chapter 6). While the importance of practical learning to these students may have been influenced by the course they studied, it supports the life-centred orientation of adult learners (Knowles et al., 2011) and the recent emphasis on work-integrated learning in higher education in efforts to improve graduate employability (e.g. Bamber, 2008; Knight and Yorke, 2004; Oliver, 2010). This has particular relevance to students from diverse backgrounds given the economic imperatives driving universal education in many countries. Consequently, there are strong implications for academic staff to design curricula that include authentic learning activities such as those mentioned in the students' stories.

A number of students also mentioned the importance of feedback in supporting and directing their learning, including Sesh (Chapter 3), Lam and Zelin (Chapter 4), Virginia (Chapter 5), and Harriet (Chapter 6). Harriet's comments particularly emphasise the importance of curriculum design that includes small learning activities which begin early and provide regular feedback, while Virginia's comments about the isolation of off-campus study and the unexpected and motivational impact of being offered a place in the Honours program, also highlight the importance of this issue. While feedback is important for all students, the development of early, regular, and comprehensive feedback strategies may be seen as especially important for students who enter higher education with disrupted educational backgrounds and lack confidence in their abilities.

Students who benefited from flexible study options included Miranda and Rochelle (Chapter 2), Sesh and Shannon (Chapter 3), and Virginia (Chapter 5), as well as Lillian, Marie, and Harriet (Chapter 6) who changed their study mode to suit changes in their circumstances. While individual academic staff members may not have direct control over the study modes that are available at their institutions, or institutional arrangements for intermitting and returning to study, they are well positioned to provide flexibility at course or subject level, such as being flexible in relation to assessment scheduling (Hockings, 2010) and practicum arrangements (Ferrier et al., 2010). If you are in a position to influence the establishment and marketing of more flexible pathways into your institution, for example, from the vocational education and training sector, this is a very important aspect of increasing flexibility for students from non-traditional backgrounds. Flexible access arrangements have the potential of assisting students' transition to university and creating a vital starting point in facilitating their success.

Personal support provided by members of teaching staff who were known to them contributed to the success of Rochelle (Chapter 2), Zelin (Chapter 4), Virginia (Chapter 5), and Marie and Harriet (Chapter 6). Given that students may approach different staff members, this further suggests the importance of *all* staff members being equipped to assist students. This is especially relevant since a notable feature of the comments made by students was the limited reference to support sought from university areas beyond the immediate study context, including central university support services (with some comments made on the deficiency of these services), despite the obvious need for assistance by some of them such as Marie (Chapter 6). Sesh (Chapter 3) avoided university support services because, during previous university study attempts, she had not found them helpful. Lam and Zelin (Chapter 4) had approached learning skills advisers and Zelin received support from information technology and library staff, but Lam had found learning skills advisers 'not completely helpful' because she needed assistance with proof reading and 'they only have a very limited consultation time'. This suggests a need to rethink how support services are organised and delivered, which has implications for both academic and professional staff. Lam's comment on proof reading also emphasises the need to raise students' awareness of the roles of different services to avoid misunderstandings, in this case because learning skills advisers are concerned with developing students' approaches to study, rather than performing 'housekeeping' duties on students' work.

The existing contact that departmental teaching and professional staff have with students positions them to provide assistance or direct students to available services, potentially anticipating the support required, of which students may be unaware or feel unable – or not entitled – to request. This, in turn, suggests a broad, proactive role in supporting students, which, for academic staff, means an expanded notion of good teaching beyond classroom pedagogy, to include advocacy and practical and emotional support, guiding students towards learning skills support and other university support services. In all, it suggests a helpful rather than purely bureaucratic approach.

The value of this approach to support can be illustrated in relation to making students aware of opportunities for financial support. Financial security was one of the circumstances contributing to the academic success of Sesh (Chapter 3), Virginia (Chapter 5), and Lillian (Chapter 6), with other students reporting significant hardship. Many mature age students also need to negotiate their financial arrangements with their partners before undertaking university studies (see Harriet's story in

Chapter 6). While having to forgo an income in order to study may not be financially possible for mature age students from low socio-economic backgrounds, Virginia felt that having a government-supported place that allowed her to defer her tuition fees until her earnings reached a certain threshold made all the difference. Both Shannon (Chapter 3) and Harriet (Chapter 6) and their families made considerable sacrifices to meet the 'hidden' costs associated with study, such as the cost of borrowing books from the university library and finding the money to attend residential schools. Neither received practicum bursaries to assist with the costs of their placements, but Harriet did receive financial support from an equity bursary. An academic staff member advised her of the availability of this support. This highlights the role of scholarships and bursaries and other small-scale forms of financial assistance, in retaining students who have to give up paid work to undertake professional placements required by their course (see Aitken et al., 2004; Ferrier et al., 2010).

Bringing services such as these to the attention of all students emphasises the value of integrating information on forms of support into mainstream teaching and learning activities and programs, rather than providing them as an adjunct to the educational program (Dodgson and Bolam, 2002; McInnis, 2001) in the context of evaluation of various models of academic and pastoral support such as separate, semi-integrated, and integrated curriculum models (Warren, 2002). It also suggests the need to be proactive in supporting all students, by linking student support, teaching, and learning (Thomas et al., 2002), and has the potential to address the complexities of students' help-seeking behaviours (Clegg et al., 2006) by emphasising the relationship between teaching staff and students in enhancing academic endeavour, successful progression, and students' help-seeking (Kinnear et al., 2008). This indicates that the 'everybody's business' approach to transition pedagogy suggested by Kift et al. (2010) is relevant to all aspects of student support.

Among the students' comments, there were also references to deficiencies in course or careers information by Rochelle (Chapter 2), Sesh and Shannon (Chapter 3), Lam and Zelin (Chapter 4), and Lillian and Harriet (Chapter 6), highlighting the importance of conveying this information to students both pre- and post-enrolment. More broadly, highlighting the experiences of successful mature age students who have come to university by alternative pathways in marketing materials is an important aspect of information that can be provided for prospective students. Also, given the importance of support by families who often have limited understanding of higher education, there is value in considering channels to convey information about the nature and demands of study to the families of first generation students.

These implications highlight the importance of professional development with a focus on social inclusion. To manage and provide a uniform approach to support at central and departmental levels, professional development programs could assist academic and professional staff to provide academic and administrative support to students and to direct students to appropriate services, anticipating the support required. Although the provision of professional development activities may not be a part of your role, you could contribute to developing awareness of this need among your colleagues and to facilitating its arrangement. As part of this, the development of guidelines for support at departmental level that are closely linked to broader university support services would inform staff responses to complex situations that arise in assisting students from non-traditional backgrounds to succeed. If you are a departmental staff member, all staff in your department could be involved in this process. A further factor supporting a consistent departmental approach is that students facing difficulties associated with features of their backgrounds are not always easily identifiable, which increases the potential value of a proactive approach in supporting all students, not just those identified as needing assistance (Thomas et al., 2002).

If you have a role in courses designed to improve the academic practice of university teachers, it is important to review the course, ensure that participants are well informed about the principles of social inclusion, and in particular develop the skills of new university teachers to support the learning of a diverse student community. This includes understanding the complexities of some students' lives, and recognising that students who are first in their family to go to university often lack confidence in their academic abilities, and that non-traditional pathways can deliver academically gifted students.

Key implications

The key implications from the above students' comments are summarised below.

1. Facilitate peer interaction:
    - Provide orientation and subsequent group activities for all students, which might not have an explicit pedagogical role but seek to build peer interaction. These also need to be provided

virtually, to address the needs of mature age students studying remotely or those who may not have time to attend face-to-face activities.
- Design learning environments that facilitate students interacting with each other, preferably in small groups.

2. Facilitate practical learning:
   - Offer learning environments that allow students to learn from real or simulated experiences. This includes the use of practicums and class activities such as role plays.

3. Offer feedback and encouragement:
   - Provide prompt, regular, and comprehensive feedback on assignments.
   - Provide personal support through feedback and encouragement.

4. Offer flexibility:
   - Implement or influence the design of flexible admissions and selection processes. At an immediate level, advise and support students to change their mode of study and study load when required.
   - Provide flexibility for assessment arrangements, sick leave, deferment and intermittence, together with family-friendly timetabling and recognition of prior learning.

5. Facilitate student-centred access to information and services:
   - Contribute to practices that provide pre- and post-entry course and careers information to all students, and examples of the experiences of students who have entered higher education via non-traditional pathways and succeeded in their studies. Given the importance of family support, consider the preparation of targeted information for families of first generation students, explaining what university study involves.
   - Contribute to practices that bring academic and technological literacy services, financial advice, and support and counselling to where students are, and provide services based on students' perception of what they need.
   - Contribute to professional development so that both teaching and professional staff are able to work together to provide a consistent approach to student support.

- Regularly update your knowledge of your institution's harassment and discrimination policies and procedures, contribute to their review where necessary, and communicate them to your students.

The above list includes factors that are relevant to both teaching and professional staff. When considering those that are applicable to your role, also think about the issues that provided a focus for the implications from students' stories in Chapters 2–6 to help guide the particular strategies you might consider. For example:

- All of the above factors are relevant to supporting the *transition* and *retention* of students.
- If supporting *international students* is your primary role, it is important that you ensure that the students have accurate information about living conditions and cultural practices in their new country, as well as accurate course information, and that you contribute to policies and practices to assist in their orientation and socialisation. If you also teach these students, then the design of curricula and the use of teaching strategies that will assist them (as well as other students) is especially important.
- If you have a teaching role, awareness of adult learning principles can help you think through ways of supporting *mature age students* and encouraging *transformative learning* that will enhance the learning of all students.

The importance of practical learning was a particularly notable implication suggested by the students' stories. An emphasis on this is consistent with the life-centred orientation to learning of adult students, influencing their readiness to learn and their motivation (Knowles et al., 2011), and it has close links to the potential for transformative learning (Mezirow et al., 2009), particularly in professional courses, as a means of changing the way that students think about themselves.

The value of the cases in this book is that they allow university staff to perceive the issues affecting the students who have shared their stories, from the students' point of view. These in-depth accounts provide a rich source of data that you can draw on to consider implications for the support of students, whatever your role. There are many further aspects of the students' stories that you could consider, beyond those that we have addressed. Stories such as these are also often powerful resources for recruiting and supporting other students from non-traditional backgrounds (see Trotman et al., 2009). You may find it helpful to use them in this way.

Summary

In this final chapter we have reviewed the stories of how students from diverse backgrounds succeeded in higher education and identified the main factors that contributed to their success, placing these factors in the context of some of the literature presented in Chapter 1. We then considered the implications for university staff suggested by these stories, identifying five key areas of focus: facilitating peer interaction; facilitating practical learning; offering feedback and encouragement; offering flexibility; and facilitating student-centred access to information and services.

'Unpacking' these implications will provide a wealth of further, specific ideas, depending on your role and context, and you may wish to consider these along with other indicators of success that can be found in the literature. We have suggested that you also consider the implications in the context of issues related to transition, retention, supporting international students, supporting mature age students, and encouraging transformative learning, with the last two of these offering directions from adult education which may be particularly useful in enhancing the learning of all students if you have a teaching role.

In their own words, these students from non-traditional backgrounds have articulated the personal and structural factors which helped them succeed, as well as those which worked against them. Their perspectives and insights provide a timely agenda for discussion and action, as universities adapt to the changing demographics of higher education in order to better serve a diverse student population and community.

Chapter 7: discussion topics

1. From your experience, brainstorm some of the ways that you have seen students from non-traditional backgrounds succeed in higher education. Make a note of any factors affecting students' success that you as an individual, or as a group or team of staff, are in a position to influence.
2. Now consider the implications for managing and supporting student diversity that we have summarised in this chapter. Think about these implications in the context of your role in your institution, together with any factors assisting students' success which you could influence that you identified above. Make a short list of five strategies (more, if you wish) that you will implement in the near future to help students from diverse backgrounds at your institution succeed in higher education. Develop an action plan for how you will implement these strategies.
3. Sometimes factors affecting students may preclude success at a particular time. Think about one or two students you have encountered where you felt success was unlikely. What were the reasons that this was the case? Is there anything further you could have done to assist them? If not, what strategies should you and your colleagues implement for dealing with such students?
4. At the end of Chapter 1 we asked you to consider how your institution could improve the way it supports the success of students from diverse backgrounds. Look back at your response to that question, and note any changes or further ideas that you would now consider after reading the students' stories in this book.

Chapter 7 discussion topics

References

Aitken, D., Schapper, C. and Skuja, E. (2004) 'Do scholarships help? Preliminary results of a case study of students in scholarship programmes at Monash University, 1997–2001', *Widening Participation and Lifelong Learning* 6(1): 15–24.

Australian Government (2009) *Transforming Australia's Higher Education System*. Canberra, ACT: Commonwealth of Australia.

Australian Government (2011) *Strategic Review of the Student Visa Program 2011 Report* (the Knight Review). Canberra, ACT: Commonwealth of Australia.

Bamber, J. (2008) 'Maximising potential in higher education: a curriculum response to student diversity', in G. Crosling, L. Thomas and M. Heagney (eds.), *Improving Student Retention in Higher Education: The Role of Teaching and Learning* (pp. 57–65). Abingdon: Routledge.

Berger, J., Motte, A. and Parkin, A. (eds.)(2009) *The Price of Knowledge Access and Student Finance in Canada*, Montreal: The Canada Millennium Scholarship Foundation.

Bologna Process Website (2007–2010) *Social dimension*. Retrieved 17 September 2012 from. http://www.ond.vlaanderen.be/hogeronderwijs/bologna/actionlines/socialdimension.htm.

Bourdieu, P. (1986) 'The forms of capital', in J. Richardson (ed.), *Handbook of Theory and Research for the Sociology of Education* (pp. 241–258). Chicago, IL: Greenwood Press.

Bradley, D. (Chair) (2008) *Review of Australian Higher Education: Final Report*. Canberra, ACT: Commonwealth of Australia.

Browne, J. (Chair) (2010) *Securing a sustainable future for higher education: an independent review of higher education and student finance* (The Browne Report). Retrieved 17 September 2012 from http://www.bis.gov.uk/assets/biscore/corporate/docs/s/10-1208-securing-sustainable-higher-education-browne-report.

Burke, P.J. and Hayton, A. (2011) 'Is widening participation still ethical?', *Widening Participation and Lifelong Learning* 13(1): 8–26.

Butcher, J., Corfield, R. and Rose-Adams, J. (2012) 'Contextualised approaches to widening participation: a comparative case study of two UK universities', *Widening Participation and Lifelong Learning* 13(special issue): 51–70.

Campbell, N. (2012) 'Promoting intercultural contact on campus: a project to connect and engage international and host students', *Journal of Studies in International Education* 16(3): 205–27.

Carroll, J. (2005) 'Strategies for becoming more explicit', in J. Carroll and J. Ryan (eds.), *Teaching International Students: Improving Learning for All* (pp. 26–34). Abingdon: Routledge.

References

Clarke, J., Zimmer, B. and Main, R. (1999) 'Review of under-representation in Australian higher education by the socioeconomically disadvantaged and the implications for university planning', *Journal of Institutional Research in Australasia* 8(1): 36–55.

Clegg, S., Bradley, S. and Smith, K. (2006) '"I've had to swallow my pride": help seeking and self-esteem', *Higher Education Research and Development* 25(2): 101–13.

Connelly, F.M. and Clandinin, D.J. (1990) 'Stories of experience and narrative inquiry', *Educational Researcher* 19(5): 2–14.

Cook, A. and Rushton, B.S. (eds.) (2009) *How to Recruit and Retain Higher Education Students: A Handbook of Good Practice*. Abingdon: Routledge.

Corbett, J. (1998) '"Voice" in emancipatory research: imaginative listening', in P. Clough and L. Barton (eds.), *Articulating with Difficulty: Research Voices in Inclusive Education* (pp. 54–63). London: Sage.

Cranton, P. (2002) 'Teaching for transformation', *New Directions for Adult and Continuing Education* 93: 63–71.

Cranton, P. (2006) *Understanding and Promoting Transformative Learning* (2nd edn.). San Francisco, CA: Jossey-Bass.

Crosling, G. (2003) 'Connecting new students: a faculty academic transition programme', *Widening Participation and Lifelong Learning* 5(1): 40–2.

Crosling, G., Thomas, L. and Heagney, M. (eds.) (2008) *Improving Student Retention in Higher Education: The Role of Teaching and Learning*. Abingdon: Routledge.

Department of Employment, Education and Workplace Relations (DEEWR) (2011a) *Education investment fund*. Retrieved 17 September 2012 from http://www.deewr.gov.au/HigherEducation/Publications/HEStatistics/Publications/Pages/2010StudentFullYear.aspx.

Department of Employment, Education and Workplace Relations (DEEWR) (2011b) *Higher education base funding review: Final report*. Retrieved 17 September 2012 from http://www.deewr.gov.au/HigherEducation/Policy/BaseReview/Documents/HigherEd_FundingReviewReport.pdf.

Devlin, M., Kift, S., Nelson, K., Smith, L. and McKay, J. (2012) *Effective teaching and support of students from low socioeconomic backgrounds: resources for Australian higher education*. Retrieved 17 September 2012 from http://www.lowses.edu.au/files/resources.htm.

Devlin, M. and O'Shea, H. (2012) 'Effective university teaching: views of Australian university students from low socio-economic backgrounds', *Teaching in Higher Education* 17(4): 385–97.

Devos, A. (2011) 'Learning to labour in regional Australia: gender, identity and place in lifelong learning', *International Journal of Lifelong Education* 30(4): 437–50.

Dobson, I., Sharma, R. and Ramsay, E. (1998) *Designated Equity Groups in Australian Universities: Performance of Commencing Undergraduates in Selected Course Types 1996*. Canberra, ACT: Australian Vice-Chancellors' Committee (AVCC).

Dobson, I. and Skuja, E. (2005) 'Secondary schooling, tertiary entry ranks and university performance', *People and Place* 13(1): 53–61.

Dodgson, R. and Bolam, H. (2002) *Student Retention, Support and Widening Participation in the North East of England*. Sunderland: Universities for the North East.

Edwards, R., Crosling, G., Lazarevic-Petrovic, S. and O'Neill, P. (2003) 'Internationalisation of business education: meaning and implementation', *Higher Education Research and Development* 22(2): 183–92.

Engle, J. and O'Brien, C. (2007) *Demography is not Destiny: Increasing the Graduation Rates of Low-income College Students at Large Public Universities*. Washington, DC: The Pell Institute for the Study of Opportunity in Higher Education.

Ferrier, F. (2012) *Higher Education in Urban Areas Case Study: Greater Merseyside, UK*. London: European Access Network (mimeo).

Ferrier, F. and Heagney, M. (2000) 'Dealing with the dynamics of disadvantage: options for equity planning in higher education institutions', *Widening Participation and Lifelong Learning* 2(1): 5–13.

Ferrier, F., Heagney, M. and Lee, M.F. (2010) *Increasing and Sustaining Diversity in Higher Education: Ideas, Information and Resources*. London: European Access Network.

Ferrier, F. and North, S. (2009, 18 March) *Social inclusion in VET and higher education*. Paper presented at a CEET/Faculty of Education Seminar, Monash University, Melbourne, VIC.

Foley, G. (ed.) (2000) *Understanding Adult Education and Training* (2nd edn.). Sydney, NSW: Allen & Unwin.

Forneng, S. (2003) *Swedish national report. International comparative research: under-represented groups in tertiary education*. Retrieved 17 September 2012 from http://www.staffs.ac.uk/access-studies/research/res18.html.

Freire, P. (1972) *Pedagogy of the Oppressed*. Harmondsworth: Penguin.

Gillard, J. (2009, 9 March) Speech to Australian Financial Review Higher Education Conference, Canberra, ACT. Retrieved 17 September 2012 from http://ministers.deewr.gov.au/gillard/australian-financial-review-higher-education-conference-9-march-2009.

Greer, L. and Tidd, J. (2006) 'You need someone to share with: taking the fear out of the transition into higher education for mature students', *Widening Participation and Lifelong Learning* 8(1): 44–51.

Habermas, J. (1971) *Knowledge and Human Interests*. Boston, MA: Beacon Press.

Handel, S. and Herrera, A. (2003) 'Access and retention of students from educationally disadvantaged backgrounds: insights from the University of California', in L. Thomas, M. Cooper and J. Quinn (eds.), *Improving Completion Rates among Disadvantaged Students* (pp. 33–52). Stoke-on-Trent: Trentham Books.

Heagney, M. (2011) 'Equitable selection: dream or reality?', in C. Prachalias, Research and Training Institute of East Aegean (INEAG) (ed.), *Proceedings of the 7th International Conference on Education, Samos Island, Greece, 7–9 July 2011. Volume 1* (pp. 436–40). Athens, Greece: National and Kapodistrian University of Athens.

Heggen, K. (2000) 'Marginalisation: on the fringe of the periphery – youth as a risky life stage?', *Young* 8(2): 45–62.

Heggen, K., Jorgensen, G. and Paulgaard, G. (2003) *De andre: Ungdom, risikosoner og marginalisering [The Others: Youth, Risk Zones and Marginalization]*. Oslo: Fagbokforlaget.

Higher Education Funding Council for England (HEFCE) (2009) *HEFCE strategic plan 2006–11*. Retrieved 17 September 2012 from http://www.hefce.ac.uk/pubs/year/2009/200921/.

Hockings, C. (2010) *Inclusive learning and teaching in higher education: a synthesis of research*. The Higher Education Academy, UK. Retrieved 17 September 2012 from http://www.heacademy.ac.uk/assets/EvidenceNet/Syntheses/inclusive_teaching_and_learning_in_he_synthesis_200410.pdf.

Jackson, S. (ed.) (2011) *Lifelong Learning and Social Justice: Communities, Work and Identities in a Globalised World*. Leicester: NIACE.

James, R. (2008) *Participation and Equity: A Review of the Participation in Higher Education of People from Low Socioeconomic Backgrounds and Indigenous People*. Melbourne, VIC: Centre for Study of Higher Education, University of Melbourne.

James, R., Baldwin, G., Coates, H., Krause, K.-L. and McInnis, C. (2004) *Analysis of Equity Groups in Higher Education 1991–2002*. Canberra, ACT: Department of Education, Science and Training.

James, R., Krause, K.-L. and Jennings, C. (2010) *The First Year Experience in Australian Universities: Findings from 1994–2009*. Melbourne, VIC: Centre for the Study of Higher Education, The University of Melbourne.

Jones, R. (2008) *Student retention and success: a synthesis of research*. Retrieved 17 September 2012 from http://www.heacademy.ac.uk/assets/EvidenceNet/Syntheses/wp_retention_synthesis_for_pdf_updated_090310.pdf.

Josselson, R. (2006) 'Narrative research and the challenge of accumulating knowledge', *Narrative Inquiry* 16(1): 3–10.

Kift, S., Nelson, K. and Clarke, J. (2010) 'Transition pedagogy: a third generation approach to FYE – a case study of policy and practice for the higher education sector', *International Journal of the First Year in Higher Education* 1(1): 1–20.

Kinnear, A., Boyce, M., Sparrow, H., Middleton, S. and Cullity, M. (2008) *Final Report. Diversity: a longitudinal study of how student diversity relates to resilience and successful progression in a new generation university*. Sydney, NSW: Edith Cowan University and Australian Learning and Teaching Council. Available at http://www.chs.ecu.edu.au/org/tlo/projects/CG638/index.php.

Kirk, K. (2006) 'Diversity and achievement: how non-traditional students succeed in higher education', *Learning and Teaching in Action* 5(1): 10–13.

Kitchenham, A. (2008) 'The evolution of John Mezirow's transformative learning theory', *Journal of Transformative Education* 6(2): 104–23.

Klinger, C. and Murray, N. (2012) 'Tensions in higher education: widening participation, student diversity and the challenge of academic language/literacy', *Widening Participation and Lifelong Learning* 14(1): 27–44.

Knight, P. and Yorke, M. (2004) *Learning, Curriculum and Employability in Higher Education*. London: RoutledgeFalmer.

Knowles, M., Holton, E.F. and Swanson, R.A. (2011) *The Adult Learner* (7th edn.). Oxford: Butterworth-Heinemann.

Krause, K.-L. and Coates, H. (2008) 'Students' engagement in first-year university', *Assessment and Evaluation in Higher Education* 33(5): 493–505.

Krause, K.-L., Hartley, R., James, R. and McInnis, C. (2005) *The First Year Experience in Australian Universities: Findings from a Decade of National Studies*. Canberra, ACT: Commonwealth of Australia.

Kuh, G.D., Kinzie, J., Buckley, J., Bridges, B. and Hayek, J.C. (2006) *What matters to student success: a review of the literature. Final Report for the National Postsecondary Education Cooperative and National Center for Education Statistics*. Bloomington, IN: Indiana University Center for Postsecondary Research. Available at http://nces.ed.gov/npec/papers.asp.

Kuh, G.D., Kinzie, J., Cruce, T., Shoup, R. and Gonyea, R.M. (2007) *Connecting the dots: multifaceted analyses of the relationships between student engagement results from the NSSE and the institutional policies and conditions that foster student success. Final Report to the Lumina Foundation for Education*. Bloomington, IN: Indiana University Center for Postsecondary Research. Available at nsse.iub.edu/pdf/Connecting_the_Dots_Report.pdf.

Land, R., Meyer, J.H.F. and Smith, J. (eds.) (2008) *Threshold Concepts within the Disciplines*. Rotterdam, Netherlands: Sense.

Leask, B. (2009) 'Using formal and informal curricula to improve interactions between home and international students', *Journal of Studies in International Education* 13(1): 205–21.

Leathwood, C. and Francis, B. (eds.) (2006) *Gender and Lifelong Learning: Critical Feminist Engagements*. Abingdon: Routledge.

Leathwood, C. and O'Connell, P. (2003) '"It's a struggle": the construction of the "new student" in higher education', *Journal of Education Policy* 18(6): 597–615.

Leichsenring, H. (2011a) 'Diversity in German higher education and an economic rationale for equity', *Widening Participation and Lifelong Learning* 13(1): 39–56.

Leichsenring, H. (2011b) 'Lack of skilled workers and equity in higher education: the astonishing effects of demographic change in Germany', in M. Cooper (ed.), *From Access to Success: Closing the Knowledge Divide. Higher Education for Under-represented Groups in the Market Economy* (pp. 129-144). Papers from the 19th Annual Conference of the European Access Network, Södertörn University, Stockholm, Sweden, 14–16 June 2010. London: European Access Network.

Levy, S. and Murray J. (2005) 'Tertiary entrance scores need not determine academic success: an analysis of student performance in an equity and access program', *Journal of Higher Education Policy and Management* 27(1): 129–41.

Long, M., Ferrier, F. and Heagney, M. (2006) *Stay, Play or Give it Away? Students Continuing, Changing or Leaving University Study in Their First Year*. Canberra, ACT: Department of Education, Science and Training.

Marginson, S. (2011, 15 February). 'The Chair', *The Age*, p. 19.

Marks, G., McMillan, J. and Hillman, K. (2001) *Tertiary Entrance Performance: The Role of Student Background and School Factors*. Melbourne, VIC: ACER.

Marr, E. (2011) 'Editorial', *Widening Participation and Lifelong Learning* 13(1): 3–7.

Marr, E. and Jary, D. (2011) 'Editorial: Higher education and employability', *Widening Participation and Lifelong Learning* 13(2): 3–7.

References

Martin, L.M. (1994) *Equity and General Performance Indicators in Higher Education, Volume 1*. Canberra, ACT: Department of Employment, Education and Training.

Marton, F. and Booth, S. (1997) *Learning and Awareness*. Mahwah, NJ: Lawrence Erlbaum.

Maslow, A.H. (1970) *Motivation and Personality*. New York: Harper & Row.

May, H. and Bridger, K. (2010) *Developing and Embedding Inclusive Policy and Practice in Higher Education*. York: The Higher Education Academy.

McGivney, V. (2006) 'Attracting new groups into learning: lessons from research in England', in J. Chapman, P. Cartwright and E.J. McGilp (eds.), *Lifelong Learning, Participation and Equity* (pp. 79–91). Dordrecht: Springer.

McInnis, C. (2001) *Signs of Disengagement? The Changing Undergraduate Experience in Australian Universities*. Melbourne, VIC: Centre for the Study of Higher Education, The University of Melbourne.

McInnis, C. (2002) 'Signs of disengagement: responding to the changing work and study patterns of full-time undergraduates in Australian universities', in J. Enders and O. Fulton (eds.), *Higher Education in a Globalising World* (pp. 175–89). Dordrecht: Kluwer Academic Publishers.

McLean, P. and Holden, W. (2004, 14–16 July) *Investing in cultural capital: a partnership enhancing transition for equity students*. Paper presented at the First Year in Higher Education Conference: Dealing with Diversity, Queensland University of Technology in conjunction with Monash University, Melbourne.

McLean, P. and Ransom, L. (2005) 'Building intercultural competencies: implications for academic skills development', in J. Carroll and J. Ryan (eds.), *Teaching International Students: Improving Learning for All* (pp. 45–62). Abingdon: Routledge.

Merriam, S.B., Caffarella, R.S. and Baumgartner, L.M. (2007) *Learning in Adulthood: A Comprehensive Guide* (3rd edn.). Hoboken, NJ: Jossey-Bass.

Meyer, J.H.F. and Land, R. (2006) *Overcoming Barriers to Student Understanding: Threshold Concepts and Troublesome Knowledge*. New York: Routledge.

Mezirow, J. (1978) 'Perspective transformation', *Adult Education* 28(2): 100–9.

Mezirow, J., Taylor, E.W. and Associates (eds.) (2009) *Transformative Learning in Practice: Insights from Community, Workplace and Higher Education*. San Francisco, CA: Jossey-Bass.

Moissidis, S., Schwarz, J., Yndigegn, C., Pellikka, L. and Harvey, M. (2011) 'Tuition fees and funding – barriers for non-traditional students? First results from the international research project Opening Universities for Lifelong Learning (OPULL)', *Widening Participation and Lifelong Learning* 13(1): 71–87.

Murphy, B. (2009) 'Great expectations? Progression and achievement of less traditional entrants to higher education', *Widening Participation and Lifelong Learning* 11(2): 4–14.

O'Dowd, M. (1996) *Access and Equity Issues for Mature Age Students at Monash University*. Report to the Equity Consultative Committee and the Equal Opportunity Committee, Monash University. Melbourne, VIC: Mature and Part Time Students' Association, Monash University.

Oliver, B. (2010) *Teaching Fellowship: Benchmarking Partnerships for Graduate Employability. Final Report*. Strawberry Hills, NSW: Australian Learning and Teaching Council.

O'Shea, S. (2007) '"Well I got here . . . but what happens next?" – exploring the early narratives of first year female students who are first in the family to attend university', *Journal of the Australia and New Zealand Student Services Association* 29: 36–51.

Palmer, N., Bexley, E. and James, R. (2011) *Selection and Participation in Higher Education: University Selection in Support of Student Success and Diversity of Participation*. Melbourne, VIC: Centre for the Study of Higher Education, The University of Melbourne.

Patton, M.Q. (2002) *Qualitative Research and Evaluation Methods* (3rd edn.). Thousand Oaks, CA: Sage.

Pinnegar, S. and Daynes, J.G. (2007) 'Locating narrative inquiry historically: thematics in the turn to narrative', in D.J. Clandinin (ed.), *Handbook of Narrative Inquiry: Mapping a Methodology* (pp. 3–34). Thousand Oaks, CA: Sage.

Radloff, A. and Coates, H. (2010) *Doing More for Learning: Enhancing Engagement and Outcomes. Australasian Student Engagement Report*. Camberwell, VIC: ACER.

Read, B., Archer, A. and Leathwood, C. (2003) 'Challenging cultures? Student conceptions of "belonging" and "isolation" at a post-1992 university', *Studies in Higher Education* 28(3): 261–77.

Rogers, C. (1969) *Freedom to Learn*. Columbus, OH: Merrill.

Ryan, J. (2005) 'Improving teaching and learning practices for international students', in J. Carroll and J. Ryan (eds.), *Teaching International Students: Improving Learning for All* (pp. 92–100). Abingdon: Routledge.

Skyrme, J. and Crow, M. (2008) 'Targeting outreach activity: a prioritisation model', in F. Ferrier and M. Heagney (eds.), *Higher Education in Diverse Communities: Global Perspectives, Local Initiatives* (pp. 76–82). London: European Access Network and the Higher Education Authority of Ireland.

Soltis, J.F. (1992) 'Inquiry paradigms', in M.C. Alkin (ed.), *Encyclopedia of Educational Research* (pp. 620–2). New York: Macmillan.

Statistics Finland (2013) *Employment of Students*. Retrieved 4 March 2013 from http://tilastokeskus.fi/til/opty/index_en.html?tulosta.

Stone, C. (2008) 'Listening to individual voices and stories – the mature-age student experience', *Australian Journal of Adult Learning* 48(2): 263–90.

Tedder, M. (2007) 'Making a choice? Insights from using a life history approach to researching access students', *Widening Participation and Lifelong Learning* 9(2): 26–35.

Teoh, K.S. (2008) 'My father wanted me to study engineering!', in G. Crosling, L. Thomas and M. Heagney (eds.), *Improving Student Retention in Higher Education: The Role of Teaching and Learning* (pp. 52–6). Abingdon: Routledge.

Thomas, L. (2006) 'The impact of first generation entry on access and success in higher education', *Widening Participation and Lifelong Learning* 8(3): 2–5.

Thomas, L., Cooper, M. and Quinn, J. (eds.) (2003) *Improving Completion Rates among Disadvantaged Students*. Stoke-on-Trent: Trentham Books.

Thomas, L. and Quinn, J. (2003) *International Insights into Widening Participation: Supporting the Success of Under-represented Groups in Tertiary Education*. Stoke-on-Trent: Institute for Access Studies, Staffordshire University.

Thomas, L., Quinn, J., Slack, K. and Casey, L. (2002) *Student Services: Effective Approaches to Retaining Students in Higher Education*. Stoke-on-Trent: Institute for Access Studies, Staffordshire University.

Tinto, V. (2012) *Completing College: Rethinking Institutional Action*. Chicago, IL: University of Chicago Press.

Trotman, C., Kop, R., Jones, R. and Jenkins, A. (2009) 'The Community University of the Valleys model: "Reaching the students other recruitment strategies can't reach"', in A. Cook and B. Rushton (eds.), *How to Recruit and Retain Higher Education Students: A Handbook of Good Practice*. London: Routledge.

Trow, M. (2000) *From Mass Higher Education to Universal Access: The American Advantage*. Berkeley, CA: University of Berkeley Center for Studies in Higher Education.

Warren, D. (2002) 'Curriculum design in a context of widening participation in higher education', *Arts and Humanities in Higher Education* 1(1): 85–99.

Wheelahan, L. (2009, 25 February) *What kind of access does VET provide to higher education for low SES students? Not a lot*. Paper presented to the National Student Equity Research Centre Forum, University of South Australia, Adelaide, SA.

Yorke, M. (1999) *Leaving Early: Undergraduate Non-completion in Higher Education*. London: Falmer Press.

Yorke, M. (2008) 'Is the first year experience different for disadvantaged students?', in F. Ferrier and M. Heagney (eds.), *Higher Education in Diverse Communities: International Perspectives, Local Initiatives* (pp. 113–20). London: European Access Network and the Higher Education Authority of Ireland.

Index

academic literacy, 88, 122, 201–202
academic writing requirements/skills, 44, 62–63, 65, 87–88, 97, 100, 109, 111, 114–115, 122–123, 169, 180, 187, 202
access (to higher education/university), 2–4, 6–11, 13–18, 127, 148, 165–166, 216
adult learners, learning, 88, 155–157, 202, 216, 221
anxiety, 15, 123, 166, 178, 183, 189, 199–200, 212
assessment, 17–18, 43, 65, 86, 156, 199, 203, 216, 220

class (social), 3, 8, 13, 137, 157, 162, 190, 192–193, 208
computer literacy, 166, 179–180, 201–202
course/career guidance/information, 15, 18, 34–35, 38–40, 74, 85–86, 97–98, 109, 120, 164, 194–195, 197, 202, 211, 213, 218, 220–221
Cranton, 202–203
critical social theory, 12–13, 19, 156, 202
cultural, social capital, 3, 8, 44–45, 86,
curricula, curriculum, 16–18, 45–46, 121, 123, 198, 211, 213–214, 216, 218, 221

disability, on-going medical condition, illness 4,172, 185, 201
disadvantage, 2–4, 8–10, 13–14, 45, 71, 88, 134, 211
distance education, *see* study modes
diverse – *see* non-traditional

English as a second language – *see* English language
English language, 4, 87, 98–100, 109–111, 114–115, 122
equity, 11, 14
  equity bursaries, 86, 197, 202, 213, 218
  equity categories, 3–4
ethnic, ethnicity, 4, 10, 13, 45, 173–174, 178, 213

family support, see student support
feedback 18, 46, 64, 82, 88, 104, 118, 147–149, 156, 198, 201, 210, 213–214, 216, 220
field work – *see* placements
finances
  bursaries, grants, scholarships (value of) 18, 86, 199, 202, 213, 218
  costs, 15, 18, 41, 61, 78–80, 82–83, 86, 218
  financial assistance 11, 211, 218
  financial security/support, 17, 44–45, 62, 86, 116, 197, 210, 214, 217–218

233

Index

first generation, first in family, 4, 10, 26, 34, 36, 44, 53, 64, 86–87, 94,128, 136, 162, 213, 219–220
first year experience, 44–45, 154, 208
flexible/flexibility, 17, 45, 81, 135. 142, 155–156, 204, 209, 212–214, 216, 220
Freire, 13, 156

gender, 13, 53, 57, 106, 113, 120, 127, 164, 193, 200, 209, 213
group work/activities, 67, 88, 102, 104, 110, 121–123, 133, 156, 198, 204, 211, 213–215, 219–220
global competitiveness, 7

harassment
   sexual harassment 201, 205
   harassment and discrimination policies and procedures 221
help-seeking, 16–17, 87, 218
Honours, 143, 147, 149, 156, 167, 172, 197, 212–213, 216

Identity – *see* self-concept
Indigenous, 4–5
individual factors – *see* personal factors
institutional factors – *see* structural factors
international students, 6, 12, 18, 87, 94, 105, 116–117, 120–124, 210–211, 215, 221
interpretivism, 12

Knowles, 155, 216, 221

library use/access 43, 78, 83, 86, 197

mature age students, 15, 18, 60, 132, 154–157, 166, 168–169, 213, 217–218, 220–221

Mezirow, 202, 204, 221
migrant/migration, 128–129, 140, 172, 184, 190, 212
motivation, *see* personal factors

narrative enquiry, 20
non-English-speaking background (NESB) – *see* English language
non-traditional, xii, 3–4, 8, 10, 13–15, 44–45, 122, 208, 214–216, 219–221

off-campus study – *see* distance education
online learning, support, 5, 18, 63, 82, 133, 156, 165, 198, 210–211, 213–215

participatory research, 19–20
personal factors, 3, 14–17, 85, 87, 144, 153–154(?), 208, 210–213
   motivation, 17, 52, 64–65, 67, 82, 86, 104, 148, 150, 170, 176, 178, 187–188, 196–199, 209–213, 216, 221
practicums – *see* placements
placements – professional/work placements, 18, 42, 44, 65, 79, 82, 84, 86, 88, 110–111, 118–119, 123, 132, 134, 142–3, 149, 168,189, 197, 204, 209–212, 215–216, 220

race, racism, 10, 13, 177–178, 190
remote, 9, 20, 36, 41, 43, 209
retention, 4, 11, 14–15, 18, 85–88, 221
role models, 28–29, 56, 136–137, 147, 152, 178, 194, 209 role plays, 110, 134, 186, 204, 211, 215, 220
rural, 4–5, 9, 26, 43, 51–52, 58, 68, 85–86, 209

Index

self-concept, 128, 155, 163–4, 174, 200–201
self doubt, 42–43, 183
self-esteem/confidence, 15, 35, 83–84, 87, 104, 109, 118–119, 134, 149, 151, 165, 168–170, 177, 187, 198–200, 209
serendipitous events or encounters, 16, 26, 44, 128, 201, 209, 211
social inclusion, 1–6, 11–15, 19, 219
socio-economic status (SES)/background 190
  low socio-economic status/background 4–5, 7, 9–11, 13, 17–18, 218
  high socio-economic status/background 9, 13
structural factors, xii, 3, 13–18, 86–88, 208–209, 212–214, 216
student engagement, 5, 16–17, 88
student success, 4–5, 14–18, 21, 32, 36, 44–46, 52, 67, 88, 119–121, 123, 142–146, 170, 197, 199–201, 208–218
  obstacles to success, 56–57
student support
  employer support, 17, 34, 35, 133–5, 209, 214
  family support, 17, 34, 38, 44, 87, 94, 103, 116, 133, 136, 146–147, 154, 184–185, 197, 215, 220
  lecturer/staff support, 16–17, 34–35, 42, 45, 87, 103, 120–121, 123, 147, 155–157, 184–185, 197, 201–203, 209, 211–221.
  peer support, 15, 17, 18, 63, 87, 103, 116, 121 147, 156, 209–210, 215
  support services, 15–16, 43, 45–46, 63–64, 83, 85, 87, 102, 115, 122, 133, 147, 156, 169, 185, 197, 202, 217, 219
study modes
  distance education, 5, 20, 26, 31, 33–34, 39, 41, 43, 45, 74, 78, 82–83, 117, 131, 141–143, 148–150, 156, 166, 199, 209–212, 216
  on-campus study, 5, 156, 166, 198
  part-time study, 4–5, 32, 34, 78, 134, 141, 166, 183-, 186–187, 195, 197, 212–213

threshold concepts, 203–204
transformation, transformative, 199–204, 221
transition, 15, 44–45, 58–59, 85, 88, 99, 103, 120–121, 216, 218, 221

visas, 111, 117, 123–124
voice, 20, 193–194, 198, 200–201

widening participation, 2–12, 15, 18